Excel for Teachers

by

Colleen Conmy, Bill Hazlett, Bill Jelen, Adrienne Soucy

Holy Macro! Books

Excel for Teachers
© 2006 Holy Macro! Books

Written by:
Colleen Conmy, Bill Hazlett, Bill Jelen, Adrienne Soucy

Edited by:
Linda DeLonais

On the Cover:
Design by Shannon Mattiza, 6Ft4 productions

Published by:
Holy Macro! Books
PO Box 82
Uniontown, Ohio, USA 44685

Distributed by:
Independent Publishers Group

First printing:
November 2005
Printed in the United States of America

Library of Congress Data
Excel for Teachers / Bill Jelen, Adrienne Soucy, Bill Hazlett, Colleen Conmy
Library of Congress Control Number: 2005929675

ISBN: 1-932802-11-8

Excel for Teachers

Table of Contents

Dedications

Colleen Conmy:

Dedicated to Catherine and Brigid Conmy.

Bill Hazlett:

Dedicated to Benjamin, Nathan, Ryan, and Caitlin.

Bill Jelen:

Dedicated to Joan Jelen.

Adrienne Soucy:

Dedicated to Matt, AJS, and TS.

Acknowledgements

Bill Jelen:

Bill Jelen wishes to thank co-authors Bill, Colleen and Adrienne for their dedication to this project. Thanks to Linda DeLonais for care in editing and formatting this book. Thanks to Tyrone Willingham for bringing the project together and to Charlie Weis for general improvements. Thanks to the entire 4B crew, specifically Matt Soucy and John Conmy for contributing authors to the project. Thanks to Dan Bricklin and Bob Frankston for inventing the computer spreadsheet. Thanks to Josh Jelen, Zeke Jelen and Mary Ellen Jelen for putting up with late nights of writing. Thanks to everyone at Rogers Media and the crew of Call for Help – this very page is being written on a flight to Toronto. Thanks to the continuing education department at the University of Akron. Thanks to Mary Rottenborn for advice on some chapters – I think I can now write off the ND-Pitt tailgate party as a business meeting. Thanks to Lora White for running the office while I finished this book. I thank my dad, Robert F. Jelen for providing the first computer, my sister Barb Jelen for shipping this book to you and handling bookkeeping, my brother Bob Jelen for being a great venture capitalist. Thanks to Matt Gagnon and the media class at Uniontown Lake High School – their assistance made the podcasts from this book possible.

Bill Hazlett

Bill Hazlett would first of all like to thank Bill Jelen for the invitation to assist in this book and for his encouragement as we went through the process. A thank you also to Adrienne for her acceptance in allowing me to join in mid-project, and to Colleen whose assistance as we approached deadline was invaluable. Thanks to Marsha Hershey for encouraging my curiosity with the new-fangled gadget called a desktop computer (hard to believe it's only been 15 years!), and thanks to Mike McCarthy for early instruction and help with MultiPlan and the TRS Model 4P (even though he tried to switch me to Lotus!). Thank you to the staff of Vermilion (OH) Sailorway Middle School who will always have a place in my heart. And finally, thanks to my wife, Arlene, who OK'd the purchase of the Amstrad and who finally dragged me out of the rut I had dug and got me to use Excel!

Adrienne E. Soucy

Adrienne Soucy wishes to give a huge thank you to Bill, Bill, and Colleen for answering my questions and showing me new and exciting ways to use Excel in my teaching. I have become a student to these great teachers. I owe each of you a chili dinner. Thank you to Christina Kaler for opening the world of Excel to an elderly teacher. Your enthusiasm for teaching inspires many. Thank you to Mike Stout for your listening ear, understanding and optimism. Thank you to the entire Jimtown South staff for welcoming change.

My need to understand Excel was born out of my desire to make our jobs a little easier. May the solutions in this book help all of us spend less time doing paperwork and thus, have more time for teaching. Thanks to Chris Khodl for solving my hardware problems and upgrading our home network. You have helped bring technology to the Soucy household. Thank you to my parents, Mary and Peter Poell, for giving me the support and opportunities to become the person I am today. Thank you to Gladys Hoff for being the best grandmother in the world and showing me that learning is a lifetime endeavor. Thank you to AJ Soucy for sleeping soundly on my lap as I finished and showing me a new level of love. Thank you to Matt Soucy for giving me a daily dose of joy and laughter, helping me "tone it down a bit" and urging me to think beyond the boundaries. And a final thank you to all teachers for choosing a career dedicated to helping others reach their goals. May you continue to inspire lifelong learning in your students.

Colleen Conmy

Colleen Conmy would like to thank Bill Jelen for his patience. Thanks to my parents, John and Eileen Conmy, for letting me know that girls can do anything boys can do. Thanks to my brother John Conmy for suggesting that I help and for passing along my e-mail address. Thanks to Mary P. Boyle for giving me my first job as a technology teacher. Thanks to the Middle School faculty at Kent Place School for letting me bounce ideas off of them.

About the Authors

Colleen Conmy

Colleen Conmy graduated from East Stroudsburg University in 1993 with a bachelor's degree in Elementary Education. In 2002 she received a Master of Arts in Education with a focus in Instructional Design & Technology from Seton Hall University. Colleen has worked as an elementary school technology teacher, a fifth/sixth grade classroom teacher, and in the technology services industry as a Project Coordinator. Currently, Colleen is working as the Middle School Instructional Technology Coordinator at Kent Place School in Summit, New Jersey.

Bill Hazlett

Wm. J. (Bill) Hazlett graduated from the Ohio State University in 1971, earning a B.S. of Ed. degree with a double major in industrial arts and mathematics. In 1982, he received the M.Ed. degree from Bowling Green State University. Most of his career was as a middle school/high school teacher in Vermilion, Ohio, teaching industrial arts, mathematics, and computer classes in grades 7-12. Prior to that, he taught industrial arts in the Elyria, Fairview Park, and Midview school districts in northeast Ohio.

His first experience with spreadsheets was in devising a basic grade book for his high school math classes, using MultiPlan and a Tandy TRS 4P computer.

After 30 years in the classroom, he retired in 2001. He now teaches part-time developmental algebra for the University of Akron, and works part-time as a props carpenter for Cleveland Opera.

Adrienne E. Soucy

Adrienne E. Soucy graduated in 1990 from the Ball State University with a bachelor's degree in elementary education with a specialization in reading. In 1999, she received a degree of Master of Arts in Education and a gifted and talented license endorsement from Ball State University. Adrienne began her educational career in 1990 by working with special education students and gifted and talented classes at the sixth, seventh, and eighth grade levels. She then moved to the elementary level where she taught first grade students for 13 years. Currently, Adrienne is working as the literacy coordinator and the reading specialist for at-risk students at Jimtown South Elementary located in Elkhart, Indiana.

Bill Jelen

Bill Jelen is the host of MrExcel.com – a leading website for Excel knowledge. He is the author of nine books about Microsoft Excel.

Preface

This book is written by three teachers and a guy who teaches Excel. As the latter, I give all of the credit for this book to Adrienne, Bill H. and Colleen – it was their logic of classroom needs that made the book what it is. The population of teachers writing this book mirrors the real population – some know Excel well and some are new to Excel.

If you learn every concept in the 25 examples in this book, you will be an Excel guru. Even if you only use a few of the topics, you will find yourself comfortable with Excel. If you don't want to learn anything about Excel, then just download the sample applications and use them in the classroom. Sample files can be downloaded from this secret page: http://www.MrExcel.com/teacherfiles.html.

The concepts in this book apply equally well to every version of Excel from Excel 97 through Excel 2003. As this book goes to press, pre-beta copies of Excel 12 are available. I've reviewed these and many concepts will be different in Excel 12. While Excel 12 threatens to make every Excel book obsolete, most public school districts are in financial trouble and will not be upgrading to Excel 12 soon. If you happen to live in a district that upgrades to Excel 12, check the aforementioned web page for information about an e-book upgrade for Excel 12 users.

– Bill Jelen

Windows vs. Mac

Screen shots in this book are taken with the Windows version of Excel 2003. Instructions for the Mac should be similar, with one important distinction. When the book says to Right-click, hold down the Control key on the keyboard while clicking the right mouse button.

Introduction

There are endless tasks that can be made easier with Excel. Excel can be used to track classroom management from grade books, class rosters, attendance, testing results, assessment measurement charts, and more. Excel can be used as an aide in teaching. Use Excel to generate random fact worksheets. Use Excel to create graphs to help teach math standards. Finally, your students can use Excel to develop models and homework.

Skills Required

We will assume that you have Excel 97 or newer running on Windows or Macintosh. You should know how to start Excel and navigate from cell to cell.

Before You Start

There is an annoying feature in Excel 2000 and later. In an effort to make Excel "simpler", Microsoft hides many menu items and toolbar items. The annoying factor is that the menus will be different on every computer. If you accidentally discover the AutoFilter command on one computer, Excel will start showing the Filter command on the Data menu on that computer. As you move from computer to computer, you will find different options on each menu.

For the purposes of this book and to minimize frustration, please turn off this annoying feature. This will ensure that your screen looks like the figures in this book and that when the book suggests that you select Filter from the Data menu, it will actually be there.

1. Start Excel. Select the Tools menu. If there is not a Customize option, then keep the Tools menu open for several seconds until Excel decides to show you the entire menu. Select Customize from the Tools menu.

2. As shown in Figure 1, the Customize dialog box offers three tabs. Select the Options tab on the right. Choose the checkbox for Always show full menus.

3. Similarly, Excel 2000 and newer will combine the Standard and Formatting toolbars on one row. This means that you only see 60% of each bar, and again, the icons visible will vary from computer to computer. On the same dialog shown in Figure 1, choose Show Standard and Formatting toolbars on two rows. (In Excel 2000, you need to uncheck "Combine Standard and Formatting Toolbars on One Row".)

Figure 1

Showing Standard and Formatting toolbars on two rows allows all of the icons to be visible on these toolbars.

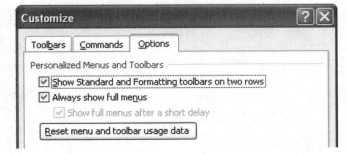

How the Book Is Set up

This book will present 25 tools that you can use in your classroom. We will show you exactly how to set up the spreadsheet in order to build the sample as shown in the book. We will walk you through how to use the sample file.

 Tip:

You can also download the 25 sample spreadsheets from this site:
HTTP://www.mrexcel.com/teacherfiles.html

Some of the more complex Excel details will be presented in a section called Excel Details in some chapters. It is possible for you to use and enjoy the template without knowing these details. However, if you wish to dramatically further your understanding of Excel and build new applications, you might want to review the details section. By learning how to build each spreadsheet, you will master several essential skills that will allow you to build your own tools to meet your classroom needs.

Introduction to Excel

Rows and Columns

When you open an Excel workbook, you have a neat array of rows and columns. Your opening screen of Excel might show columns A, B, C, and so on. Depending on your monitor size, you might see out through column H or column Q or, if you are in an incredibly wealthy district, out through column T. Similarly, you might see rows 1, 2, 3, down to 20, 31, or 40 depending on your monitor size.

Figure 2

Excel's opening workbook screen

	A	B	C	D
1				
2				
3				
4				
5				
6				
7				

The intersections of these rows and columns form boxes known as cells. Each cell is given a name that is a combination of the column letter followed by the row number. In the image above, the box in Cell A1 is called the cellpointer. Cell A1 is called the active cell. Anything that you type will be placed in the active cell.

Each cell can contain a number, some words, a date, a time, or a formula that calculates a value. You can format the cells to be left justified, center justified, or right justified. You can change the color of the letters in a cell, the background color, and even the style of the borders. Excel is up to the job whether you are trying to get data organized into rows and columns like Figure 3...

Figure 3

Data organized into neat rows and columns

	A	B	C	D	E	F
1		Mon	Tue	Wed	Thurs	Fri
2	1st	Reading	Reading	Reading	Reading	Reading
3	2nd	Math	Writing	Math	Writing	Math
4	3rd	Gym	Music	Art	Gym	Art
5	4th	Lunch	Lunch	Lunch	Lunch	Lunch
6	5th	Science	Science	Science	Science	Science
7	6th	Soc.St	Soc.St	Soc.St	Soc.St	Soc.St
8	7th	A.R	Math	Computer	Math	Computer
9						

...or if you want to create visually stunning tables suitable for presentations or newsletters.

Figure 4

Artistically formatted table

	A	B	C	D	E	F
1		*Mon*	*Tue*	*Wed*	*Thurs*	*Fri*
2	1st	Reading	Reading	Reading	Reading	Reading
3	2nd	Math	Writing	Math	Writing	Math
4	3rd	Gym	Music	Art	Gym	Art
5	4th	Lunch	Lunch	Lunch	Lunch	Lunch
6	5th	Science	Science	Science	Science	Science
7	6th	Soc.St	Soc.St	Soc.St	Soc.St	Soc.St
8	7th	A.R	Math	Computer	Math	Computer

To Infinity and Beyond

Well, that isn't quite true, but there are more cells than those that you can see on your computer monitor. If you use the right arrow key, you can scroll out past column Z. After column Z, Excel starts over at AA, AB, AC. The alphabet repeats over and over all the way out to column IV – which is the 256th column. Use the PgDn key to move down to new rows. You will eventually arrive at row 65,536 – the final row. Considering that there is a cell at the intersection of every row and column, that gives you 16,777,216 places to store information on one single worksheet! And an Excel workbook can have many Excel worksheets. It might sound as though you would never fill up a single worksheet, but in some industries, even this isn't enough rows or columns. Many predict that, in 2006, the new version of Excel will offer even more cells on a worksheet.

Calculating, Always Calculating

Remember that cells in Excel can contain formulas that calculate values from other cells. Every time that you change a value in any cell in Excel, the computer instantly recalculates every formula on the worksheet. The values in row 24 and column C of the table shown in Figure 5 are actually formulas.

Figure 5

The values in row 24 and column C are actually formulas rather than the values shown.

	A	B	C	D	E
1	Money Collected For Field Trip				
2					
3	Name	Turned In	Still Due		
4	Joey		3.25		
5	Billy		3.25		
6	Amber	3.25	0		
7	Andy		3.25		
8	Roni	3.25	0		
9	Thelma	3.25	0		
10	Eddy		3.25		
11	Carol	3.25	0		
12	Cathy	3.25	0		
13	Danny		3.25		
14	Ray		3.25		
15	Tracy	3.25	0		
16	Elly	3.25	0		
17	Denise	3.25	0		
18	Eddy R.		3.25		
19	Jimmy		3.25		
20	Jessica	3.25	0		
21	Laura	3.25	0		
22	April	3.25	0		
23					
24	Total	$35.75	$26.00		
25					

When Eddy turns in his money, simply type the value in cell B10; the formulas in C10, B24, and C24 will all update, as shown in Figure 6.

Figure 6

Formulas update automatically when any cell associated with them changes

	A	B	C	D	
1	**Money Collected For Field Trip**				
2					
3	**Name**	**Turned In**	**Still Due**		
4	Joey		3.25		
5	Billy		3.25		
6	Amber	3.25	0		
7	Andy		3.25		
8	Roni	3.25	0		
9	Thelma	3.25	0		
10	Eddy	3.25	0		
11	Carol	3.25	0		
12	Cathy	3.25	0		
13	Danny		3.25		
14	Ray		3.25		
15	Tracy	3.25	0		
16	Elly	3.25	0		
17	Denise	3.25	0		
18	Eddy R.		3.25		
19	Jimmy		3.25		
20	Jessica	3.25	0		
21	Laura	3.25	0		
22	April	3.25	0		
23					
24	**Total**	$39.00	$22.75		

The ability to recalculate was the original purpose for the electronic spreadsheet. You can set up formulas to calculate grades, absences, and tardies. There are over 400 functions available in Excel that make it handy for use in accounting, science, engineering, and in the classroom.

Excel also comes with a host of tools to make it easier to wrangle data. If you need to alphabetize a list, just use the Sort command. It takes one click to turn Figure 7 into a sorted list.

Figure 7

Data can be sorted alphabetically by name

	A	B	C	D	E
1	**Money Collected For Field Trip**				
2					
3	**Name**	**Turned In**	**Still Due**		
4	Amber	3.25	0		
5	Andy		3.25		
6	April	3.25	0		
7	Billy		3.25		
8	Carol	3.25	0		
9	Cathy	3.25	0		
10	Danny		3.25		
11	Denise	3.25	0		
12	Eddy	3.25	0		
13	Eddy R.		3.25		
14	Elly	3.25	0		
15	Jessica	3.25	0		
16	Jimmy		3.25		
17	Joey		3.25		
18	Laura	3.25	0		
19	Ray		3.25		
20	Roni	3.25	0		
21	Thelma	3.25	0		
22	Tracy	3.25	0		
23					
24	**Total**	$39.00	$22.75		

Excel can create charts from your data: bar charts, column charts, surface charts, pie charts and more. You can insert clipart or digital photos of your students on the worksheet.

The examples in this book will walk you through doing all of these tasks. The book will cover things to make your life much easier. However, even after working through the 25 examples, there will still be far more power in Excel left for you to discover.

1

Chapter 1 – Calculation Basics

Opportunity

Excel is great at doing math. When Dan Bricklin conceived of the first spreadsheet in 1978, he envisioned a calculator where you could set up a math problem, but then scroll backwards in time and change the terms in the problem to see a new answer. Along with Bob Frankston, he developed VisiCalc – a Visible Calculator. Since VisiCalc in 1979, all spreadsheets have been able to calculate.

Solution and Overview

This section will teach you the basic math operators and functions available for demonstrating classroom math.

There are also at least three common methods of entering formulas. In the first three examples below, you will learn the three methods of entering formulas. You can choose whichever method is the easiest for you.

Using the Touch-Typing Method (Addition)

Figure 8 shows a story problem. You want to enter a formula in cell B6 that will add cells B4 and B5.

Figure 8

Solving an addition story problem in Excel with touch-typing

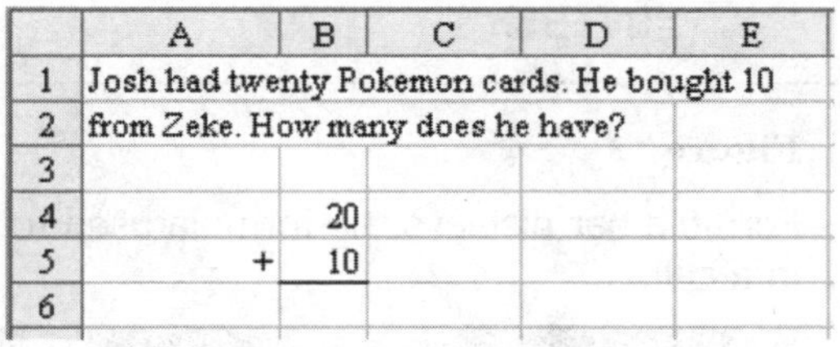

	A	B	C	D	E
1	Josh had twenty Pokemon cards. He bought 10				
2	from Zeke. How many does he have?				
3					
4		20			
5	+	10			
6					

1. With the mouse, single click in cell B6 to move the cellpointer to that cell. Every formula must start with an equals sign, so type the equals sign to start entering the formula.

Figure 9

Always start a formula with an equals sign.

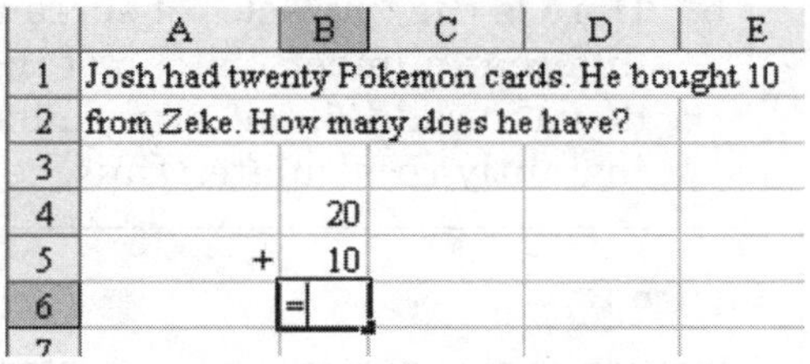

	A	B	C	D	E
1	Josh had twenty Pokemon cards. He bought 10				
2	from Zeke. How many does he have?				
3					
4		20			
5	+	10			
6		=			
7					

1

2. In this example, you will use the touch-typing method of entering the formula. Without typing any spaces, finish typing the formula as **B4+B5**. When your screen looks like Figure 10, type the Enter key on the keyboard.

Figure 10

Using a formula to add values in two cells

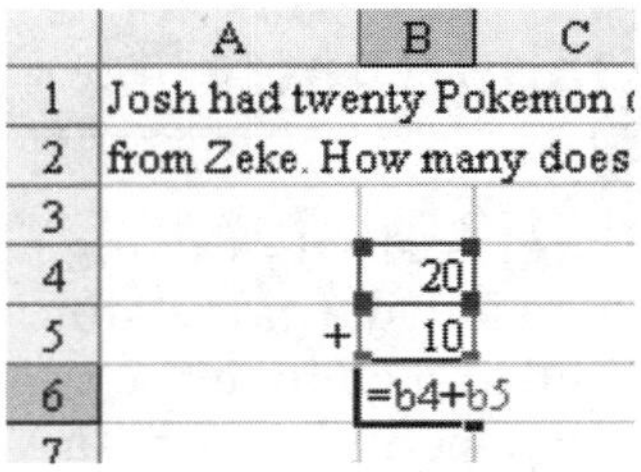

	A	B	C
1	Josh had twenty Pokemon		
2	from Zeke. How many does		
3			
4		20	
5	+	10	
6		=b4+b5	
7			

3. After you type Enter, Excel will calculate that the sum is 30. Excel will also move the cellpointer down one cell to B7.

Figure 11

Pointer automatically moves down one cell when calculation is done.

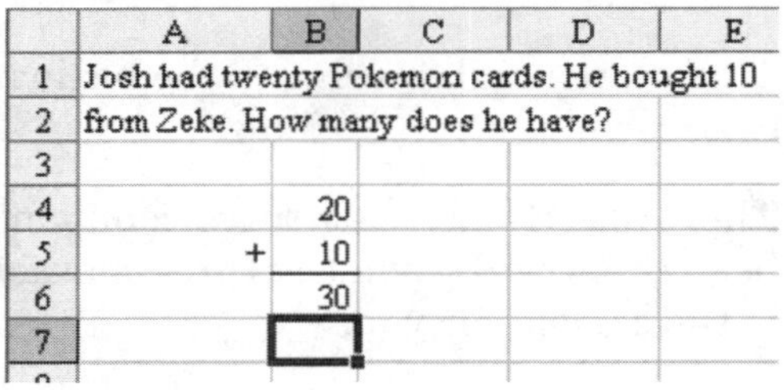

	A	B	C	D	E
1	Josh had twenty Pokemon cards. He bought 10				
2	from Zeke. How many does he have?				
3					
4		20			
5	+	10			
6		30			
7					

4. Press the Up-Arrow 1 time to move the cellpointer back to cell B6. When B6 is selected, look at the formula bar just above the spreadsheet. Although the spreadsheet shows a value of 30 in the cell, the formula bar reveals that this cell really contains a formula of =B4+B5.

Figure 12

Formula bar displays the formula used to derive value in a cell.

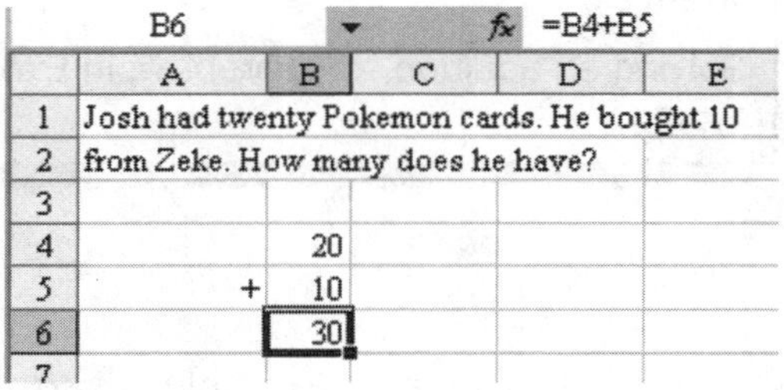

B6 ▼ *fx* =B4+B5

	A	B	C	D	E
1	Josh had twenty Pokemon cards. He bought 10				
2	from Zeke. How many does he have?				
3					
4		20			
5	+	10			
6		30			
7					

5. Here is the "miracle" of spreadsheets. Move the cellpointer up to cell B4 and type a different number instead of the 20. Type 200, type Enter. The cellpointer will move down to cell B5, but all formulas that reference B4 in the entire worksheet would instantly recalculate. Thus, cell B6 becomes 210.

Figure 13

A formula's value automatically updates when any cells referenced in that formula change.

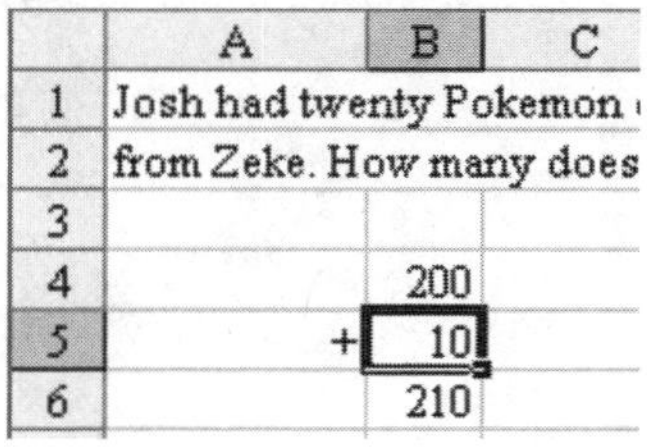

	A	B	C
1	Josh had twenty Pokemon		
2	from Zeke. How many does		
3			
4		200	
5	+	10	
6		210	

Using the Mouse Method (Subtraction)

Figure 14 shows a subtraction story problem. In this case, you will want to set up a formula that subtracts B5 from B4. In this example, you will use the mouse for entering parts of the formula.

1

1. As before, you will have to type the equals sign on the keyboard to start the formula.

Figure 14			A	B	C	D
		1	Athena fed 50 cats. 30 of them got full.			
Formulas start with an equals sign		2	How many are still eating?			
		3				
		4		50		
		5		-	30	
		6		=		
		7				

2. After typing the equals sign, use the mouse to touch cell B4. Because you are in formula entry mode, the formula in cell B6 automatically types B4 for you.

Figure 15	COUNTA ▼ ✗ ✓ ƒx =B4
	A	B	C	D
Solving a subtraction problem in Excel using the mouse	1	Athena fed 50 cats. 30 of them got full.
	2	How many are still eating?
	3	
	4	50
	5	- 30
	6	=B4
	7	

3. Now, back on the keyboard, type the minus sign. Notice that when you type the minus sign, the flashing dots around B4 become a solid blue color. Excel is waiting for you to touch another cell with the mouse.

Figure 16	
	50
A solid blue box indicates that Excel is waiting for your input.	- 30
	=B4-

 Tip:

If your keyboard has a numeric keypad, the upper right keys on the keypad will let you type the common operator keys without using the Shift key.

4. With the mouse, touch the 30 in cell B5. Excel will enter B5 in the formula.

Figure 17	COUNTA ▼ ✗ ✓ ƒx =B4-B5
	A	B	C	D
Excel automatically enters the cell location you click on with the mouse.	1	Athena fed 50 cats. 30 of them got full.
	2	How many are still eating?
	3	
	4	50
	5	- 30
	6	=B4-B5
	7	

1

5. You can now type the Enter key to have Excel calculate the result.

Figure 18

Excel calculates the result and automatically moves the cursor down one cell.

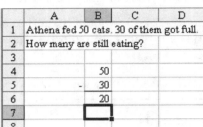

	A	B	C	D
1	Athena fed 50 cats. 30 of them got full.			
2	How many are still eating?			
3				
4		50		
5	-	30		
6		20		
7				

If you are comfortable using the mouse, this technique of entering formulas is fairly quick and easy

Using the Arrow Key Method (Addition and Subtraction)

The next story problem requires both addition and subtraction. The arrow key method was introduced in 1981 by Lotus 1-2-3. The method became very popular for accountants who hated typing obscure cell references like B4 and AJ62. This was before computers typically had a mouse (the first Macintosh didn't come out until late 1983).

1. As shown in the image below, start by typing an equals sign in cell B7.

Figure 19

Solving a subtraction problem in Excel using the arrow keys

	A	B	C	D
1	There were two ducks at a pond. Three			
2	ducks joined and two left. How many			
3	are left?			
4		2		
5	+	3		
6	-	2		
7		=		

2. Next, using the arrow keys on your keyboard, type the Up-Arrow key three times. After the first press of the Up-Arrow key, the screen will think that you want to start your formula as =B6.

Figure 20

Screen after pressing Up-Arrow key once

2a. That is OK. Ignore the screen and type the Up-Arrow key a second time. Now the screen thinks that you must want to start your formula with =B5.

Figure 21

Screen after pressing Up-Arrow key twice

2b. Again, ignore what is on the screen and type the Up-Arrow key one more time. Now the screen suggests that your formula should start with **=B4**. This is correct.

Figure 22		A	B	C	D
	1	There were two ducks at a pond. Three			
Screen after pressing Up-Arrow key three times	2	ducks joined and two left. How many			
	3	are left?			
	4		2		
	5	+	3		
	6	-	2		
	7		=B4		

3. The next part is a little tricky. In your formula, you want to add B5 to the formula. Type the plus sign on your keyboard. This tells Excel that you are accepting the B4 portion of the formula and that you are ready to enter another cell. Instead of a flashing box around B4, you now have a solid box around B4. Here is the tricky part: as soon as you type the plus sign, Excel returns the focus back to the original cell location of B7.

Figure 23		COUNTA	▾ ✕ ✓ *fx*	=B4+	
		A	B	C	D
The flashing box turns solid blue when you accept a portion	1	There were two ducks at a pond. Three			
of the formula by typing the plus sign	2	ducks joined and two left. How many			
	3	are left?			
	4		2		
	5	+	3		
	6	-	2		
	7		=B4+		
	8				

4. You want to point to the 3 in cell B5 now. Many people trying this method for the first time think that they should type the Down-Arrow to move down from B4. This is not correct. You actually have to type the Up-Arrow twice to move up from cell B7 to B5. Type the Up-Arrow twice and Excel will propose a formula of **=B4+B5**.

Figure 24	
Excel proposes the next element in the formula	

5. Next, type the minus sign on the keyboard. Excel will return the focus to the original location of B7. Press the Up-Arrow one time to subtract B6 from the formula.

Figure 25	
Selecting the next element	

6. Type Enter and Excel will calculate an answer of 3. Move the cellpointer back to B7 to examine the formula in the formula bar.

1

Figure 26
Completed formula

	B7	▼		*fx*	=B4+B5-B6
	A	B	C	D	E
1	There were two ducks at a pond. Three				
2	ducks joined and two left. How many				
3	are left?				
4		2			
5	+	3			
6	-	2			
7		3			
8					

Now that you have learned the three methods for entering formulas, you can use whichever method suits you the best. In the remaining sections of this chapter, you will see the formulas to use for various mathematical operations. You can use whichever method you prefer for entering these formulas.

 Note:

Once you get used to the arrow key method, it is the absolute fastest way to enter formulas. The act of moving your hands from the keyboard to the mouse then back to the keyboard is relatively slow. The process to enter the formula above requires only nine keystrokes, and many of those are repetitive strokes of the Up-Arrow.

Entering Multiplication Problems

Problems requiring multiplication use the Asterisk key for the multiplication operator. Type an asterisk using either the Shift-8 key, or the Asterisk key on the numeric keypad. Yes – it would be a lot easier if they used the X key for multiplication, but then we could get confused whether the X was referencing a cell location, as in X2, or was meant to multiply by 2.

Figure 27
Multiplication problems use an asterisk

	B7	▼		*fx*	=B5*B6
	A	B	C	D	
1	There are twelve cookies in a				
2	package. How many are in				
3	five packages?				
4					
5		12			
6	x	5			
7		60			
8					

Entering Division Problems

There are two slash signs on the keyboard. File paths in Windows typically require the backslash located above the Enter key. Luckily, division problems require the forward slash located on the same key as the question mark. The image on the following page shows a division problem.

Figure 28

Division problems use a forward slash

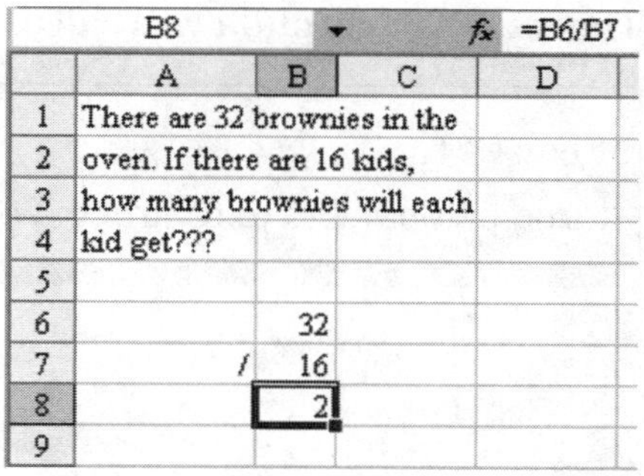

B8			f_x =B6/B7
	A	B	C	D
1	There are 32 brownies in the			
2	oven. If there are 16 kids,			
3	how many brownies will each			
4	kid get???			
5				
6		32		
7	/	16		
8		2		
9				

Entering Fraction Problems

Sometimes Excel expects our students to understand higher mathematical concepts, such as that a fraction is really a division problem. That is, one-ninth is actually one divided by nine. For fractions in Excel, enter the numerator, the forward slash, and the denominator, as seen in the formula bar in Figure 29.

Figure 29

Expressing fractions as division problems

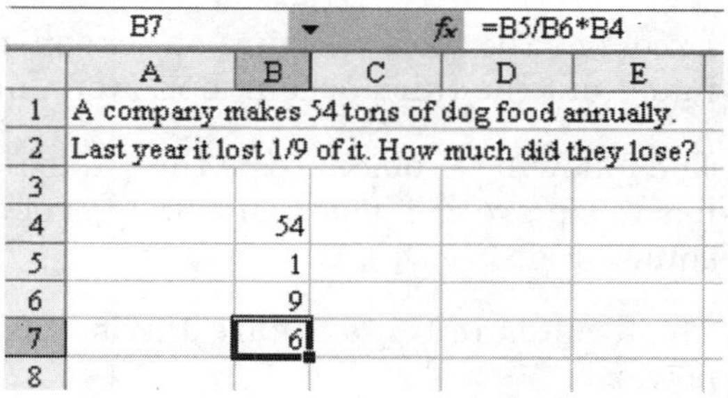

B7			f_x =B5/B6*B4	
	A	B	C	D	E
1	A company makes 54 tons of dog food annually.				
2	Last year it lost 1/9 of it. How much did they lose?				
3					
4		54			
5		1			
6		9			
7		6			
8					

Using Parentheses to Control the Order of Operations

The formula for the next problem produces an incorrect result. If three club members are going to split 12 candy bars, they should each get four candy bars instead of eight.

Figure 30

The order of operations causes a wrong result for this formula

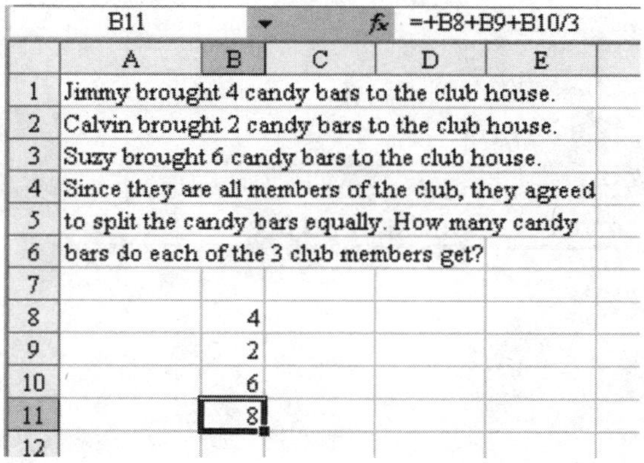

B11			f_x =+B8+B9+B10/3	
	A	B	C	D	E
1	Jimmy brought 4 candy bars to the club house.				
2	Calvin brought 2 candy bars to the club house.				
3	Suzy brought 6 candy bars to the club house.				
4	Since they are all members of the club, they agreed				
5	to split the candy bars equally. How many candy				
6	bars do each of the 3 club members get?				
7					
8		4			
9		2			
10		6			
11		8			
12					

You need to understand Excel's order of operations. In a formula, Excel performs calculations in this order:

1. Unary Minus
2. Exponents
3. Division and Multiplication, left-to-right
4. Addition and Subtraction, left-to-right

Thus, Excel will first divide B10 by 3 to get an intermediate result of 2. It will then add B8 to B9 to get 6. Finally, Excel will add the 6 and the 2 to get 8. For problems that don't follow the Associative law of mathematics, you will want your students to enter parentheses to override Excel's default order of operations.

1

The following formula will calculate the correct result: =(B8+B9+B10)/3

Figure 31

Using parentheses to control the order of operations

	B11	▼		fx	=(B8+B9+B10)/3	
	A	B	C	D	E	
1	Jimmy brought 4 candy bars to the club house.					
2	Calvin brought 2 candy bars to the club house.					
3	Suzy brought 6 candy bars to the club house.					
4	Since they are all members of the club, they agreed					
5	to split the candy bars equally. How many candy					
6	bars do each of the 3 club members get?					
7						
8		4				
9		2				
10		6				
11		4				
12						

Calculating Squares, Cubes, Square Roots, Cube Roots

Excel has the tools to figure out exponents and roots. However, it might be a bit confusing to figure out the third or fourth root of a number.

The following problem tests the student's knowledge of the Pythagorean theorem. The student has to square the length of both legs of a right triangle, sum the squares, and then take the square root.

The formula in C6 to square 122 is =B6^2. In Excel, the carat (^) is used to raise a number to a power.

Figure 32

Using a carat to raise a number to a power

	C6	▼		fx	=B6^2		
	A	B	C	D	E	F	
1	It is 122 miles from B to A. It is 60 miles						
2	from B to C. How far is from A directly						
3	to C?						
4							
5			Squares				
6		122	14884				
7		60	3600	A			
8	Sum of Squares:						
9	Square Root:						
10							
11							
12							
13							
14							
15							
16				B		C	
17							

Tip:

You can type a carat by holding down the Shift key and pressing 6.

Look at Figure 33. The formula in C7 is =B7^2. The formula in C8 is =C6+C7. In cell C9, you want to take the square root of cell C8. There are two ways to do this.

First, Excel offers a built in function to calculate square roots.

1. Type **=SQRT** followed by an open parentheses to start the function.

2. Using the mouse, touch cell C8. Type the closing parentheses.

This formula suggests that it is about 136 miles from A to C.

	Figure 33
	Taking a square root using SQRT

	C9			fx	=SQRT(C8)
	A	B	C	D	E
1	It is 122 miles from B to A. It is 60 miles				
2	from B to C. How far is from A directly				
3	to C?				
4					
5			Squares		
6		122	14884		
7		60	3600	A	
8	Sum of Squares:		18484		
9	Square Root:		135.9559		
10					

At some point in the future, much later than eighth grade, your students may learn that taking the square root of a number is the same as raising the number to the one-half (1/2) power.

Thus, the alternate formula for C9 is =C8^(1/2), as shown in Figure 34.

	Figure 34
	Taking a square root using exponents

	C9			fx	=C8^(1/2)
	A	B	C	D	
1	It is 122 miles from B to A. It is 60 miles				
2	from B to C. How far is from A directly				
3	to C?				
4					
5			Squares		
6		122	14884		
7		60	3600	A	
8	Sum of Squares:		18484		
9	Square Root:		135.9559		
10					

In the next problem, the student is to determine the volume of a cube that is 25 feet on each side. The volume is the length raised to the third power. Again, the carat is used for an exponent.

To raise B6 to the third power, use =B6^3.

	Figure 35
	Raising to the third power using a carat

	B7			fx	=B6^3
	A	B	C	D	
1	Ralph rents a storage space that is 25				
2	feet tall, 25 feet wide, and 25 feet long.				
3	How many cubic feet of cookies can				
4	he store in the space?				
5					
6		25			
7		15625			
8					
9					

The converse problem is trickier. In the following problem, the student would have to take the cube root of 3375. Excel does not offer a Cube Root function like the SQRT function for square roots.

Thus, your student is going to have to use the alternative form of =B5^(1/3) in order to take a cube root. This may be confusing for the student, but it is easier than figuring out cube roots by hand!

	Figure 36
	Taking a cube root using a carat and a fraction

	B6			fx	=B5^(1/3)
	A	B	C	D	
1	A customer needs to store				
2	3375 cubic feet of oatmeal.				
3	How large of a cube does he need?				
4					
5		3375			
6		15			
7					

1

Adding a Column of Numbers

Consider the problem in the next image. You might be tempted to use a very long formula such as =B5+B6+B7+B8+B9+B10+B11 to calculate the total.

Figure 37

Adding a column of numbers

	A	B	C	D	E
1	Wendy Woods had not done very well in her				
2	astronomy classes. Her grades were 72, 81, 70, 79,				
3	75, 84, and 97. What are her total points?				
4					
5		72			
6		81			
7		70			
8		79			
9		75			
10		84			
11		97			
12					

There is a much faster way. Excel offers a SUM function for totaling several cells. Because summing a column of numbers is such a popular task among accountants, Microsoft gave us a shortcut key to enter sums.

1. Place the cellpointer in cell B12. Look on the Standard toolbar for a Greek letter Sigma. This is the AutoSum button. See Figure 38 below.

Figure 38

AutoSum button shortcut for summing cells

2. With the cellpointer in B12, press the AutoSum button. Excel will use its Intellisense and propose a formula to sum the range from B5:B11. The program even draws a flashing box around the range that it is proposing to sum.

Figure 39

Proposed range to sum

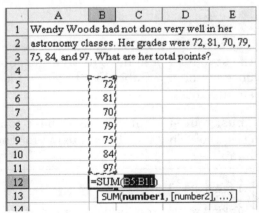

3. This is the correct range, so simply type Enter to sum this column.

| Figure 40 | | B12 | ▼ | *fx* =SUM(B5:B11) |
| Summing of a column of numbers | | | | |

	A	B	C	D	E
1	Wendy Woods had not done very well in her				
2	astronomy classes. Her grades were 72, 81, 70, 79,				
3	75, 84, and 97. What are her total points?				
4					
5		72			
6		81			
7		70			
8		79			
9		75			
10		84			
11		97			
12		558			
13					

Calculating an Average

In the next problem, you need to figure out the Average of a column of numbers.

| Figure 41 |
| Taking the average of a column of numbers |

	A	B	C	D	E
1	Wendy Woods had not done very well in her				
2	astronomy classes. Her grades were 72, 81, 70, 79,				
3	75, 84, and 97. What is her average score?				
4					
5		72			
6		81			
7		70			
8		79			
9		75			
10		84			
11		97			
12					

Take a look at the AutoSum button in Figure 42. To the right of the button is a dropdown-Arrow. This dropdown-Arrow will allow you to quickly enter formulas that will let you Average, Count, and find the smallest or largest value.

Put the cellpointer in B12. Select the dropdown arrow next to the AutoSum button and choose Average.

| Figure 42 |
| Selecting Average from the AutoSum dropdown menu |

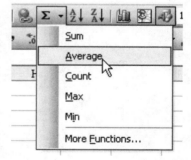

The result: Excel will enter a formula using the AVERAGE function to calculate the average.

1

Figure 43

Average of a column of numbers

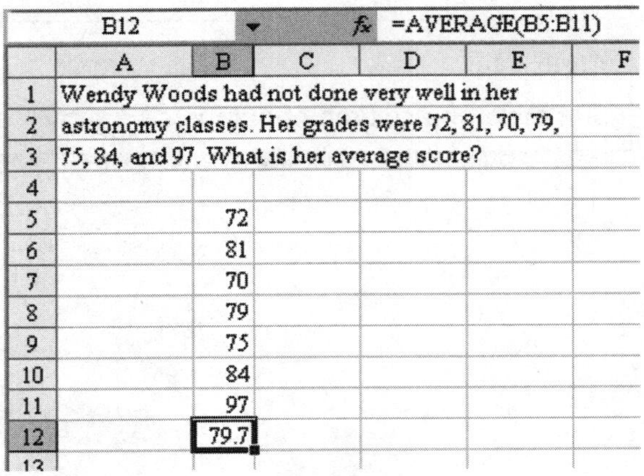

B12		▼		f_x =AVERAGE(B5:B11)		
	A	B	C	D	E	F
1	Wendy Woods had not done very well in her					
2	astronomy classes. Her grades were 72, 81, 70, 79,					
3	75, 84, and 97. What is her average score?					
4						
5		72				
6		81				
7		70				
8		79				
9		75				
10		84				
11		97				
12		79.7				
13						

Chapter 2 – Multiplication Tables

Opportunity

My classic example for demonstrating the various types of mixed references is to create a multiplication table. Although you probably have access to a multiplication table that you can photocopy, this exercise will demonstrate both the AutoFill option and how to use mixed cell references.

Solution and Overview

You will use some efficient tools to create the multiplication table. AutoFill lets you type the first few cells in a series and then extend the series. Transpose lets you turn a range on its side. Finally, you will build one formula that handles the entire multiplication table.

Creating the Solution

Start with a blank Excel workbook. Leave cell A1 blank.

Using the Fill Handle to Extend a Series

In cells A2 and A3, type the numbers "1" and "2". Select a range containing both cells. In the lower right corner of the selection, there is a square dot known as the Fill Handle. With the mouse, grab the fill handle and drag down to row 13.

Figure 44

Selecting the fill handle

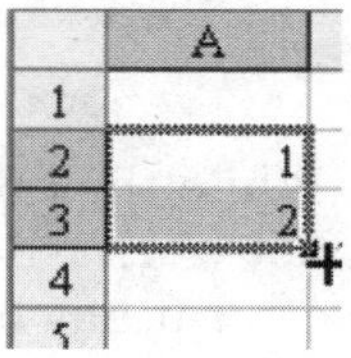

As you drag, a tooltip appears showing the numbers that will be entered in the last cell. When you get to row 13, the tooltip indicates that the series will extend to 12. Release the mouse button to enter 1 through 12 in the cells.

Copying a Range on its Side

After using the fill handle, the range of A2:A13 will be selected. Use Ctrl+C to copy that range. Move to cell B1.

From the menu, select Edit – Paste Special. In the Paste Special dialog box, choose the checkbox for Transpose. The process of transposing will turn data that goes down a column to data that goes across a row.

Figure 45

Transposing a column into a row

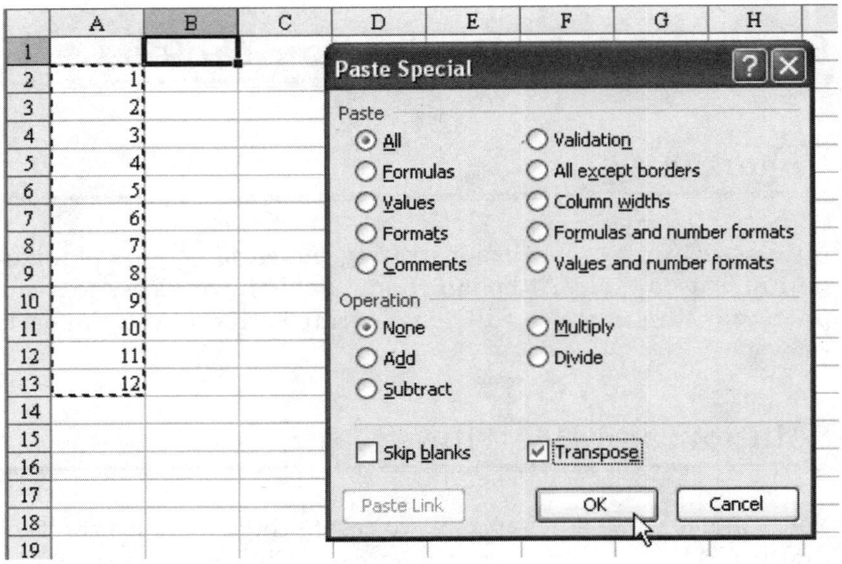

Entering a Single Formula for Many Cells

With a little thought, you can usually write one formula that can be copied to many cells. If you think about the formula that is needed to populate the interior of the multiplication table, it can be expressed this way: "For any cell, multiply the number found in row 1 above the cell with the number found in column A to the left of the cell."

One such formula would be =C1*A5, as shown in cell C5.

Figure 46

Formula multiplying two cells

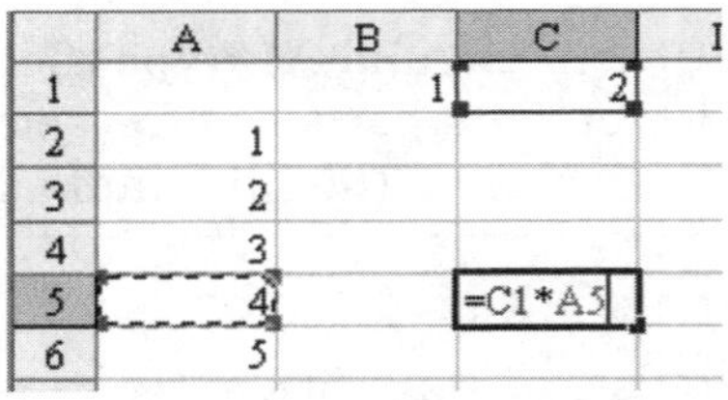

While the preceding formula will work just fine in cell C5, it will not work when you copy the formula to any other cell in the table. Figure 47 shows the formula after it has been copied to D6. The reference that used to point to C1 is now pointing to D2. The reference that used to point to A5 is now pointing to B6. This behavior is called relative references and it is by design in Excel.

Figure 47

Relative references

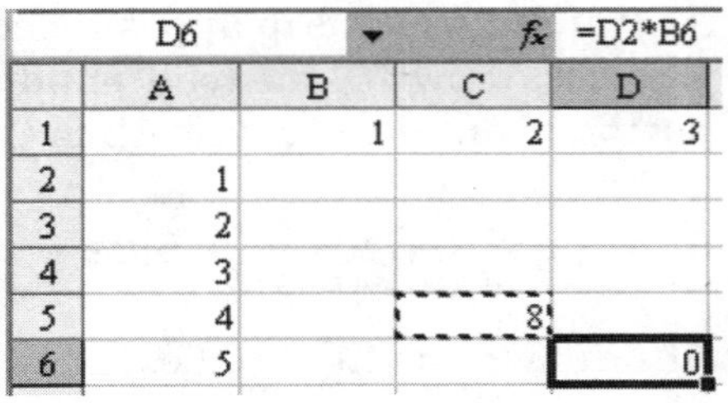

If you change C1 to $C$1, this is called an absolute reference. When you copy a formula with this reference, the formula will always point to cell C1. The dollar signs ($) before C and 1 ensure that neither the C nor the 1 will change as the formula is copied to other cells.

2

Sometimes, you need a reference that is partially absolute. This is called a mixed reference and has only a single dollar sign.

If you place the dollar sign before the column letter, then the column letter will be fixed but the row number will change as you copy the formula down the rows. In our current example, the portion of the formula pointing at column A would need a dollar sign before the A.

If you place the dollar sign before the row number, then the row number will be fixed, but the column letter will change as you copy the formula across a range. In our current example, the portion of the formula pointing at row 1 would need a dollar sign before the 1.

Move the cellpointer to cell B2. While holding down the Shift key, use the Down- and Right-Arrow keys to select the range of B2:M13.

Any formula that you type will start to appear in cell B2. Type =B$1*$A2. Instead of hitting Enter by itself, type Ctrl+Enter to put a similar formula in the entire selected range.

Figure 48

Mixed references

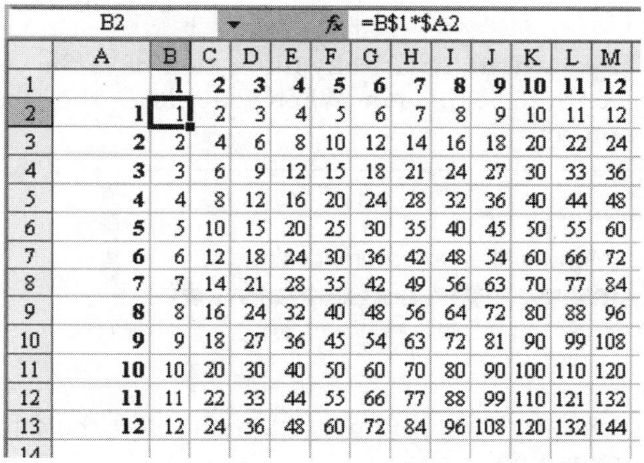

	B2				fx	=B$1*$A2							
	A	B	C	D	E	F	G	H	I	J	K	L	M
1		1	2	3	4	5	6	7	8	9	10	11	12
2	1	1	2	3	4	5	6	7	8	9	10	11	12
3	2	2	4	6	8	10	12	14	16	18	20	22	24
4	3	3	6	9	12	15	18	21	24	27	30	33	36
5	4	4	8	12	16	20	24	28	32	36	40	44	48
6	5	5	10	15	20	25	30	35	40	45	50	55	60
7	6	6	12	18	24	30	36	42	48	54	60	66	72
8	7	7	14	21	28	35	42	49	56	63	70	77	84
9	8	8	16	24	32	40	48	56	64	72	80	88	96
10	9	9	18	27	36	45	54	63	72	81	90	99	108
11	10	10	20	30	40	50	60	70	80	90	100	110	120
12	11	11	22	33	44	55	66	77	88	99	110	121	132
13	12	12	24	36	48	60	72	84	96	108	120	132	144
14													

Using the Application

Print the sheet out and allow your students to study from it.

Excel Details

Simplifying Dollar Sign Entry in Absolute and Mixed References

The process of entering the dollar signs in a reference can be simplified by using the F4 key. As you are entering the formula, pressing F4 immediately after typing the reference will change the reference from relative to absolute; that is, A2 would change to $A$2. Press F4 again to change to a mixed reference where only the row is held constant – A$2. Press F4 again to change to a reference where only the column is fixed – $A2. Press F4 again to toggle back to the relative reference of A2.

Thus, the shortcut for entering the formula in B2 is as follows.

Type an equals sign. Type the Up-Arrow to move to B1. Press F4 twice to lock just the row. Type the Asterisk key on the numeric keypad. Type the Left-Arrow to move to A2. Type the F4 key three times to lock just the column number.

More Cool Fill Handle Tricks

At the start of this chapter, you used the fill handle to extend a series starting with 1, 2. The fill handle can automatically enter many types of data in a range of cells.

Type "Sep" into a cell. Select the cell. Click on the fill handle and drag down or to the right.

Figure 49

Dragging the fill handle

Excel will automatically fill in months of the year. As you drag, a tooltip will indicate the last month to be filled in. When you release the mouse button, the selected number of months will appear.

Figure 50

Months filled in automatically

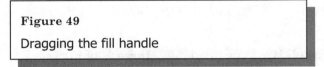

Type "1st Period" into a cell, then select the cell and drag the fill handle; Excel will type the remaining periods.

Figure 51

Class periods filled in automatically

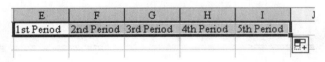

There is a neat trick with days or dates. If you type "Monday" into a cell and drag the fill handle, you will get the days of the week.

Figure 52

Days of the week filled in automatically

As a teacher, though, try this trick. Type "Monday" into a cell. Select the cell. Right-click the fill handle and drag. Initially, the tooltip shows Tuesday, Wednesday, Thursday, Friday, Saturday, Sunday, etc. However, when you release the mouse pointer, you are given a menu. Choose Fill Weekdays from the menu.

Figure 53

Selecting Weekdays from Fill dropdown menu

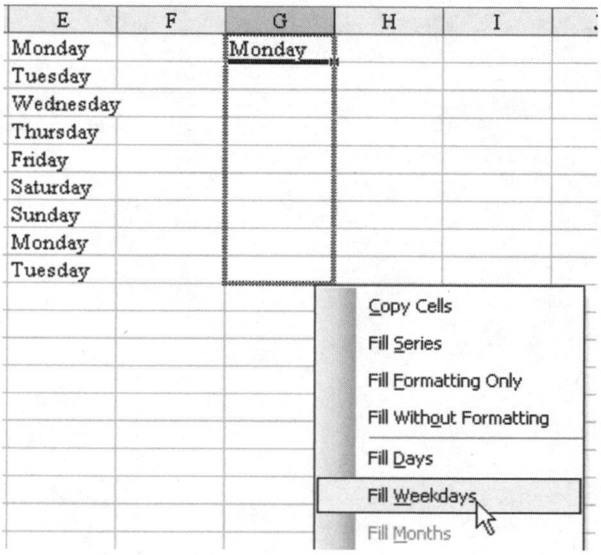

2

Instead of giving you the days of the week, Excel will repeat Monday through Friday.

Figure 54

Weekdays filled in automatically

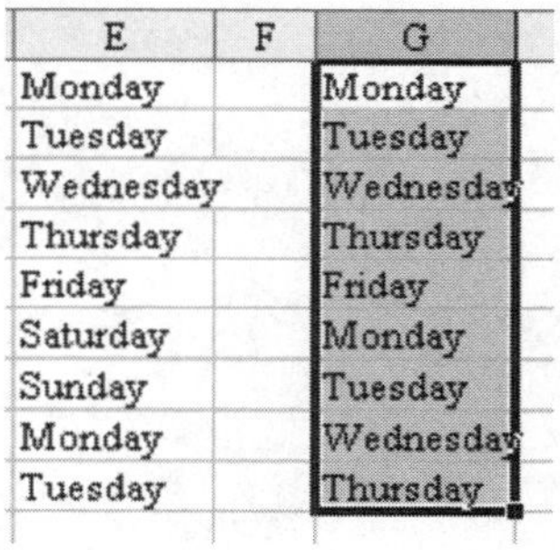

The right-click and drag trick for the fill handle also works with dates.

Figure 55

Dates filled in automatically

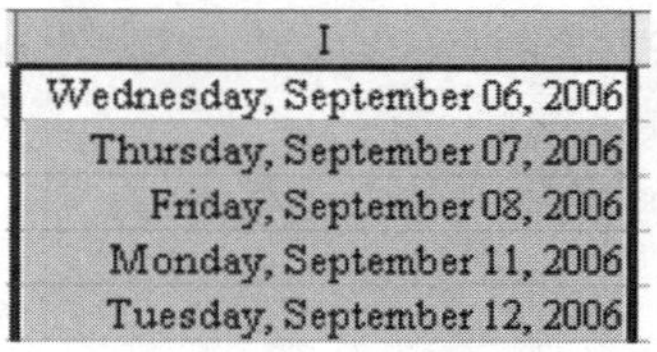

2

Chapter 3 – Calculating with Times

Opportunity

In gym class, students run a 400-yard dash once a week. Times are recorded in Excel. You would like to determine the total time for the class in order to see net improvement.

Although you have 15 students who recorded times of about one minute and 50 seconds each, the total formula shows a time of 2 minutes and 23 seconds, which is clearly wrong. Does Excel not handle times correctly?

3

		B20		▼	*fx*	=SUM(B4:B18)

Figure 56

Adding times in Excel requires proper formatting

	A	B	C	D	E
1	Quarter Mile Times				
2					
3	Student	9/3	9/10	9/17	
4	Eleanor	1:25	1:24	1:21	
5	Alicia	1:37	1:34	1:30	
6	Kathleen	1:35	1:32	1:30	
7	Peter	1:59	1:56	1:54	
8	Marian	1:46	1:44	1:42	
9	Josh	1:37	1:34	1:30	
10	Jonathan	2:00	1:59	1:55	
11	Gerald	1:32	1:29	1:28	
12	Zeke	1:48	1:46	1:43	
13	Richard	1:32	1:28	1:25	
14	Harriet	1:50	1:46	1:43	
15	Cassie	1:48	1:47	1:47	
16	Jason	2:02	1:59	1:58	
17	April	1:48	1:46	1:43	
18	Jesse	2:04	2:01	1:58	
19					
20	Total	2:23	1:45	1:07	

Solution and Overview

Dates and Times in Excel

Excel stores all dates as a number representing the number of elapsed days since 1900 (or 1904 on a Macintosh). Although the numeric formatting makes the value in the cell appear as a date, the value really stored in the cell is a strange number such as 38,964 for September 4, 2006.

Try it – enter a number in the range of 38,000 to 39,000 in a cell. Then use Format – Cells and choose a date format. The number will convert to a recent date.

Excel carries this analogy forward and stores times as a decimal portion of a day. Six hours is the same as 0.25. Enter 0.25 in a cell and use Format Cells to choose a time format. The cell will change to 6:00 AM.

This method allows Excel to do some excellent calculations with dates. You can figure out the number of days between two dates or total a series of hours.

There are some gotchas, though, that can trip you up. Most often, errors come about from one of three formatting problems:

- The result is not formatted properly
- The result is a time that exceeds 24 hours and is converted to a date and time
- The time looks like minutes and seconds, but Excel is storing hours and minutes

3

How Many Days Until Winter Break?

This should be a simple question. Enter the first day of winter break in cell A2. Enter =TODAY() in cell A1. The formula for A3 is =A2-A1. Excel gives a bizarre answer of April 17, 1900.

Figure 57

Subtracting dates gives the right answer but in the wrong format

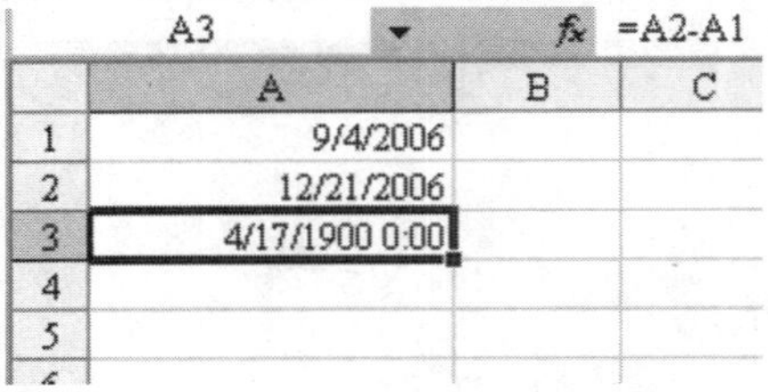

	A	B	C
1	9/4/2006		
2	12/21/2006		
3	4/17/1900 0:00		
4			
5			

A3   *fx* =A2-A1

There are 108 days from now until break. Because you are doing math with dates, Excel automatically formats the answer as a date. The number 108 corresponds to April 17, 1900. To convert the worksheet to a useful answer, select cell A3. Select Format Cells and format the answer as a number with zero decimal places.

Figure 58

Apply a number format to reveal the correct answer

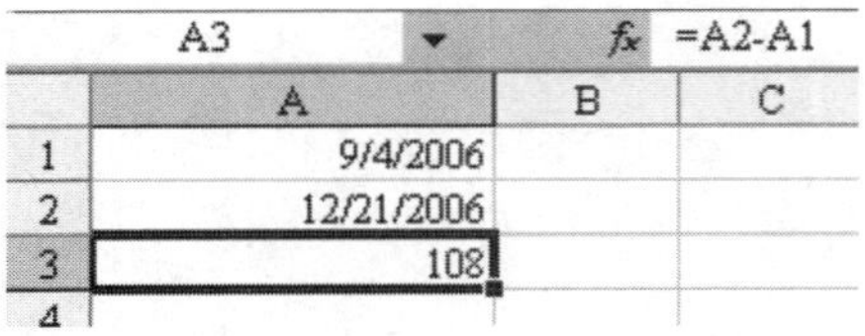

	A	B	C
1	9/4/2006		
2	12/21/2006		
3	108		
4			

A3   *fx* =A2-A1

How Many Hours Did the Class Read?

Your students are trying to read 300 hours in the first nine weeks. You build this table to track reading hours per student per week. The students add total formulas, but the total in K20 shows that they've only completed 2 hours and 15 minutes.

Figure 59

Adding times to include days requires some secret formatting

	A	B	C	D	E	F	G	H	I	J	K
1	Reading Journey										
2											
3	Student	3-Sep	10-Sep	17-Sep	24-Sep	1-Oct	8-Oct	15-Oct	22-Oct	29-Oct	Total
4	Alicia	3:45	3:45	3:45	3:45	3:45	3:45	3:45	3:45	3:45	9:45
5	April	3:45	3:45	3:45	3:45	3:45	3:45	3:45	3:45	3:45	9:45
6	Cassie	3:45	3:45	3:45	3:45	3:45	3:45	3:45	3:45	3:45	9:45
7	Eleanor	3:45	3:45	3:45	3:45	3:45	3:45	3:45	3:45	3:45	9:45
8	Gerald	3:45	3:45	3:45	3:45	3:45	3:45	3:45	3:45	3:45	9:45
9	Harriet	3:45	3:45	3:45	3:45	3:45	3:45	3:45	3:45	3:45	9:45
10	Jason	3:45	3:45	3:45	3:45	3:45	3:45	3:45	3:45	3:45	9:45
11	Jesse	3:45	3:45	3:45	3:45	3:45	3:45	3:45	3:45	3:45	9:45
12	Jonathan	3:45	3:45	3:45	3:45	3:45	3:45	3:45	3:45	3:45	9:45
13	Josh	3:45	3:45	3:45	3:45	3:45	3:45	3:45	3:45	3:45	9:45
14	Kathleen	3:45	3:45	3:45	3:45	3:45	3:45	3:45	3:45	3:45	9:45
15	Marian	3:45	3:45	3:45	3:45	3:45	3:45	3:45	3:45	3:45	9:45
16	Peter	3:45	3:45	3:45	3:45	3:45	3:45	3:45	3:45	3:45	9:45
17	Richard	3:45	3:45	3:45	3:45	3:45	3:45	3:45	3:45	3:45	9:45
18	Zeke	3:45	3:45	3:45	3:45	3:45	3:45	3:45	3:45	3:45	9:45
19											
20	Total	8:15	8:15	8:15	8:15	8:15	8:15	8:15	8:15	8:15	2:15
21											

Three hours and 45 minutes is 15.6% of a day. Thus, each of those cells above really contains the value of 0.156. The total for each student is 0.156 x 9 or 1.40. Excel treats the value of 1.40 as 1 day, 9 hours, and 45 minutes. Because you are adding times, Excel applied a time format to the totals. The time format says that you would only like to see hours and minutes. Excel leaves off any seconds, and also leaves off any whole days!

There is a secret time format that tells Excel to roll any whole days up into the hours figure. Select the entire range of the table starting in row 4. From the menu, select Format – Cells. First, select a time format such as 13:30. Then, select the Custom choice in the Category box. This will reveal that the custom format for 13:30 is really the formatting code of "h:mm".

Figure 60

The default time format causes the problem

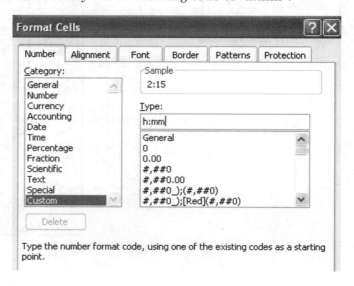

The dialog suggests using one of the existing codes as a starting point. This is a good suggestion. Add square brackets around the "h" in the numeric code.

Figure 61

Adding square brackets around "h" will show total hours

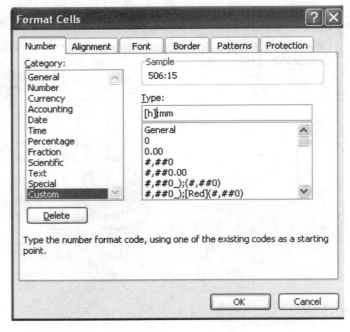

You can see from the sample that the students have read 506 hours this grading period. When you choose OK, chaos will result. All of your totals will be replaced by pound signs (#). This means that the column is not wide enough to display the result.

Figure 62

Total column too narrow to display results

	A	B	C	D	E	F	G	H	I	J	K
1	Reading Journey										
2											
3	Student	3-Sep	10-Sep	17-Sep	24-Sep	1-Oct	8-Oct	15-Oct	22-Oct	29-Oct	Total
4	Alicia	3:45	3:45	3:45	3:45	3:45	3:45	3:45	3:45	3:45	####
5	April	3:45	3:45	3:45	3:45	3:45	3:45	3:45	3:45	3:45	####
6	Cassie	3:45	3:45	3:45	3:45	3:45	3:45	3:45	3:45	3:45	####
7	Eleanor	3:45	3:45	3:45	3:45	3:45	3:45	3:45	3:45	3:45	####
8	Gerald	3:45	3:45	3:45	3:45	3:45	3:45	3:45	3:45	3:45	####
9	Harriet	3:45	3:45	3:45	3:45	3:45	3:45	3:45	3:45	3:45	####
10	Jason	3:45	3:45	3:45	3:45	3:45	3:45	3:45	3:45	3:45	####
11	Jesse	3:45	3:45	3:45	3:45	3:45	3:45	3:45	3:45	3:45	####
12	Jonathan	3:45	3:45	3:45	3:45	3:45	3:45	3:45	3:45	3:45	####
13	Josh	3:45	3:45	3:45	3:45	3:45	3:45	3:45	3:45	3:45	####
14	Kathleen	3:45	3:45	3:45	3:45	3:45	3:45	3:45	3:45	3:45	####
15	Marian	3:45	3:45	3:45	3:45	3:45	3:45	3:45	3:45	3:45	####
16	Peter	3:45	3:45	3:45	3:45	3:45	3:45	3:45	3:45	3:45	####
17	Richard	3:45	3:45	3:45	3:45	3:45	3:45	3:45	3:45	3:45	####
18	Zeke	3:45	3:45	3:45	3:45	3:45	3:45	3:45	3:45	3:45	####
19											
20	Total	56:15	56:15	56:15	56:15	56:15	56:15	56:15	56:15	56:15	####
21											

Select column K. From the menu, choose Format – Column – AutoFit to make the column wide enough to display the data.

Figure 63

Using AutoFit to adjust column width

	A	B	C	D	E	F	G	H	I	J	K
1	Reading Journey										
2											
3	Student	3-Sep	10-Sep	17-Sep	24-Sep	1-Oct	8-Oct	15-Oct	22-Oct	29-Oct	Total
4	Alicia	3:45	3:45	3:45	3:45	3:45	3:45	3:45	3:45	3:45	33:45
5	April	3:45	3:45	3:45	3:45	3:45	3:45	3:45	3:45	3:45	33:45
6	Cassie	3:45	3:45	3:45	3:45	3:45	3:45	3:45	3:45	3:45	33:45
7	Eleanor	3:45	3:45	3:45	3:45	3:45	3:45	3:45	3:45	3:45	33:45
8	Gerald	3:45	3:45	3:45	3:45	3:45	3:45	3:45	3:45	3:45	33:45
9	Harriet	3:45	3:45	3:45	3:45	3:45	3:45	3:45	3:45	3:45	33:45
10	Jason	3:45	3:45	3:45	3:45	3:45	3:45	3:45	3:45	3:45	33:45
11	Jesse	3:45	3:45	3:45	3:45	3:45	3:45	3:45	3:45	3:45	33:45
12	Jonathan	3:45	3:45	3:45	3:45	3:45	3:45	3:45	3:45	3:45	33:45
13	Josh	3:45	3:45	3:45	3:45	3:45	3:45	3:45	3:45	3:45	33:45
14	Kathleen	3:45	3:45	3:45	3:45	3:45	3:45	3:45	3:45	3:45	33:45
15	Marian	3:45	3:45	3:45	3:45	3:45	3:45	3:45	3:45	3:45	33:45
16	Peter	3:45	3:45	3:45	3:45	3:45	3:45	3:45	3:45	3:45	33:45
17	Richard	3:45	3:45	3:45	3:45	3:45	3:45	3:45	3:45	3:45	33:45
18	Zeke	3:45	3:45	3:45	3:45	3:45	3:45	3:45	3:45	3:45	33:45
19											
20	Total	56:15	56:15	56:15	56:15	56:15	56:15	56:15	56:15	56:15	506:15

The Gym Class Problem

At the beginning of the chapter, the gym teacher had a series of times entered and the calculations were not working properly. If you select cell B4 and look in the formula bar, you will see the problem. Although you entered 1:25 in the cell, Excel interpreted this to mean 1 hour and 25 minutes.

Figure 64

Representing minutes and seconds correctly

B4		▼	fx	1:25:00 AM
	A	B	C	D
1	Quarter Mile Times			
2				
3	Student	9/3	9/10	9/17
4	Eleanor	1:25	1:24	1:21
5	Alicia	1:37	1:34	1:30
6	Kathleen	1:35	1:32	1:30
7	Peter	1:59	1:56	1:54
8	Marian	1:46	1:44	1:42

Microsoft would like you to instead enter 0:01:25 to represent 1 minute and 25 seconds. This is fairly annoying. You don't want to have to re-enter all of these values.

There is a cool function called the TIME function. The syntax is =TIME(Hours,Minutes,Seconds). You can strip out the hours from cell B4 with =HOUR(B4). You can strip out the minutes from cell B4 with =MINUTE(B4).

Because Excel has the minutes in the hour position and the seconds in the Minute position, you can solve this by entering =TIME(0,HOUR(B4),MINUTE(B4)) in cell E4. Format the cell as h:mm:ss. Copy the formula down to the other rows and columns.

Figure 65

Copying down the formula to represent minutes and seconds correctly

 Note:

3

Before you delete the wrong numbers in columns B through D, you need to change the formulas in E through G to values. Select those columns and type Ctrl+C to Copy. Then select Edit – Paste Special – Values.

	A	B	C	D	E	F	G
1	Quarter Mile Times						
2							
3	Student	9/3	9/10	9/17			
4	Eleanor	1:25	1:24	1:21	0:01:25	0:01:24	0:01:21
5	Alicia	1:37	1:34	1:30	0:01:37	0:01:34	0:01:30
6	Kathleen	1:35	1:32	1:30	0:01:35	0:01:32	0:01:30
7	Peter	1:59	1:56	1:54	0:01:59	0:01:56	0:01:54
8	Marian	1:46	1:44	1:42	0:01:46	0:01:44	0:01:42
9	Josh	1:37	1:34	1:30	0:01:37	0:01:34	0:01:30
10	Jonathan	2:00	1:59	1:55	0:02:00	0:01:59	0:01:55
11	Gerald	1:32	1:29	1:28	0:01:32	0:01:29	0:01:28
12	Zeke	1:48	1:46	1:43	0:01:48	0:01:46	0:01:43
13	Richard	1:32	1:28	1:25	0:01:32	0:01:28	0:01:25
14	Harriet	1:50	1:46	1:43	0:01:50	0:01:46	0:01:43
15	Cassie	1:48	1:47	1:47	0:01:48	0:01:47	0:01:47
16	Jason	2:02	1:59	1:58	0:02:02	0:01:59	0:01:58
17	April	1:48	1:46	1:43	0:01:48	0:01:46	0:01:43
18	Jesse	2:04	2:01	1:58	0:02:04	0:02:01	0:01:58
19							
20	Total	26:23	25:45	25:07			9/4/2006

You can now safely enter totals and averages to see that the class has managed to shave over a minute off their collective time after a few weeks.

Figure 66

Once the times are entered correctly, you can use any function and get the right result

	A	B	C	D
1	Quarter Mile Times			
2				
3	Student	9/3	9/10	9/17
4	Eleanor	0:01:25	0:01:24	0:01:21
5	Alicia	0:01:37	0:01:34	0:01:30
6	Kathleen	0:01:35	0:01:32	0:01:30
7	Peter	0:01:59	0:01:56	0:01:54
8	Marian	0:01:46	0:01:44	0:01:42
9	Josh	0:01:37	0:01:34	0:01:30
10	Jonathan	0:02:00	0:01:59	0:01:55
11	Gerald	0:01:32	0:01:29	0:01:28
12	Zeke	0:01:48	0:01:46	0:01:43
13	Richard	0:01:32	0:01:28	0:01:25
14	Harriet	0:01:50	0:01:46	0:01:43
15	Cassie	0:01:48	0:01:47	0:01:47
16	Jason	0:02:02	0:01:59	0:01:58
17	April	0:01:48	0:01:46	0:01:43
18	Jesse	0:02:04	0:02:01	0:01:58
19				
20	Total	0:26:23	0:25:45	0:25:07
21	Average	0:01:46	0:01:43	0:01:40

Converting Times to Hours

In the following worksheet, a student is tracking his community service hours. He records a start time and an end time each day. In cell D4, he writes a formula to record how many hours he worked today. The answer given by the spreadsheet is 1:15 AM. Sometimes, Excel seems like a student who just doesn't quite get the concept.

Figure 67

Converting times to hours

D4 fx =C4-B4

	A	B	C	D
1	Community Service Log			
2				
3		Start	End	Hours
4	Monday	2:30 PM	3:45 PM	1:15 AM
5	Tuesday	2:30 PM	3:35 PM	
6	Wednesday	2:30 PM	3:55 PM	
7	Thursday	2:30 PM	4:00 PM	
8	Friday	2:30 PM	3:15 PM	
9				
10				

You might be tempted to use the HOUR function to find the number of hours.

However, this function will capture the whole hours but will throw out any fractional hours.

Figure 68

Using the HOUR function leaves off minutes

D4 fx =HOUR(C4-B4)

	A	B	C	D
1	Community Service Log			
2				
3		Start	End	Hours
4	Monday	2:30 PM	3:45 PM	1.00
5	Tuesday	2:30 PM	3:35 PM	1.00
6	Wednesday	2:30 PM	3:55 PM	1.00
7	Thursday	2:30 PM	4:00 PM	1.00
8	Friday	2:30 PM	3:15 PM	0.00

The solution is to subtract the earlier time from the later time, multiply the result by 24, and format the result as numeric with two decimal places.

Figure 69

Multiply the result by 24 to get a decimal number of hours

D4 fx =24*(C4-B4)

	A	B	C	D
1	Community Service Log			
2				
3		Start	End	Hours
4	Monday	2:30 PM	3:45 PM	1.25
5	Tuesday	2:30 PM	3:35 PM	1.08
6	Wednesday	2:30 PM	3:55 PM	1.42
7	Thursday	2:30 PM	4:00 PM	1.50
8	Friday	2:30 PM	3:15 PM	0.75
9	Total			6.00
10				

3

Chapter 4 - Classroom Libraries

Opportunity

I need help remembering all of the different books I have available for use in my classroom. I can spend hours trying to remember and locate the books I need to use with lesson planning and activity center usage. When ordering classroom books, I often order books already in my library because I have forgotten which books I have there for classroom use. Can Excel help me keep track of my extensive classroom library? Is it possible to use Excel to manage a large list of books?

I have a huge library (over 3,000) of student books that I keep in my classroom for many purposes. I would like to categorize the books I have and to easily access the books for specific lessons and theme planning. For example, if I were going to highlight the author Eric Carle, I'd like to be able to sort my student library by author to list all books authored or illustrated by Eric Carle. Then, I could print off the list and look for all the Eric Carle books in my library. I would also like to type in a key word, such as space, and be able to get a list of all books relating to the topic of space. I know that this would require me to enter all relevant book data, such as author, illustrator, and subject matter or related themes.

Solution and Overview

You will create a database on a worksheet in Excel. The worksheet will be designed to allow you to easily sort, filter, and search your library.

Creating the Solution

1. Start with a blank worksheet. Type these values in row 1 as shown in Figure 70:

    ➢ A1: Title
    ➢ B1: Author
    ➢ C1: Illustrator
    ➢ D1: Location
    ➢ E1: Subject
    ➢ F1: Notes

Figure 70

Keeping track of a classroom library

	A	B	C	D	E	F
1	Title	Author	Illustrator	Location	Subject	Notes
2						
3						
4						

2. Grab a book from your bookshelf and key in its information in row 2. As you key in this data, think about the rules you will use for the data. Perhaps you want to store the

author name as Carle, Eric or perhaps as Eric Carle. Make that decision now and stick to it. Your library will be more useful if you keep it consistent.

Figure 71

Using rules for entering book data

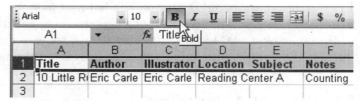

 Note:

As you type the book data in row 2, many of the entries will be wider than the standard 8.5 column width. You will have a chance to fix that soon.

3. Configure Excel to always show the headings as you scroll.
Select row 1 by using the mouse to click on the 1. Apply bold by choosing the B icon in the Formatting toolbar.

Figure 72

Making headings bold

3a. Select cell A2 by clicking on the cell. From the menu, select Window – Freeze Panes.

Figure 73

Selecting Freeze Panes

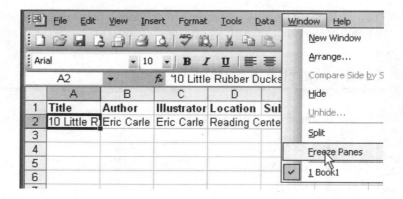

3b. Select all cells by clicking on the square above and to the left of cell A1. From the menu, select Format – Column – AutoFit Selection.

Figure 74

Selecting AutoFit

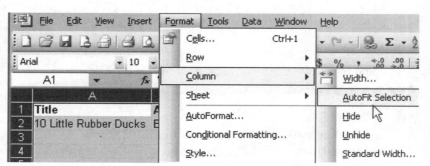

Tip:

The AutoFit command will make the columns wide enough to hold the widest value in each column at the time you use the command. After entering more books, it is a good idea to repeat the AutoFit command.

4. Enter more books. If you have a number of Eric Carle books to enter, you don't have to type Eric Carle again. Move the cellpointer up to the cell above. The fill handle is a square dot in the lower right corner of the cell.

Figure 75

Locating the fill handle

	A	B
1	Title	Author
2	10 Little Rubber Ducks	Eric Carle
3	The Grouchy Ladybug	

4a. With the mouse, click on the fill handle and drag down one cell. This will copy Eric Carle from B2 to C2.

Figure 76

Copying by dragging down on the fill handle

Author	Illustrator
Eric Carle	Eric Carle
Eric Carle	
	Eric Carle

You can use AutoComplete to help you complete entries. As you start typing, you may notice, after typing a few letters, that Excel will propose a complete entry for you. In this example, if you start to type E in cell B4, Excel will immediately offer to fill in Eric Carle. This figure shows Excel after typing the "E" in Eric Carle.

Figure 77

AutoComplete suggests an entry based on the first letter(s) you type

	A	B	
1	Title	Author	Ill
2	10 Little Rubber Ducks	Eric Carle	E
3	The Grouchy Ladybug	Eric Carle	E
4	1, 2, 3 to the Zoo	Eric Carle	

4b. To accept this entry, simply press Enter (or type the Right-Arrow to move to the next cell). This feature is called AutoComplete. It is a nice feature that can save you a fair amount of typing. What if you don't want to accept the proposed entry? Just keep typing the complete name.

 Tip:

AutoComplete offers complete entries when you have keyed in sufficient letters to offer a unique choice.

The AutoComplete feature may seem to work intermittently. Here is why. Figure 78 shows the worksheet after five books have been entered. You will notice that Eric Carle is in rows two through four. Erin Whalen is in row 5.

4c. In cell B6, type "Er". Pause, waiting for Excel to offer an auto completion.

Figure 78

Excel is unable to propose an AutoEntry because of more than one possible match

	A	B
1	Title	Author
2	10 Little Rubber Ducks	Eric Carle
3	The Grouchy Ladybug	Eric Carle
4	1, 2, 3 to the Zoo	Eric Carle
5	Charlie Goes to Sea	Erin Whale
6	Very Hungry Caterpillar	Er

4d. However, Excel won't offer to AutoComplete. Excel isn't sure if you mean Erin or Eric, so until you type the "c" in Eric, the AutoComplete will not work. Once you type the "c", then the entry is unique enough for Excel to propose Eric Carle.

Figure 79

Excel proposes Eric Carle when it is the only possible match

Erin Whale Ni
lar Eric Carle

This limitation can be especially frustrating if you have books by John Jacob Jingleheimer Schmidt and John Jacob Jingleheimer Scott. You must type 27 letters before Excel figures out where you are going with the entry. It might be better to use copy and paste, instead.

5. Make sure that you've selected any cell within your data. From the menu select, Data – Filter – AutoFilter. This will add a dropdown arrow to each heading. These dropdowns allow you to easily filter the data to find all books by one author.

Using the Application

Entering Data

To make data entry easier, choose Data – Form from the menu. An easy-to-use form will appear for entering your data.

Figure 80

Form for entering data easily

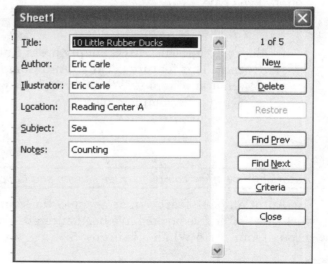

Sorting Data

To sort your database by author, choose one cell in the B column and click the AZ button in the Standard toolbar.

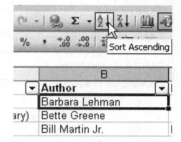

Figure 81

Selecting the AZ button to sort data

To sort by title, choose one cell in the A column and click AZ button. When there is a tie, Excel remembers the previous sequence. If you sort by title first and then by author, the result will be an alphabetical list by title within each author.

Figure 82

List sorted alphabetically by author's first name using the AZ button

	A	B
1	Title	Author
2	The Red Book (Caldecott Honor Book)	Barbara Lehman
3	Philip Hall Likes Me. I Reckon Maybe. (Puffin Newberry Library)	Bette Greene
4	Brown Bear, Brown Bear, What Do You See?	Bill Martin Jr.
5	Polar Bear, Polar Bear, What Do You Hear?	Bill Martin Jr.
6	Freight Train Board Book (Caldecott Collection)	Donald Crews
7	The Bronze Bow: Newberry Medal	Elizabeth George Speare
8	Adam of the Road (Puffin Newberry Library)	Elizabeth Gray Vining
9	Moccasin Trail (Puffin Newberry Library)	Eloise Jarvis McGraw
10	1, 2, 3 to the Zoo	Eric Carle
11	1,2,3 To the Zoo: A Counting Book	Eric Carle
12	10 Little Rubber Ducks	Eric Carle
13	10 Little Rubber Ducks	Eric Carle

You must select just one cell when sorting. If you select a single cell, Excel will use IntelliSense to extend the selection in all directions until it encounters a blank row and blank column. If you accidentally select two cells or a single column, older Excel versions will sort just the selected cells. Imagine if the entire author column was sorted alone when the rest of the list was sorted by title. The result shown in Figure 83 is a bit of a disaster.

Figure 83

Data partially sorted due to selection of more than one cell when pressing the AZ button

	A	B
1	Title	Author
2	1, 2, 3 to the Zoo	Barbara Lehman
3	1,2,3 To the Zoo: A Counting Book	Bette Greene
4	10 Little Rubber Ducks	Bill Martin Jr.
5	10 Little Rubber Ducks	Bill Martin Jr.
6	A Girl Named Disaster (Newberry Honor Books)	Cynthia Kadohata
7	Adam of the Road (Puffin Newberry Library)	Donald Crews
8	Brown Bear, Brown Bear, What Do You See?	Elizabeth George Speare
9	Charlie Goes to Sea	Elizabeth Gray Vining
10	Freight Train Board Book (Caldecott Collection)	Eloise Jarvis McGraw
11	From Head to Toe Board Book	Eric Carle
12	In the Night Kitchen (Caldecott Collection)	Eric Carle

 Caution!

Be sure to select only one cell when doing a sort to avoid inadvertently sorting only part of your data.

Immediately after realizing the problem in Figure 83, type Ctrl+Z to undo the sort option. If you fail to realize the problem until later, your list will be ruined, so always get in the habit of selecting just one cell when sorting.

Figure 84

Excel 2003's IntelliSense detects adjacent data and alerts you to a possible sorting disaster before it happens.

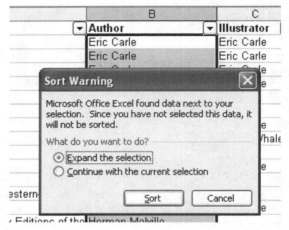

 Tip:

Excel 2003 has IntelliSense that detects adjacent data and offers to extend the range.

4

Filtering Data

Say that you want to find all of the Eric Carle books. From the dropdown in B1, select Eric Carle.

Figure 85

Selecting an author by which to filter the books to be displayed

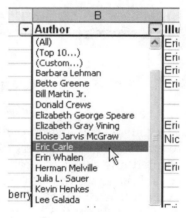

You will be presented with all of the Eric Carle books.

Figure 86

Filtering out all books except those by the selected author

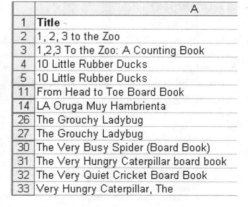

You can combine filters on two columns by selecting a filter on a second column. Later, you can remember which columns have been filtered by taking note of the blue dropdown arrows. To turn off a filter for a column, select the dropdown and choose (All).

Copying Filtered Records

Once you've filtered the list to see just the Eric Carle books, you can print the list. However, if you try to copy the records, you will find that Excel copies the hidden rows as well. This is very frustrating. There are a couple of ways to handle this.

1. Select your data. From the menu, select Edit – Go To. In the Go To dialog, choose Special.

Figure 87

Displaying the Go To dialog to access the Special option

2. In the Go To Special dialog, choose Visible cells only and choose OK.

Figure 88

Selecting Visible cells only to avoid copying hidden cells

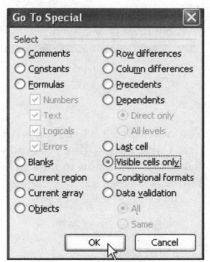

It is barely perceptible, but Excel draws white lines at certain rows. This tells you that there are hidden rows that are not selected.

Figure 89

Hidden rows indicated by white lines

	A	B
1	Title ▾	Author
2	1, 2, 3 to the Zoo	Eric Carle
3	1,2,3 To the Zoo: A Counting Book	Eric Carle
4	10 Little Rubber Ducks	Eric Carle
5	10 Little Rubber Ducks	Eric Carle
11	From Head to Toe Board Book	Eric Carle
14	LA Oruga Muy Hambrienta	Eric Carle
26	The Grouchy Ladybug	Eric Carle
27	The Grouchy Ladybug	Eric Carle
30	The Very Busy Spider (Board Book)	Eric Carle
31	The Very Hungry Caterpillar board book	Eric Carle
32	The Very Quiet Cricket Board Book	Eric Carle
33	Very Hungry Caterpillar, The	Eric Carle

3. If you are following the exercise, make sure that you have a blank workbook open.
Choose the New icon from the Standard toolbar.

Figure 90

New icon on the Standard toolbar

4. Switch back to the original workbook with Ctrl+Tab.

5. Use Edit – Copy to copy the visible cells to the clipboard. Use Ctrl+Tab to switch to the blank workbook. Type Ctrl+V or use Edit – Paste to paste the visible cells to a new sheet.

Figure 91

Visible rows only copied

	A	B	C	D	E	F
1	Title	Author	Illustrator	Location	Subject	Notes
2	1, 2, 3 to t	Eric Carle	Eric Carle	Reading C	Zoo	Counting
3	1,2,3 To th	Eric Carle	Eric Carle	Bins		
4	10 Little Ri	Eric Carle	Eric Carle	Reading C	Sea	Counting
5	10 Little Ri	Eric Carle	Eric Carle	Reading Center B		
6	From Heac	Eric Carle	Eric Carle	Bins		
7	LA Oruga I	Eric Carle	Eric Carle	Bins		
8	The Grouc	Eric Carle	Eric Carle	Reading C	Ladybug	Manners &
9	The Grouc	Eric Carle	Eric Carle	Reading Center B		
10	The Very E	Eric Carle	Eric Carle	Bins		
11	The Very F	Eric Carle	Eric Carle	Reading Center B		
12	The Very C	Eric Carle	Eric Carle	Bins		
13	Very Hung	Eric Carle	Eric Carle	Reading C	Caterpillar	Gluttony

You now have a workbook with just the Eric Carle books. Use Format – Column – AutoFit Selection to make the columns wider.

Locating Data

The AutoFilter command doesn't work if you need to find partial cell values. If you want to find all cells that contain a value of "Ladybug", AutoFilter is not the way to go.

In this case, you will want to use the Find command.

1. From the menu, select Edit – Find. Type ladybug and choose Find Next.

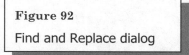

Figure 92

Find and Replace dialog

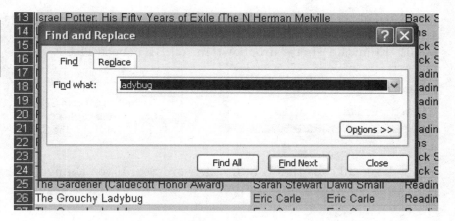

 Tip:

There are some choices hidden behind the Options>> button. If you share a computer with someone else and they most recently selected Match entire cell contents, Excel will remember this setting and your Find command won't find The Grouchy Ladybug even when you know it is there. If Find doesn't seem to be working, choose the Options dialog and see if either Match case or Match entire cell contents is selected.

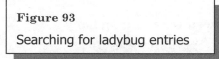

Figure 93

Searching for ladybug entries

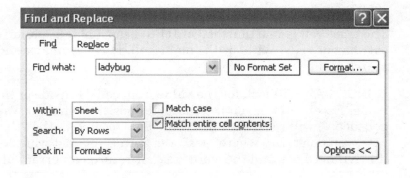

Each time you choose Find Next, Excel will show you the next cell containing "ladybug". This may not be an effective way to search if you have hundreds of ladybug books.

Using a Formula to Find

If you are hooked on the AutoFilter and want to find all books with Sea in the title, it can be done. Follow these steps.

1. Insert a new column B. Select cell B1 and choose Insert – Column from the menu.

2. Label this column "There?"

3. Type the word "sea" in an out of the way cell such as J1. Use lower case.

4. In cell B2, use this formula =NOT(ISNA(FIND(LOWER($J$1),LOWER(B2)))).

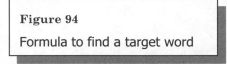

Figure 94

Formula to find a target word

5. Double click the fill handle to copy the formula down to all cells.

6. From the There? dropdown in cell B1, choose TRUE.

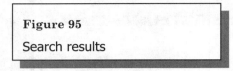

Figure 95

Search results

	A	B	C	
1	Title ▼	There? ▼	Author ▼	Illu:
8	Tim and Lucy Go to Sea	TRUE	E. Ardizzone	
24	Charlie Goes to Sea	TRUE	Erin Whalen	Nic(
25	The Old Man and The Sea	TRUE	Ernest Hemingway	

You will see all cells that contain the word Sea. If you change J1 from sea to ladybug and then re-select TRUE from the B1 dropdown, the list will filter to just books with Ladybug in the title.

Excel Details

In Step 1 above, you should choose to put the new column in B instead of G because you can assume that every book has a title. The trick of double clicking the fill handle to copy a formula only works when the column to the left has no blank cells.

In Step 3, I used sea in J1. I could have typed this into the formula =FIND("sea", A2), but then the find wouldn't be as flexible. I would have to change the formula and re-copy it for each new search.

The "sea" cell is in J1 instead of H1 to keep a blank column between your data and any extraneous cells. Without the blank cell, Excel would extend the AutoFilter list to include the search term.

=FIND(J1,A2) will look for the value from cell J1 inside of the value in cell A2. If it finds this value, Excel will tell you the character position where it was found. =FIND("of", "board of education") will return a 7 because "of" is located in the 7th character (including spaces). In your case, you don't care where "sea" was found; you just want to know if it was found. Well, luckily, if FIND does not find the word "sea", it returns an error value as shown in Figure 96.

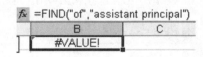

Figure 96

#VALUE! error displays when target word is not found

	=FIND("of","assistant principal")	
	B	C
	#VALUE!	

Using ISERR will convert the error values to TRUE and non-error values to FALSE. This would require you to have your heading called NotThere? Using the NOT function changes the TRUEs to FALSEs and the FALSEs to TRUEs.

Chapter 5 – Grade Books

Opportunity

Although I have a traditional paper grade book at my disposal, I find that when it comes time for report cards or progress charts to go home, punching in recorded grades on a calculator takes too much time and I am prone to mistakes. (I am constantly rechecking my calculations!) Is it possible to use Excel to set up a grade book that would calculate the grades (percentages) for students in my class? Can I have different worksheets for different subject matters so that all my spelling scores will be kept separate from addition math scores? Can Excel also calculate grades for individual students as well as give me class averages for the entire class in each subject matter?

Some schools do offer their teachers an on-line grade book. This is usually incorporated into their student information files/attendance tracking/computerized report card software that is used corporation wide. Many districts use a program that fails miserably. Teachers are not trained, the program is not user friendly, it loses information, and so on. Some schools might use the program to generate report cards, but not necessarily use it for their grade books. There will be schools where teachers are required to enter grades on a program adopted by the corporation. Many teachers still won't use the on-line or corporation-wide computerized grade book because of reliability reasons. They would prefer to have some control over where the data is stored. If the data is lost, you are up a creek without a paddle! Having a worksheet in Excel that a teacher could easily back-up and save data to secure places (like removable disks/thumb drives) would be extremely helpful. Also, the computerized grade books can be rather rigid in their make-up and if the teacher needs to record student progress data in a different category and/or subject matter that does not "fit" into the computerized grade book pre-set categories, being able to set up an individualized worksheet using Excel will be very useful!

Teachers that I have encountered (including myself!) usually have different sections in a grade book for different subjects, which usually goes right along with required elements found on the report card. For a first grader in my corporation, I would need to record grades in the "large" subject matters such as reading, spelling, phonics, writing, math, social studies, science, physical education, music, art, as well in areas such as work habits and social development. Many of the "large" subject matters would need subheadings. For example, phonics would need smaller categories for grades such as knows letter names, knows letter sounds, knows short vowels sounds, knows long vowel sounds, etc.

Most teachers record grades to be averaged using a percentage scale. Different schools will have different percentage scales to determine the grades. One school may say 95% and higher is an "A", while another school may say 90% and higher. So, it is important for teachers setting up a grade book worksheet to be able to incorporate their own percentage scales for determining grades. Also, some subject matters might warrant a different percentage scale within the same grade book. For example, because I was working with first time spellers in first grade, my spelling scale was easier (or more lenient) than my addition and subtraction scales.

Solution and Overview

An Excel workbook can contain many Excel worksheets. This chapter will walk you through the process of setting up a grade book workbook with one worksheet for each subject area.

In the process of setting up the grade book, you will encounter many new and essential Excel skills. Tasks that seem minor, such as turning assignment names on their side, will make the grade book much easier to use so that an entire grading period can be seen at a glance. You will see how to enter a formula and copy it to many cells. You will also learn the essential skill of setting up a formula that can be copied and that always points to the cell with the totals for the grading period. Finally, you will see the trick for creating copies of a completed worksheet many times within a workbook.

Creating the Solution

When you open a blank workbook, you might notice that it automatically starts with several worksheet tabs along the bottom. You might have Sheet1, Sheet2, and Sheet3. Microsoft does this because they think that you are not smart enough to use the Insert – Worksheet command. In my opinion, it is a waste to always start with three worksheets. (Those of you using Excel 95 may always start with 16 worksheets – a real waste!) How often do you really create a workbook with exactly three worksheets? In this case, we will eventually need one worksheet for each grading subject. However, your strategy will be to set up a perfect grade book on Sheet1 and then copy Sheet1 multiple times for each subject. In reality, you will never use Sheet2 or Sheet3. If you agree that having extra blank sheets is a confusing waste, they can easily be turned off. From the Excel menu, select Tools – Options. On the General tab, change the Sheets in New Workbook setting from three down to one.

Figure 97

Setting number of sheets in a new workbook to one

1. Start with a blank workbook with a single blank worksheet. You can set up a working grade book for math first and then copy this worksheet multiple times for each subject area.

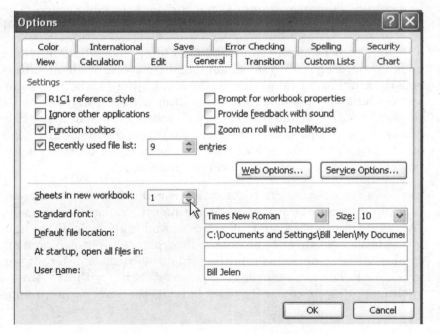

2. Change the worksheet name from Sheet1 to the appropriate subject name. If you double-click on the Sheet1 tab, Excel will allow you to edit the sheet name.

Figure 98 Double-clicking on worksheet name

2a. Change the worksheet name to Math. Click anywhere in the spreadsheet to accept the new sheet name.

Figure 99 Renaming new worksheet

3. If you like using colors, it is possible in Excel 2002 and later to change the color of the tab. Right-click (Ctrl+Click for Macintosh) on the sheet tab to access a menu where you can change the tab color.

Figure 100

Right-click a worksheet tab to access the Tab Color command

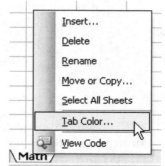

After you choose a color, Excel will add a tiny swath of color to the edge of the active sheet tab. When you add additional worksheets, the color of the non-active tabs will reflect the chosen color.

4. Changing the worksheet name is useful for viewing the grade book on the computer screen, but the sheet name does not usually print in the printed worksheet. Thus, start the worksheet by typing the subject name in cell A1 of the worksheet.

Entering Student Names

You always want to leave a blank row between the title of the worksheet and the headings for the data section. The blank row will help Excel's Intelisense technology to figure out where your data starts. Follow these steps:

1. In cell A3, enter a heading for Student.

2. If you have your class roster, type the student names going down column A. To make alphabetizing easier, type in the format of Last Name, First Name.

3. Many of the names will be wider than the column. That is OK for now. Leave a blank row at the end. The blank row will be used to separate your student data from the totals. New students can be added above this blank row.

4. After the blank row, add a cell with the words Points Possible. Add another cell with the words Class Average.

	A	B	C
1	Math - 2006/2007		
2			
3	Student		
4	Barnby, Eric		
5	McGinnis, Courtney		
6	Mullen, Ashley		
7	Dutton, Meredith		
8	Boxler, Austin		
9	Flaherty, Wes		
10	Hupp, Allison		
11	Slack, Steve		
12	Wells, Meredith		
13	Zelich, Milan		
14	Peters, Joe		
15	Poling, Brittany		
16	Hastings, Madelyn		
17	Horning, Mike		
18	Huff, Sarah		
19	Cairns, Mike		
20	Coerver, Nate		
21	Robert, Courtney		
22	Scott, Doug		
23	Boyes, Julie		
24			
25	Points Possible		
26	Class Average		
27			

Figure 101

Adding sum (Points Possible) and average (Class Average) headings

5. You will want to make column A wide enough to handle any of the names in column A, but not necessarily wide enough to handle the title in cell A1. With the mouse, select cells A3:A26. From the menu, select Format – Column – AutoFit Selection. The width of column A will adjust to allow for the longest student name in the selected area.

6. You will also notice that for some inexplicable reason, your classroom roster was not printed in alphabetical order. It is very easy in Excel to alphabetize a list. This process is called Sorting.

   6a. Select a single name in the list. From the menu, select Data – Sort.

Because your data contains only a single column, Excel initially assumes that you do not have a header row. This is a bad assumption, because Excel would then sort the "Student" cell down to be alphabetically after Slack, Steve.

Figure 102

Excel mistakenly assumes that there is no header row

   6b. In the lower left portion of the Sort dialog, choose the option button for Header Row.

Notice that after telling Excel that you have a header row, Excel changes the sort column from the generic "Column A" to the heading of "Student". Also, the range selected for sorting will start one cell lower.

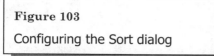

Figure 103

Configuring the Sort dialog

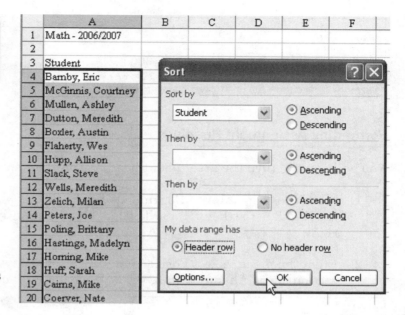

6c. Choose OK; within less than a second, the names will be placed in alphabetical order.

Entering Assignment Names

1. In cell B3, start entering assignment names going across the page. Use short names such as "HW1" for Homework 1 or "Quiz 3" for the third quiz. It is not critical at this point that you know every assignment as it will happen. You are trying to get some data in so that the grade book can be easily formatted. You can always change the assignment names later, or insert new columns or delete unnecessary columns.

Figure 104

Entering assignment names

	A	B	C	D	E	F	G
1	Math - 2006/2007						
2							
3	Student	HW1	HW2	HW3	Quiz 1	HW4	Test
4	Bamby, Eric						
5	Boxler, Austin						
6	Boyes, Julie						
7	Cairns, Mike						

 Tip:

After typing HW1 in cell B3, type the right arrow to accept the entry in B3 and automatically move the cellpointer one cell to the right.

In a typical grading period, you will find that there are more assignments going across the worksheet than will fit on the screen. Eventually, the worksheet will scroll to the right and you will not be able to see the student names anymore. You will correct this problem in a few steps.

2. After you have entered enough assignments going across, add three new columns labeled Total, Average, and Grade.

Figure 105

Add new columns for Total, Average, and Grade

	R	S	T	U	V	W
1						
2						
3	HW13	HW14	Test3	Total	Average	Grade
4						
5						

Formatting Assignment Headings

You will want to turn the assignment headings on their side so that they take up less room.

1. Move the cellpointer to B3. Hold down the Shift key while typing the End key and then the Right-Arrow key. This will select all of the contiguous filled cells from B3 to the right.

2. From the menu, select Format – Cells. Choose the Alignment tab. In the Orientation section of the Alignment tab, you will see a red diamond.

Figure 106

Drag the red diamond to change orientation

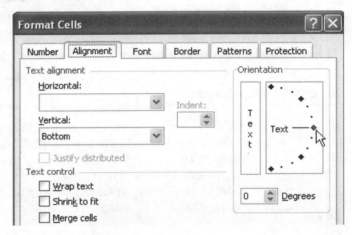

3. With the mouse, grab the red diamond and drag it from the 3 o'clock position to the 12 o'clock position.

Figure 107

Red orientation diamond rotated to turn text sideways

This causes the text in the selected cells to turn sideways. The cells will still be too wide, even though the text in the cells is now turned sideways, as shown in the following figure.

Figure 108

Cells are still too wide, even after rotating text

	A	B	C	D
1	Math - 2006/2007			
2				
3	Student	HW1	HW2	HW3
4	Barnby, Eric			
5	Boyler, Austin			

4. Assuming that you need to be able to accommodate scores of 100 in each column, use Format – Column – Width and choose a width of 3.4 for the selected range.

Figure 109

Adjusting column width to accommodate desired number of scores

After choosing this setting, you will be able to see many more assignments going across the monitor.

If your school district buys you incredibly large monitors, it is possible that you will be able to see your entire grade book in one screen of the monitor. However, assuming that you are in a school with a funding crunch, you probably have a normal size monitor and you will not be able to see all of the assignments going across the screen.

Keeping Headings Visible

There is a fantastic feature in Excel that will keep any headings visible on the screen as you scroll around the worksheet. Unfortunately, the feature is a little bit counterintuitive to use.

As you look at the grade book, you always want to be able to see the student names in column A. Even if you scroll out to the 28th assignment, you still need to be able to see the students in column A. Also, you always want to see the assignment names in row 3. Even if you have 64 students in a college classroom, you still want to see row 3 as you scroll down. Thus, you want to freeze all of the headings above and to the left of cell B4.

1. Move the cellpointer to cell B4. This is the first cell that is will not be frozen. After selecting the next command, everything visible on the screen to the left of the cellpointer and everything visible on the screen above the cellpointer will be frozen.

Figure 110

Freezing all rows and columns above and to the left of the cursor

2. From the menu, select Window – Freeze Panes.

You can now begin to scroll out past the right edge of the worksheet or past the last visible row on the worksheet. Even as you are working out in column S and row 21, you can still see the headings in the frozen section of the workbook.

	A	S	T	U	V	W
1	Math - 2006/2007					
2						
3	Student	HW14	Test3	Total	Average	Grade
21	Slack, Steve					
22	Wells, Meredith					
23	Zelich, Milan					
24						
25	Points Possible					
26	Class Average					
27						

Figure 111

Darkened lines show the areas above and to the left of the cursor that will remain in view

Entering Formulas for Total Score

In Chapter 1 – Calculation Basics, you learned how to use the AutoSum tool to sum a column of numbers. Now, you want to total a row of numbers that has not yet been entered.

1. Move the cellpointer to the total column for the first student. If you press the AutoSum icon (it looks like a Greek letter Sigma), Excel will have no clue as to what data you want to sum. It starts to enter the SUM function, but then waits for you to specify the cells to include in the total.

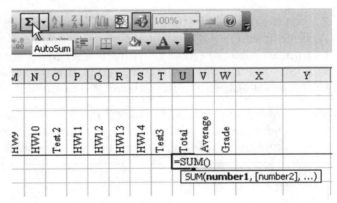

Figure 112

Excel waiting for target data input

2. Using the mouse, highlight the cells from B3 through the last assignment in row 3. In the sample grade book, this is the range from B3:T3. Press the Enter key to accept the formula. Excel will show a total of 0 for the student.

Copying Excel Formulas

The great thing about Excel is that after you have written a formula once, you can usually copy that formula to many different cells. In the step above, you created a formula of =SUM(B4:T4) to total the scores for the first student.

Figure 113

Existing formula ready to copy

U4			*fx*	=SUM(B4:T4)		
	A	S	T	U	V	W
1	Math - 2006/2007					
2						
3	Student	HW14	Test3	Total	Average	Grade
4	Bamby, Eric			0		
5	Boxler, Austin					
6	Boyes, Julie					

If you copy this cell and paste it to the other cells in column U, Excel will automatically adjust the formula. When copied from U4 to U5, the formula automatically changes to =SUM(B5:T5).

Figure 114

Copied formula automatically adjusts to new locations

	A	S	T	U	V	W
1	Math - 2006/2007					
2						
3	Student	HW14	Test3	Total	Average	Grade
4	Bamby, Eric			0		
5	Boxler, Austin			0		
6	Boyes, Julie			0		
7	Cairns, Mike			0		

Thus, you can simply copy the formula from U4 down to all of the cells in column U for your students.

There are five ways to copy the cell using copy and paste.

Select cell U4. Type Ctrl+C to copy. Select cells U5:U23. Type Ctrl+V to paste.

Select cell U4. From the menu, select Edit – Copy. Select cells U5:U23. From the menu, select Edit – Paste.

Select Cell U4. Right-click and choose Copy. Select cells U5:U23. Right-click and choose Paste.

Select Cell U4. Touch the toolbar icon for copy. Select cells U5:U23. Right-click and choose Paste.

The fifth method is the easiest.

Select cell U4; you will see a thick black border around the cell. In the lower left corner of the cell is a square black dot. This dot is called the fill handle. With the mouse, click the fill handle and drag down through cell U23 to copy the formula.

You will also have to copy the formula from the last student to the row containing points possible. Select cell U23 and type Ctrl+C to copy. Select cell U25 and type Ctrl+V to paste.

Setting up an Average Formula – Using Absolute References

 Tip:

Before setting up the remaining formulas, it might help to type in scores for the first assignment. Calculating averages requires dividing by the total points possible, and Excel will return an error value if your divisor is zero.

1. In cell B25, type in a 10 to indicate that 10 points were possible on the first homework assignment. Throughout the range of B4:B23, type in the student's scores for the homework.

Figure 115

Entering points possible and students' scores

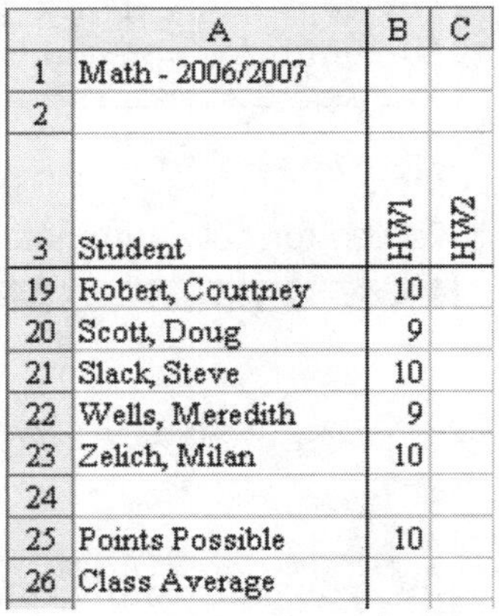
A
B
C
1 Math - 2006/2007
2
3 Student
HW1
HW2
19 Robert, Courtney 10
20 Scott, Doug 9
21 Slack, Steve 10
22 Wells, Meredith 9
23 Zelich, Milan 10
24
25 Points Possible 10
26 Class Average

The formula in U25 (see Figure 116) shows the total points possible for the grading period so far. To determine the percentage grade for the first student, you need to divide U4 by U25.

2. In cell V4, type =U4/U25. Excel gives you a result of 1.

Figure 116

Student's score divided by number of possible points

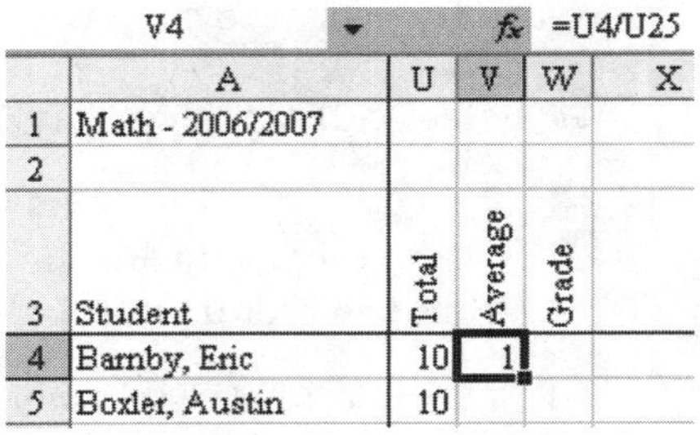
V4
=U4/U25
A
U
V
W
X
1 Math - 2006/2007
2
3 Student
Total
Average
Grade
4 Barnby, Eric 10 1
5 Boxler, Austin 10

5

3. Select cell V4 and choose the Percentage icon in the Formatting toolbar. Now the answer turns to ##. This is because the column is not wide enough to show 100%.

Figure 117

Changing the result to a percentage

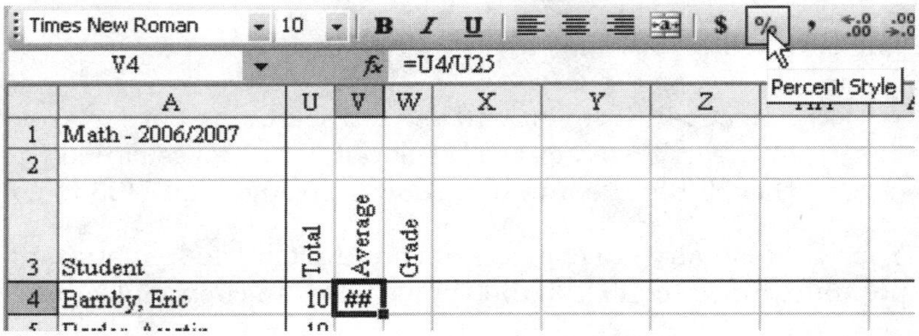
Times New Roman
10
V4
=U4/U25
Percent Style
A
U
V
W
X
Y
Z
1 Math - 2006/2007
2
3 Student
Total
Average
Grade
4 Barnby, Eric 10 ##

4. Double-click the line dividing the gray V heading from the gray W heading. The column will automatically resize to show the 100%.

Figure 118

Double-clicking between column headings automatically resizes column widths

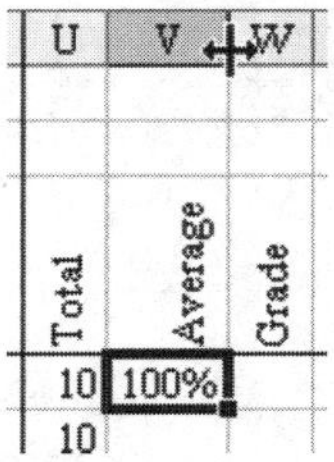
U
V
W
Total
Average
Grade
10 100%
10

Although this formula correctly calculates the first student's score, there is a problem with the formula. When you copy the formula from the first student to the second student, you get a division by zero error. What is going on?

Figure 119

Division by zero error when formula is copied to second student

	V5				fx	=U5/U26
	A			U	V	W
1	Math - 2006/2007					
2						
3	Student			Total	Average	Grade
4	Bamby, Eric			10	100%	
5	Boxler, Austin			10	#DIV/0!	
6	Boyes, Julie			10		

The original formula divided the points for student one in cell U4 by the total points possible in cell U25. When this formula was copied down, the cell reference correctly changed from U4 to U5. However, the cell reference for the divisor also changed, with U25 becoming U26. Since U25 contains the total points possible but U26 contains nothing, Excel's default method of copying formulas is working against you in part of the formula.

You need a way to specify that part of a formula should always point to one particular cell. In the early 1980's, Lotus 1-2-3 adopted a standard that is still used to this day.

5. Use a dollar sign in a cell reference to hold either the column letter and/or the row number absolute. If you change the original formula to be =U4/$U$25 and copy the formula, the divisor will always point to cell U25.

Figure 120

Using dollar signs to keep the same row and column number references

	A			U	V	W
1	Math - 2006/2007					
2						
3	Student			Total	Average	Grade
4	Bamby, Eric			10	=U4/$U$25	

There are even shortcut keys to make the entry of dollar signs easier. If you type =U4/U25 and then immediately type the F4 key, Excel will add the dollar signs before the U and before the 25.

6. Earlier in this chapter you learned how to drag the fill handle to copy a formula. At this point in building the grade book, you have a situation where you have a formula in cell V4. The adjacent column has a column of values in U4:U23. If you double-click the fill handle in V4, Excel's Intellisense will copy the formula down to all of the cells to match the neighboring column. Because the first blank cell in column U is at row 24, double-clicking the fill handle in V4 will copy the formula down to V4:V23.

 Tip:

A reference like $U$25 is called an absolute reference. It is also valid to have references like U$25 to keep the row number constant and $U25 to keep the column letter constant. These types of references are called mixed references. See Chapter 2 – Multiplication Tables on page 23 for examples of this type of reference. The normal reference of U25 is called a relative reference.

Figuring out the Classroom Average

In row 26, you have a line to calculate the classroom average. You can calculate the classroom average both for each assignment and for the entire grading period.

1. The formula for B26 is =AVERAGE(B4:B23). As you enter additional grades across the sheet, copy the B26 formula over for the new columns.

2. To find the average for the whole grading period, copy the formula from B26 to U26. Copy the Average formula from V4 to V26.

So far, after one homework assignment, the students in this fictional class have a 93% average.

Figure 121
Copying a formula to find averages for the whole class

	A	U	V	W	X	
					U26	▼	*fx* =AVERAGE(U4:U23)
1	Math - 2006/2007					
2						
3	Student	Total	Average	Grade		
20	Scott, Doug	9	90%			
21	Slack, Steve	10	100%			
22	Wells, Meredith	9	90%			
23	Zelich, Milan	10	100%			
24						
25	Points Possible	10				
26	Class Average	9.3	93%			

Assigning Letter Grades

You need to set up a table to hold your school grading scale. Excel has a quirk in its lookup tables that requires you to think about your grading scale in a slightly different way.

You school grading scale will have some system where, say, anything under a 65% is assigned a letter grade of F. 66%-69% may be assigned a D. So – while your grading scale says that anything under 65% is an F, in Excel you need to think that anything above 0% gets an F; anything above 65% gets a D; anything above 70% gets a C, and so on.

1. Off to the right of the worksheet, set up a table with two columns. The first column should contain the starting boundary for each letter grade. The second column should contain the letter grade assigned to grades above that boundary. Figure 122 shows a sample grading scale table.

Figure 122
Sample grading scale table in ascending order

0%	F
65%	D
69%	D+
70%	C
83%	C+
85%	B
92%	B+
95%	A
98%	A+

Of course, the school manual expresses the grading scale in a different manner. The school grading scale probably starts with the A+ grade and expresses ranges as follows:

➢ 98%-100%   A+

➢ 95%-97.9%   A

➢ 92%-94.9%   B+

➢ and so forth…

 Tip:

Because the Excel lookup table must be in ascending order numerically, you will have to start with the F category and progress upwards.

The lookup table in the sample workbook is in the range of AA4:AB12 (see Figure 123). Depending on the number of letter grades, your table may take up more or less rows.

The function you will use is called the VLOOKUP function. This stands for "Vertical Lookup". In the figure below, the formula bar shows the formula for the first student grade. The formula is =VLOOKUP(V4,$AA$4:$AB$12,2). In English, this formula tells Excel to take the numeric grade in cell V4 and to look through the first column of the vertical lookup table in AA4:AA12. Then, when it finds the scale boundary just smaller than that student's grade, to return the value from the second column of the table.

Figure 123

Using VLOOKUP with a vertical lookup table

Note:

The syntax for VLOOKUP is =VLOOKUP(Value to Lookup, Table Containing Values in first column, Which column of that table to return when a match is found).

	W4	▼	fx	=VLOOKUP(V4,$AA$4:$AB$12,2)				
	A	V	W	X	Y	Z	AA	AB
1	Math - 2006/2007							
2								
3	Student	Average	Grade					
4	Barnby, Eric	100%	A+				0%	F
5	Boxler, Austin	100%	A+				65%	D
6	Boyes, Julie	100%	A+				69%	D+
7	Cairns, Mike	70%	C				70%	C
8	Coerver, Nate	100%	A+				83%	C+
9	Dutton, Meredith	60%	F				85%	B
10	Flaherty, Wes	100%	A+				92%	B+
11	Hastings, Madelyn	100%	A+				95%	A
12	Horning, Mike	80%	C				98%	A+

2. Enter the VLOOKUP formula [=VLOOKUP(V4,$AA$4:$AB$12,2)] in W4, the cell for the first student's grade.

3. Copy it down for the other students. Remember to use the fill handle!

Note that the address for the Table contains dollar signs to make sure that, as the formula is copied down from W4 to other cells, Excel always looks at the lookup table.

Page Setup Settings for Printing

In case you want to print the grade book, it is best to set up the page setup settings before making copies of the worksheet. Follow these steps:

1. When you print, you will want to print all of the student information, but not necessarily the grading scale. Select the range from A1 to W26. From the menu, select File – Print Area – Set Print Area.

2. Depending on the number of assignments that you have in the grading period, the grade book will probably need to be printed in landscape mode. From the menu, select File – Page Setup.

2a. There are four tabs on the Page Setup dialog. On the Page tab, select Landscape as the orientation.

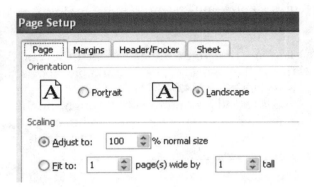

Figure 124

Changing page setup from portrait to landscape

3. On the Margins tab, set the left, right, top, and bottom margins to be 0.5". Set the Footer setting to be 0.25"

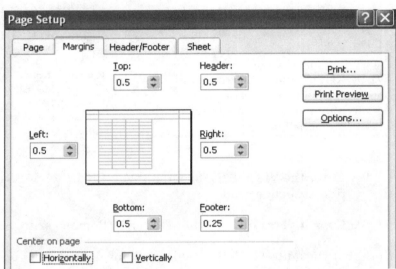

Figure 125

Setting margins and footer

It would be nice to have the date on any printed copy of the grade book. You can insert this in the header or footer of the worksheet.

4. On the Header/Footer tab of the Page Setup dialog, choose Custom Footer.

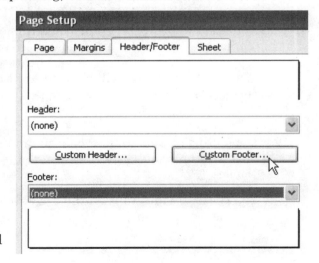

Figure 126

Selecting a custom footer

4a. In the Footer dialog, you can set up footers for the left, center, or right side of the page. Click inside the Left section.

4b. Type the words "As of ", with "of" followed by a space. Then, using the mouse, touch the Date icon. Excel will insert the special code used to insert the current date.

Figure 127

Entering text for footer with code to insert the current date

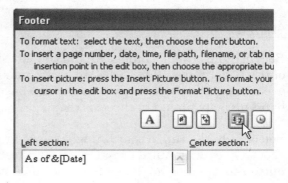

 Tip:

In Excel 2003, there are icons to automatically insert the page number, the total number of pages, the date, the time, the path & filename, just the file name, the sheet name, or a picture. Many of these options were added in Excel 2002 or later. If you are using Excel 97, you will be limited to the page number icons and the date and time icons.

4c. Choose OK to close the Footer dialog. The Header/Footer tab in the Page Setup dialog will show a sample of the footer you have set up.

5. The last tab in the Page Setup dialog is the Sheet tab. It may seem like overkill now, but in case your grade book ever grows to be more than one page wide, you should set up the Print Titles section now.

If the grade book spans more than one page, you will want the students' names to appear on each printed page. There is a setting for Columns to repeat at left. You want to specify column A in this box. While you might be tempted to type the letter A in this box, Excel will not accept that answer. Since it is hard to remember that Excel needs "A:A" in the box, use this technique:

5a. Using the mouse, click inside the textbox for Columns to repeat at left. Then, with the mouse, click on the heading for column A that is visible behind the dialog. Excel will insert the code of $A:$A in the box.

Figure 128

Selecting columns to repeat

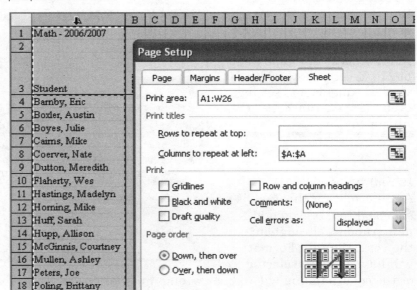

5b. If your class size should ever grow beyond 40 students, you might have more than one vertical page. In this case, you would want rows 1:3 to appear at the top of each page. In the Rows to repeat at top textbox, type 1:3.

5c. Choose OK to close the Page Setup dialog.

Applying Color Formats

Applying Color Banding Using AutoFormat

Because the student names are on the left side of the page and the grades are on the right side of the page, it would be easier to apply some form of color banding to the worksheet so that your eye can easily follow the line across the page. Excel offers 15 quick formatting options, and color banding is available in three of them.

Select only the range containing student grades (A4:W23) in your worksheet. From the menu, choose Format – AutoFormat. The AutoFormat dialog has an Options button. Choose that button to expand the dialog to show the Formats to Apply section at the bottom of the dialog.

Initially, you will see the first six formats: Simple, three versions of Classic and two versions of Accounting. Use the scrollbar on the dialog to move down to the three versions of a List format. List 1 will apply alternating shading of white and gray to each row. List 2 will alternate by applying green shading to two rows, then white shading to two rows. The 3D Effects 2 format will apply a sunken appearance to every other row.

5 You do not want the AutoFormat command to overwrite your percentage format in the grade book nor do you want it to overwrite your vertical alignment for the assignments. In the Formats to Apply section, uncheck Number, Alignment, and Width/Height. See Figure 129.

Figure 129

Selecting AutoFormat attributes

Caution!

Do not include the vertical assignment headings in your selection before choosing an AutoFormat. An apparent bug in Excel will override the vertical alignment settings even if you uncheck the Alignment tab.

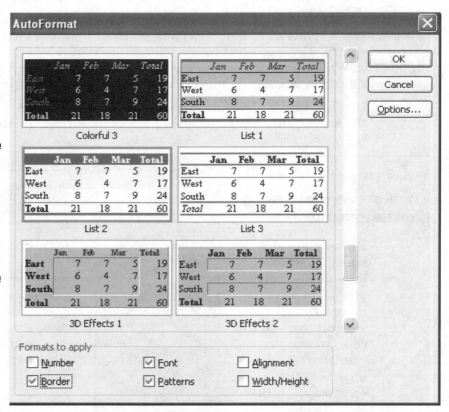

In reality, using AutoFormat for this task is shortsighted. As you add new students throughout the year, the AutoFormat will have to be re-selected or the color banding will appear wrong. Further, you have to deal with the bug that overrides the vertical alignment. The AutoFormat only offers color banding in gray or green instead of the full pallet of colors.

The next section reveals an obscure trick for dynamically adding color banding that overcomes these problems.

Applying Color Banding Using Conditional Formatting

Since you will probably be adding and deleting students throughout the year, it would be better to use this technique for adding color to alternating rows of the grade book. Also, the AutoFormat options make the Excel gridlines invisible, and this is not desirable in the grade book application.

The technique works because of some obscure functions. The ROW function returns the row number of the current cell. Combining the MOD and ROW functions, the =MOD(ROW(),2) formula divides the row number by 2 and returns just the remainder value. With a division by 2, the remainder will be zero for even-numbered rows and one for odd-numbered rows.

1. To start, select the range of students and their grades. Feel free to include the Total and Average rows. In the sample workbook, this would be A4:W26.

2. From the menu, select Format – Conditional Formatting. Initially, you will have this limited version of the Conditional Formatting dialog.

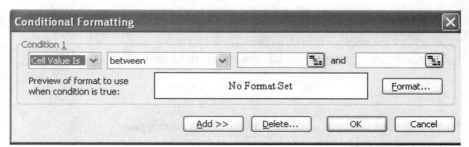

Figure 130

Default Conditional Formatting dialog box

3. Select the dropdown next to Cell Value Is and change the selection to Formula Is. This version of the tool allows you to write any formula that evaluates to 0, 1, True, or False. The conditional formatting will be applied when the result of the formula is one or True.

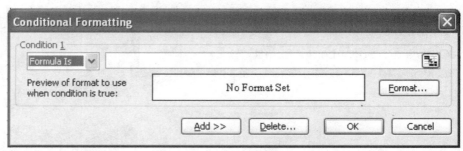

Figure 131

Selecting conditions

4. In the large textbox, type =MOD(ROW(),2).

Figure 132 Entering a formula for the condition

5. Choose the Format... button. On the patterns tab, choose any light color such as light green or light blue or light yellow. Applying a pattern causes the Excel gridlines to disappear on the selected rows. On the Border tab, use the color dropdown to select a light gray.

Figure 133

Formatting the pattern and the borders

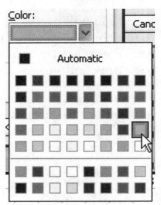

6. In the line style section, choose a solid line.

Figure 134

Selecting a solid line from the Line Style menu

In the Border section, Excel shows a thick black/gray line to indicate that the selection contains mixed borders. You want to override this setting for the left and right border only.

7. Click on the left and right borders. The mouse pointer in Figure 135 shows where to click to change the right border.

Figure 135

Changing the right border format

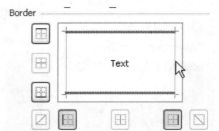

8. Choose OK to close the format dialog. Choose OK to close the Conditional Formatting dialog. The result will be a grade book with every other line highlighted in a light color. The gridlines will appear to be unbroken between the columns.

Note that even this method is not perfect. When you print the grade book, the vertical gridlines in the rows with coloring will print.

Chapter 5 – Grade Books

Copying the Math Grade Book for Other Subjects

At this point, you have created a working grade book for one subject. You will want to create an exact copy of this worksheet for each other subject.

Excel offers the Move or Copy command to create an exact copy of a worksheet. This command is better than copy and paste because it will copy the column width and print settings.

1. Right-click the worksheet tab for the Math worksheet. From the menu, select Move or Copy.

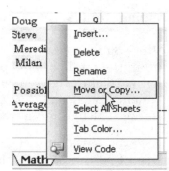

Figure 136

Selecting Move or Copy from the Right-click menu

The Move or Copy dialog box offers many powerful options. You could choose to copy a single worksheet from one workbook to a new workbook or to a certain place in another open workbook. In the present case, you just need to create a copy of the Math worksheet and move it to the end of the workbook.

2. Check the box for Create a Copy. Choose (move to end).

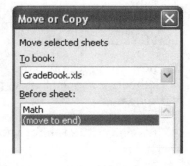

Figure 137

Selecting Move or Copy options

A new tab will be created called Math (2):

 Tip:

To copy a worksheet within a workbook, you can skip the Move or Copy dialog. While holding down the Ctrl key, click on a worksheet tab and drag it to a new place. When you release the mouse, a new worksheet will be created.

2a. Make a total of five new copies of the worksheet. You will then need to rename each tab with the appropriate subject name.

3. Right-click the tab name and choose Rename. Type the new subject name on the tab.

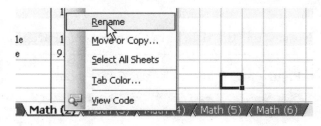

Figure 138

Renaming the new worksheet copies

4. Also, remember to change the subject name in cell A1 of each worksheet.

5. After creating the new worksheets, remember to type new assignments going across the page. Also, replace the math grades for the first assignment with the appropriate grades.

Using the Application

Adding Grades

After you have graded a new assignment, type the assignment name in row 3 of the grade book. Fill in the total possible points in row 25 of the grade book. Copy the average formula from B26 to row 26 of the current column. Fill in the individual student scores in the columns. If a student was absent, leave his or her score blank. (Blank cells will not factor into the classroom average calculation in row 26).

Once you have entered grades for all of the students for the assignment, you can see their current percentage and their letter grade if the grading period ended today.

Adding New Students

New students should be added in the middle of the grade book. This is where you would naturally add them alphabetically, unless the new student is Andy Aaaaardvark or Zeke Zzzzzumekis. Adding a new row in the interior of the grade book ensures that the ranges in the total formula will expand to include the new student.

If a new student joins your classroom, you will want to add him or her to all of the grading worksheets at once. This is possible to do. Let's say that you have six worksheets in the grading workbook.

1. Select the tab for the first worksheet.

Figure 139 Selecting the first tab

2. While holding down the Ctrl key, click the mouse on the worksheet tab for the last worksheet. If you have done this successfully, all of the tabs will turn white to indicate that they are all selected.

Figure 140 All tabs selected

Notice that the title bar changes to indicate that you are in Group mode.

Figure 141 Title bar displays Group mode

Microsoft Excel - GradeBook.xls [Group]

Group mode is a very special mode in Excel. Although you only see the active worksheet, any changes that you make will apply to all of the worksheets selected in the group.

3. To add a new student alphabetically before row 19, select cell A19 and, from the menu, choose Insert – Row.

4. Type the new student's name in column A. If (and only if) all of the worksheets have the same number of assignments, you can copy the formulas from U18:W18 down to the new row.

 Caution!

It is very important to remember to ungroup the sheets immediately after adding the student. If you forget that the sheets are grouped and start entering grades on the active sheet, you will quickly overwrite grades in all of the other subjects causing a huge mess. To ungroup the sheets, right click a sheet tab name and choose Ungroup. Alternatively, you can activate any sheet that is not the active sheet.

I can assure you that 95% of the time the new student will not appear alphabetically at the top of the class. However, the law of averages says that someone reading this book will have a new student show up who needs to be at the top of the list. Adding a new student at the top of the list will cause the total formulas to be wrong at the bottom of the worksheet. Rewriting all of the total formulas is such a hassle that I instead suggest using this method to insert the new student. Follow these steps:

1. Do not add a new blank row at the top. Instead, add a new blank row above the second student in the class. Adding interior rows makes sure that the classroom average formula expands to include the new student.

2. Copy the name, grades, and formulas for the first student to the second position in the list. You will now have two students named Barnby.

3. Type the new student, Appleby, Abby in the first position in the list. Remember to clear out the number scores for the former first student.

Adding More Room for Assignments

If you need to add new columns for assignments, add them to the interior of the list. Currently, column T contains an assignment called Test 3. Before using this column, insert new column Ts to hold additional assignments. Select cell T1 and choose Insert – Column several times to insert new columns.

 Tip:

If you want to globally insert columns in all of the grading worksheets, group the sheets first as described above.

Excel Details

The workbook currently handles grades for one grading period. You may wish to extend the functionality by adding additional sections for new grading periods. These could be added off to the right. Insert new columns before the grading scale for additional grading period sections.

5

Chapter 6 – Attendance Records

Opportunity

I would like a system to personally keep track of classroom attendance. Though my school uses a district wide computerized program to keep attendance officially, the records are accessible only through the school secretary. Many times, the office attendance records are inaccessible and unavailable to me, especially after school hours (when I do much of my work!). I find I often need my own verification for student records when a parent or student asks about specific absence dates. I also want to keep track of students who are present at special study sessions and academic team meetings. These study sessions and team meetings have optional attendance but I am interested in keeping track and recording who attends and when they attended.

Is it possible to use Excel to set up a way to track classroom attendance? It would also be useful to track by grading period and for the entire school year.

Solution and Overview

You will create a form to list the names of your students and the dates of a grading period. As you mark them absent, the spreadsheet will automatically tally the total absences for the grading period and the totals for the year.

Creating the Solution

1. Start with a blank worksheet. In A1, enter a heading of "Student". In B1, enter a heading of "Absences".

2. Select cell C1. Type in the date of the first day of school and press Enter. You can type in August 29 or Aug 29. Excel will default to display 29-Aug. If you want to display the year, simply add that when typing in the date. In older versions of Excel, you may need to change the format of the cell by right clicking, choosing Number – Date, and then selecting the date format you wish to use.

   With cell C1 selected, notice that there is a thick border around cell C1. In the lower right corner, there is a square dot. This dot is called the fill handle. When you hover your mouse over the dot, the mouse pointer changes to a plus sign.

Figure 142 Selecting the fill handle

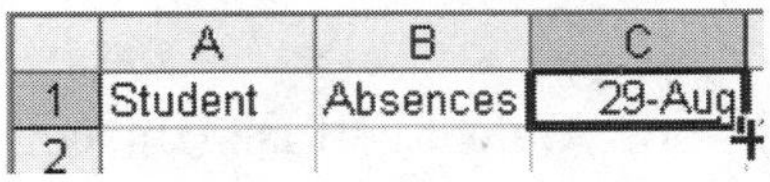

	A	B	C
1	Student	Absences	29-Aug
2			

3. Normally, you can click and drag the fill handle. However, in this case you only want to fill weekdays, so you have to right-click the fill handle and drag to the right, approximately the number of columns that would correspond to the length of the first grading period. (If you have nine-week periods, this will be somewhere around AZ1.)

Don't worry if you go too far or not far enough; you can fix that later. When you get there, let go of the mouse button and a dialog box will appear. About halfway down, you will see "Fill Weekdays".

Figure 143

Selecting Fill Weekdays from the Right-click menu

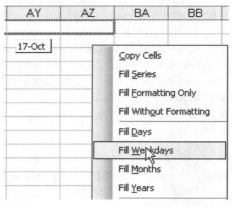

Choose Fill Weekdays from the popup menu, and the dates for the days of the week, Monday – Friday will appear. If you highlighted more dates than you need, simply delete the contents of the extra cells. To delete cell contents, highlight the cells and type the Delete key to clear the cells. If you did not go far enough, simply repeat this process, starting with the last cell that has a date in it.

The worksheet will look better if you make the headings in row 1 bold. You can apply the bold format to the entire row by selecting the row first.

4. Click on the gray "1" to the left of cell A1 to select the entire row. Look for the B icon in the Formatting Toolbar. Select this icon to apply Bold to the row.

Figure 144

Selecting the Bold icon

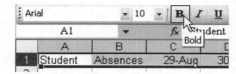

5. In column A, type in the names of all your students. To make it easier to re-alphabetize as you lose and gain students through the year, type them in as last name, first name. Most of the names will not fit in the column. Don't worry; we'll fix that later, too.

Figure 145

Entering student names

	A	B
1	Student	Absences
2	Smith, Mary	
3	Peterson, Joe	
4	Bricklin, Dan	
5	Frankston, Bob	
6	White, Josh	
7	Kohl, Jerry	

6. Select cell B2 (the cell directly beneath the word "Absences"). This is where you will enter the formula to total up the number of absences for each student. You will be using the COUNTIF function. Enter =COUNTIF(C2:??2, "X"), where ?? is the column of the last day of the grading period. Now press Enter. If your last day is in column AZ, your formula should look like this: =COUNTIF(C2:AZ2,"X")

Figure 146

Entering a formula to total absences

	B2	▼	*fx*	=COUNTIF(C2:AZ2,"X")	
	A	B	C	D	E
1	Student	Absences	29-Aug	30-Aug	31-Aug
2	Smith, Ma	0			
3	Peterson, Joe				

7. With B2 selected, double click the fill handle to copy the formula down for all your students. (It is OK to use the left mouse button to double-click the fill handle). You should now have zeroes next to all your students' names.

8. As you scroll through the worksheet, you will always want to see the names in column A and the dates in row 1. You might also want to see the absences total in B. Click on cell C2. From the Window menu, select Freeze Panes. This will add a set of lines above and to the left of C2. As you scroll to the right, columns A and B will always remain visible.

9. Select all cells by clicking on the square above and to the left of A1. From the menu, select Format – Column – AutoFit Selection. This will adjust all columns to fit the text in each cell.

This application will keep track of student absence for one grading period. If you would like to keep a cumulative record of absences and of the absences for each grading period, you have a few more steps to complete.

Extending Workbooks for Additional Grading Periods

1. After saving the workbook, delete any extra worksheets that are empty. They are probably named Sheet2 and Sheet3. To do this, select the tabs one at a time; right-click and choose Delete from the menu.

2. Right click the remaining worksheet tab and choose Rename. Give the worksheet a suitable name such as 1st Grading Period.

Figure 147

Renaming a worksheet

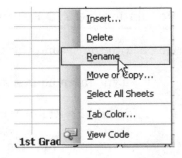

3. Now, make an exact copy of this worksheet. To do this, right-click on the worksheet tab and choose Move or Copy to display the Move or Copy dialog box. In the Before Sheet section, choose (move to end). In the lower left corner, choose Create a copy and click OK.

Figure 148

Selecting options in the Move or Copy dialog

A second tab will now appear with the same name as your other worksheet, except it will have a (2) at the end.

Figure 149 A worksheet copy has a (2) in its name

4. Right-click the new tab and choose Rename. Name the worksheet 2nd Grading Period.

5. You will want a new column before column B to hold absences from previous grading periods. In the new worksheet, select column B. Click on the B above row 1 in column B to highlight the entire column. Right-click and choose Insert. A new column B will appear. Label it YTD (for Year to Date). Adjust column width by highlighting the column and selecting Format – Column – AutoFit Selection, as you did before.

6. Make as many more copies of 2nd Grading Period worksheet as you will need for the school year. Rename each tab appropriately. In cell D1 of each new worksheet, type in the date of the first day of each grading period; right-click and fill in the weekdays, as you did before.

Populating the YTD Figures

Go back to the second worksheet and highlight cell B2. Do the following:

1. Type in an equals sign (=).

2. Press the Right-Arrow key once.

3. Type in a plus sign (+).

4. Click the tab for the first worksheet; click on cell B2 and press Enter.

5. Copy this new formula down for all your students by double clicking the fill handle in B2.

6. Repeat this for each of the remaining worksheets. When typing in the formula, you will click back to the *previous* worksheet, instead of the first.

Using the Application

On either a daily or weekly basis, enter the absences for your students using either a lower or upper case X.

If you teach anywhere in the world, your student roster is going to change (sometimes daily!) Remember that if you eliminate a student, make sure you also eliminate their absence records. On each worksheet, select the entire row, right-click, and choose Delete.

To add a student, click on a cell in the row just below the new student. From the menu, select Insert – Row. Type the new student's name in the new row. Copy down the formulas from the row above.

Before you get started, you may want to make a master copy by using Save As and saving it as a Template. That way, you will always have a fresh copy to which you can go back.

Excel Details

With a little extra work, you can make each sheet a little easier to read by inserting a column after every Friday date and adjusting its width to 1. This will give you a visual break at the end of each week.

Figure 150

Using a column as a visual break

	C	D	E	F	G	H	I	J	K
	29-Aug	30-Aug	31-Aug	1-Sep	2-Sep		5-Sep	6-Sep	7-Sep
	A	A							A
			T	A	A		A	A	A

You may also want to add color to the headings (row 1). You can do this by selecting all the cells with text in row 1 and right clicking. Choose Format cells and the Patterns tab, and then a light shade of your favorite color.

You can use this application to keep track of any event that you want to by adding another column after the student names and changing the formula that keeps track of absences. For example, if you also want to keep track of tardies, the new formula in a new column would be the same as before, except with "T" instead of "X". You could not enter both a T and an X in the same day for a student, however. (On the other hand, a student couldn't be both absent and tardy on the same day!)

Figure 151

Tracking absences and tardies

fx =COUNTIF(E2:AA2,"T")

C	D	E	F	G
Absence	Tardies	29-Aug	30-Aug	31-Aug
3	2	A	A	
5	5			T

It is also possible to change the look of the application by having two columns under each date, so that you could keep track of two events that could occur on the same day. (For example, tardy and an after school help session.) To do this, you need to have two merged columns for each day of the grading period. Highlight two columns, right-click, and select Format Cells – Alignment. Under Text control, select Merge Cells. Now type in the first day of the grading period, and fill in to the right as before.

Now you have two columns underneath each date for each student. Of course, you now need to add the extra column and formula after the student names to keep count of this event. If you are working with "either-or" events (such as absent-tardy, or detention- study session), you could actually keep track of up to four different events in two columns.

Figure 152

Tracking two either-or events in one column

	A	B	C	D	E	F	G	H	I
1	**Student**	**ID #**	**29-Aug**		**30-Aug**		**31-Aug**		**1**
2	Mary	001	A		D	W			
3	Joe	003							
4	Pete	004							
5	Susie	002							
6									
7		KEY:	A = absent						
8			T = tardy						
9			D = detention						
10			W = after school workshop						
11									

The "gotcha" here, however, is that adjusting the column width as before will not work. You will need to highlight all the columns with dates in them, right-click and select Column width, and then type in a column width. Play around with it until you get something you like, but somewhere between 3-6 ought to work. You may also want to center the dates within their combined two cells.

Chapter 7 – Lesson Plan Sheets

Opportunity

Lesson planning and organization is an important part of every teacher's day. Lesson planning is not only for teachers to refer to during the school day, but can also be used for other instances. In case of an absence, teachers are responsible for leaving adequate plans for a substitute teacher. Teachers can also use lesson plans for documentation of lessons taught and to fulfill job requirements set by their corporation. As teachers set their daily schedules and begin to lesson plan, certain times of the day need to be set aside for regular commitments such as lunch time, recess, breaks, academic subjects, etc. Teachers often find that many parts of the school day are part of a school-wide schedule set by the principal or corporation. These dictated parts of the daily schedule, over which teachers have no control, combined with their own classroom agenda, comprise the daily and weekly classroom routine. This "set schedule" or daily routine creates the backbone of a teacher's daily lesson planning.

When teachers plan their lessons, they are most often given a blank lesson plan book to fill in and chart out the day's activities. I find filling in the plan book's pages with set schedules and repetitive tasks very tedious and time consuming. Many commitments and activities are repeatedly written down day after day or week by week. I would like to find a way, using Excel, to create a lesson plan template that I could use as a blueprint for my daily lesson planning. I would like to set up the template or blank form with the daily classroom schedule and times. This template could be then filled in, printed off, and put in a three-ring binder for easy reference throughout the day. This computerized way of lesson planning would greatly cut down my planning time, allowing me to utilize my time more efficiently and effectively.

This application in Excel would not require the program to calculate any figures. It would mostly be used as a way to create a grid or form that could then be filled in by a teacher. The teacher could print off the forms with just the routine schedule and then fill in the daily activities by hand OR the teacher could open up the form daily, insert lesson activities via the computer, and then print off the schedule. Teachers like organization and the wonderful boxes that Excel provides can really help to systematize their planning.

Two years ago, I started putting my daily plans on the computer using Word. I took a lot of time to set up the beginning form, but after my weekly schedule was set and typed out, it took only a few minutes to change page numbers or activities. Word allowed me to save time, but my planning was very wordy and each daily plan sheet was 4-7 pages long. I was hoping that Excel would streamline the planning process.

Solution and Overview

The solution will create one week's worth of lesson plans in a single workbook. Each day's plan will be on a single worksheet, with five worksheets in the workbook.

The goal is to maximize the amount of information that can be put on a single sheet of paper.

Creating the Solution

Start with a blank workbook with a single worksheet. You will format this worksheet for a single day and then copy the worksheet for the remaining four days of the week.

1. Your first step is to reduce the margins to allow more columns in the worksheet. From the menu, select File – Page Setup. On the Margins tab, change the margins to 0.5" for the top, right, and bottom. Change the left margin to 0.75". The left margin of .75 allows for a three-hole punch to not affect the form.

Figure 153

Setting margins in Page Setup

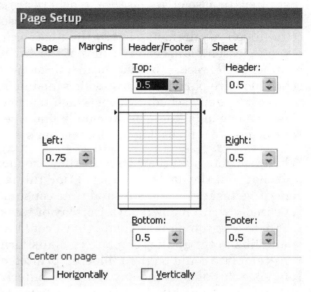

Next, you will want Excel to show you how many columns and rows can fit on a single printed page.

2. Choose the Print Preview button in the Page Setup form. Later versions of Excel may nag you that "Microsoft Excel did not find anything to print". Click OK to dismiss this dialog. The result is that Excel draws in dotted lines at the right and bottom edge of the page.

3. Determine how many class period divisions are needed and add one more for the header. Divide the number of rows by this number. If there is a remainder, it can later be added to the number of rows in the header. (i.e., 8 classes + 1 = 9. 56 rows in print area divided by 9 = 6 with remainder 2. Header will have 8 rows, (6 + 2) and each period will have 6.)

3a. Highlight the rows needed for the first period in column A. From the menu, choose Format – Cells. On the Alignment tab, choose the checkbox for Merge Cells. In the Text Alignment section, change Horizontal and Vertical to Center. Change the Orientation setting to 90.

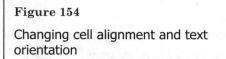

Figure 154

Changing cell alignment and text orientation

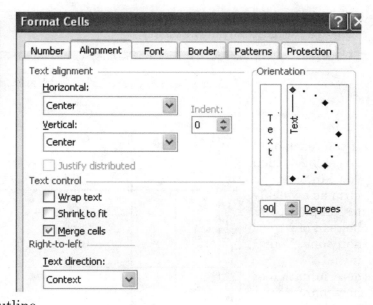

4. Still in the Format Cells dialog, select the Borders tab. On the Borders tab, select the icon for Outline.

Figure 155

Setting borders to outline

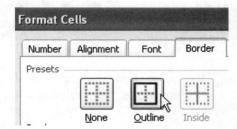

4a. Click OK to close the Format Cells dialog.

5. Your cellpointer will now be in A1 cell, which is six rows tall. You want to copy this formatting from A1 to B1. Type Ctrl+C to copy A1. Using the mouse, select cell B1 and press Enter to copy. This will copy the formatting, including the merged cells, to column B.

6. Select the rest of the columns with the same number of rows. Type Ctrl+1 to display the Format Cells dialog. On the Alignment tab, select merge cells and alignment as in Step 3, but do not change font rotation. In addition, check the box for Wrap text. This will allow you to type a paragraph in a single cell if necessary. On the Border tab, select the Outline.

7. Select all of the cells in the rows and columns that you were just working on and copy them. Select the first cell in row A that will be in the next time period, and Paste. Continue to select a new cell and Paste until you are at the end of your print area.

8. Put the time of the class in either column A or B, and the subject or class period number in the other. Use the rest of the columns to type in the instructions or simply print and write by hand.

Figure 156 Lesson plan worksheet

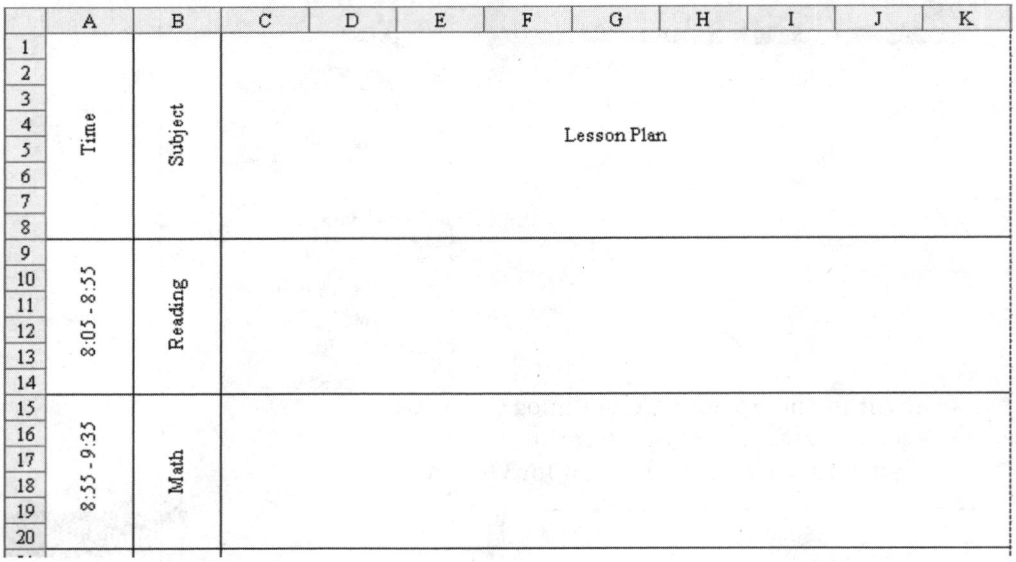

If you teach only one subject, then you can use this form as a weekly lesson plan page instead of a daily one. Your initial determination of how many rows to use will be based on six divisions (M – F, plus a heading).

	A	B	C	D	E	F	G	H	I	J	K
1											
2											
3	Time	Subject				Lesson Plan					
4											
...											
9-14	8:05 - 8:55	Reading									
15-20	8:55 - 9:35	Math									

9. Once the template is made, Ctrl+Drag the worksheet tab to make a copy. Repeat until you have five copies of the lesson plan in one workbook.

Using the Application

You will have a large space to type the lesson plan for each subject. There are a couple of ways to control the word wrap for each subject. As you type, Excel will naturally break between words at the edge of the cell.

Figure 157

Lesson plan

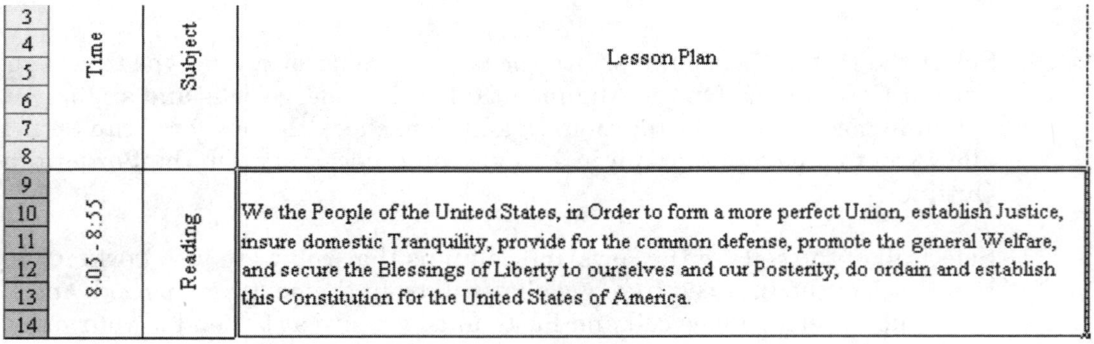

	Time	Subject	Lesson Plan
3-8			
9-14	8:05 - 8:55	Reading	We the People of the United States, in Order to form a more perfect Union, establish Justice, insure domestic Tranquility, provide for the common defense, promote the general Welfare, and secure the Blessings of Liberty to ourselves and our Posterity, do ordain and establish this Constitution for the United States of America.

However, sometimes you may want to start a new line within a cell. To start a new line, type Alt+Enter. This allows you to format your comments on several lines.

15			
16			Check Homework (Math Links 4.2)
17	8:55 - 9:35	Math	Cover pp 47-49
18			In-class worksheet
19			
20			

Figure 158

Using Alt+Enter to start a new line

Excel Details

If you have a couple of extra rows left at the bottom of the worksheet, you might want to add these to the header in row 1. Normally, you might select cell A3 and select Insert – Rows two times to insert new rows above row 3. However, because you have merged cells A1:A6, cell A3 no longer exists! To insert a new row above row 3, select a cell far to the right in row 3. For example, you might select cell Z3. From the menu, select Insert – Rows.

7

7

Chapter 8 – Random Sequence for Book Reports

Opportunity

Your students have to do oral book reports. Is there a fair way to assign the sequence? Students named Amber and Andy are hoping you don't use the alphabetical method.

Solution and Overview

Create a random sort in Excel.

Creating the Solution

1. In cell A1, type a heading of "Name". Type the student's names into a column starting in A2.

2. In cell B1, type a heading of "Random". Select cells from B2 down to B16. Type =RAND(). Although many cells are selected, the formula will be typed in only the first cell.

Figure 159

Using the RAND function

	A	B
1	**Name**	**Random**
2	Amber	=RAND()
3	Andy	
4	Ashley	
5	Brandon	
6	Chris	
7	Emily	
8	Jessica	
9	Joey	
10	Josh	
11	Matt	
12	Mikey	
13	Samantha	
14	Sarah	
15	Taylor	
16	Tyler	
17		

3. To apply the formula to all of the selected cells, type Ctrl+Enter. The column will be filled with random decimals between the value of 0 and 1. Every time that you type the F9 key, the random numbers will change.

 Tip:

You could possibly have a game with the students, with someone suggesting the number of times you press the F9 key to figure out the final sequence.

Figure 160

Column filled with random numbers

	A	B
1	**Name**	**Random**
2	Amber	0.247917
3	Andy	0.658375
4	Ashley	0.746179
5	Brandon	0.292224
6	Chris	0.068936
7	Emily	0.926134
8	Jessica	0.984246
9	Joey	0.910319
10	Josh	0.805871
11	Matt	0.763002
12	Mikey	0.657269
13	Samantha	0.00024
14	Sarah	0.473641
15	Taylor	0.714599
16	Tyler	0.234955

Using the Application

Select a single cell in column B – either B1 or B2. Press the AZ Sort button in the Standard toolbar.

> **Figure 161**
>
> AZ button located on the Standard toolbar

The students' names will sort into a random sequence. Have the students make their oral book reports in the sequence shown.

> **Figure 162**
>
> Student names sorted according to column of random numbers

	A	B
1	**Name**	**Random**
2	Samantha	0.887157
3	Chris	0.417475
4	Tyler	0.09035
5	Amber	0.505513
6	Brandon	0.791774
7	Sarah	0.627155
8	Mikey	0.172279
9	Andy	0.589539
10	Taylor	0.55209
11	Ashley	0.283238
12	Matt	0.759272
13	Josh	0.757124
14	Joey	0.781856
15	Emily	0.466303
16	Jessica	0.361156

Excel Details

It is best to delete or hide column B immediately after the sort. In Figure 160, you will notice that Samantha had the lowest value with 0.00024. Excel sorted the names based on the values in Figure 160. After the sort, Excel then performs a final calculation. This forces all of the random numbers to recalculate. If Samantha is sharp, she might protest that her new value of 0.88 is not the lowest value in the list.

For older students, it would make sense to lock the random numbers before doing the sort. Select Range B2:B16. Type Ctrl+C to copy, then Alt+ESV to choose Edit – Paste Special – Values.

Chapter 9 – Randomly Calling on a Student

Opportunity

Can the computer have a teacher's pet? Probably not. For a fun way to keep people engaged, why not let the computer decide whom you are going to call on? With the computer selecting who gets called next, everyone has an equal chance of being selected. The possibility of being selected by the computer might keep kids engaged in the discussion.

Solution and Overview

The solution is similar to that in the preceding chapter. Basically, you will add one formula with three Excel functions, MIN, MATCH, and INDEX, to identify the student who has the lowest random number.

Creating the Solution

Start with the workbook that you created in Chapter 8 – Random Sequence for Book Reports. This workbook has a list of your students in column A and a series of RAND functions in column B.

Insert seven blank rows at the top of the worksheet. Select rows one through seven by clicking on the 1 and dragging down to the 7 to the left of column A. From the menu, select Insert – Rows.

If you just want the answer, skip ahead to Putting It All Together. However, if you want to see how the functions work, then follow along.

Finding the Student with the Lowest Random Number

Excel offers functions for finding the highest or lowest number in a range. The MIN and MAX functions accept as an argument any range of cells. To see how this works, enter =MIN(B9:B23) in cell B4. Every time that you press the F9 key, new random numbers are generated and Excel shows the smallest random number from the range in B4.

9

Figure 163

Determining the smallest random number

	B4	▼	ƒx	=MIN(B9:B23)	
	A	B	C	D	
1					
2					
3					
4	Min:	0.048815			
5					
6					
7					
8	**Name**	**Random**			
9	Samantha	0.727826			
10	Chris	0.941017			
11	Tyler	0.217395			
12	Amber	0.244673			
13	Brandon	0.049424			
14	Sarah	0.23788			
15	Mikey	0.048815			
16	Andy	0.446548			
17	Taylor	0.456576			
18	Ashley	0.228043			
19	Matt	0.775596			
20	Josh	0.352341			
21	Joey	0.232175			
22	Emily	0.928784			
23	Jessica	0.604039			
24					

When I first read about the next function, I thought that it was fairly useless, but I was wrong. The MATCH function looks for a value within a range of cells. When it finds the value, it will return the relative row number of the match within the range. For example, in Figure 163 the function would look for 0.048815 within the range of B9:B23 and determine that the match occurs in cell B15. The MATCH function would tell you that B15 is the seventh cell in B9:B23. So, the result of =MATCH(B4,B9:B23,0) would be 7.

The final function also seemed useless on its own. The INDEX function returns the value from a particular row and column from a range. You have the MATCH function telling you that the lowest value in column B is happening in the seventh row of a particular range. Now – to find the student who is in the seventh row and first column of A9:A23, you would use =INDEX(A9:A23,7,1). Of course, to make this easier to use, you would put the result of the MATCH function in the formula instead of typing a "7" as the second argument.

 Note:

The MATCH function could behave in three different ways, based on the third argument passed to the function. A value of 0 requires an exact match. A value of 1 or -1 allows MATCH to return the value equal to or closest, either larger or smaller. Note that if you use -1 or 1 as the third argument, the range must be sorted in sequence.

Figure 164 shows the three individual parts of the formula. Cell B4 identifies that the smallest number after the last recalculation in 0.050842. Cell B5 identifies that this number occurs in the 14th row within B9:B23. Cell B6 identifies that Emily is the 14th student in the list. The computer suggests that you should call on Emily.

Figure 164

Worksheet with three separate formulas to determine name of student to call upon

	B6	▼	fx	=INDEX(A9:A23,B5,1)	
	A	B	C	D	
1					
2					
3					
4	Min:	0.050842	=MIN(B9:B23)		
5	Match:	14	=MATCH(B4,B9:B23,0)		
6	Index:	Emily	=INDEX(A9:A23,B5,1)		
7					
8	**Name**	**Random**			
9	Samantha	0.093782			
10	Chris	0.803118			
11	Tyler	0.953627			
12	Amber	0.524954			
13	Brandon	0.656115			
14	Sarah	0.417894			
15	Mikey	0.524153			
16	Andy	0.575049			
17	Taylor	0.945045			
18	Ashley	0.473262			
19	Matt	0.899511			
20	Josh	0.127294			
21	Joey	0.263001			
22	Emily	0.050842			
23	Jessica	0.522271			
24					

Building a Single Formula from Intermediate Formulas

When you are trying to figure out a complex formula, sometimes it is easier to build the formula in several cells, as shown in Figure 164. Now that you have the logic working, there is really no reason to leave the worksheet with three separate formulas when they can be combined into one formula.

There is a trick for copying and pasting from one formula to another.

1. The formula in cell B5 uses a value calculated in cell B4. Select cell B4. Press the F2 key to put the cell in Edit mode. With the mouse, highlight all of the characters in the formula bar except for the leading equals sign.

Figure 165 Highlighting all formula characters except the equals sign

=MIN(B9:B23)

2. Type Ctrl+C to copy these characters to the clipboard. Press the Esc key to exit the editing mode in cell B4.

3. Move to cell B5. Press F2 to put this cell in Edit mode. In the formula bar, highlight the characters "B4".

Figure 166 Highlighting characters to be replaced by a formula

=MATCH(B4,B9:B23,0)

4. Type Ctrl+V to paste the first formula, thus replacing B4 in the second formula.

Figure 167 Replacing highlighted characters with a formula

`=MATCH(MIN(B9:B23),B9:B23,0)`

5. The formula in B6 has a reference to the result from B5. Select cell B5. Press the F2 key on the keyboard to put B5 in Edit mode. With the mouse, select all of the characters in the formula bar except the equals sign. Type Ctrl+C to copy.

Figure 168 Highlighting and copying portion of a formula

`=MATCH(MIN(B9:B23),B9:B23,0)`

6. Type Esc to finish editing B5. Move to B6 and press the F2 key to put B6 in Edit mode. Highlight the characters B5 in the formula.

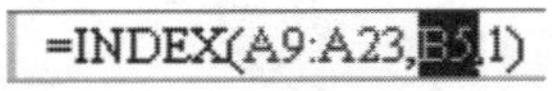

Figure 169 Highlighting characters to be replaced by a formula

`=INDEX(A9:A23,B5,1)`

7. Type Ctrl+V to replace the reference to B5 with the formula from B5.

Figure 170 Completing the formula

`=INDEX(A9:A23,MATCH(MIN(B9:B23),B9:B23,0),1)`

8. Type Enter to accept the formula.

To move the formula from B7 up to A2, it is important that you cut and paste the formula. When you cut a formula in Excel, you can paste it somewhere else and all of the cell addresses in the formula will remain unchanged.

9. Select B7. Type Ctrl+X to cut. Select cell A2. Type Ctrl+V to paste.

Putting It All Together

The formula in cell A2 should be: =INDEX(A9:A23,MATCH(MIN(B9:B23),B9:B23,FALSE),1).

Add an instruction in cell A1: "Press F9 to have the computer choose a new student".

	A2	▼	*fx*	=INDEX(A9:A23,MATCH(MIN(B9:B23),B9:B23,FALSE),1)		
	A	B	C	D	E	F	G
1	Press F9 to have the computer choose a new student					
2	Brandon						
3							
4							
5							
6							
7							
8	**Name**	**Random**					
9	Samantha	0.420266					
10	Chris	0.344195					
11	Tyler	0.368449					
12	Amber	0.573988					
13	Brandon	0.196414					
14	Sarah	0.842695					
15	Mikey	0.41346					
16	Andy	0.415407					
17	Taylor	0.991465					
18	Ashley	0.979709					
19	Matt	0.869737					
20	Josh	0.938826					
21	Joey	0.334488					
22	Emily	0.309617					
23	Jessica	0.615835					

Figure 171

Completed worksheet with three formulas combined into one

Using the Application

Press F9 and a new student name appears in cell A2.

Excel Details

It is also possible to use conditional formatting to highlight the student with the lowest random number.

1. Open the original worksheet from the Random Sort chapter. Select cell A2 and choose Format – Conditional Formatting from the menu.

2. In the Conditional Formatting dialog, change the Cell Value Is dropdown to Formula Is. Type the following formula in the formula box: =B2=MIN($B$2:$B$16). Click the Format button and choose a green color on the Pattern tab. Click OK to close the Format Cells dialog and then press OK again to close the Conditional Formatting dialog.

 Note:

95% of the time, nothing will be highlighted in green after setting up the condition for just the first cell. Don't expect to see anything change after you set up the condition in A2.

3. Select cell A2. Type Ctrl+C to copy this to the clipboard. Select the range of students in A2:A16. From the menu, choose Edit – Paste Special – Formats – OK. This will copy the conditional format from A2 to the other cells. Now, the student with the lowest random number will be highlighted in green. To select a new student, press F9.

9

Chapter 10 – Tracking Student Information

Opportunity

How can you track student information per classroom (phone numbers, addresses, parental information)? Is there something that would let you keep track of your individual students, rather like a computerized address book, that could also keep track of notes home, phone calls, and other pertinent data?

I have found it helpful to document parental contacts and/or disciplinary actions throughout the school year, especially in instances where documentation is needed to prove behavior problems, for retention, for special education services, or to accommodate doctor's requests for classroom performance (usually for counseling or medication).

Solution and Overview

A single worksheet with columns for name, address, and telephone would be fine for tracking basic information for each student. However, once you need to record information about several dated events for each student, it then makes sense to build one worksheet for each student.

The solution presented will have some fairly complex concepts such as VLOOKUPs and Hyperlinks. These features would make it easier to populate and use the address book. Both features are optional. You can easily leave these features out without a tremendous loss in functionality.

Creating the Solution

Start with a workbook with a single worksheet. Rename this worksheet "Class". Add headings across row 1 for the basic student information such as name, address, telephone, mother contact info, and father contact info. Either import student information from a school-supplied list or type this information into the worksheet.

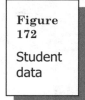

Figure 172

Student data

	A	B	C	D	E	F	G	H	I
1	Student	Street	City	ST	ZIP	Home Phone	Mother	Mother Work Phone	Mother Cell
2	BLACK, LAUREN	1894 Main Street	South Bend	IN	46556	(330) 555-1212	GLORIA BLACK	(330) 555-1212	(330) 555-121;
3	COLLINS, JOSEPH	1317 Main Street	South Bend	IN	46556	(330) 555-1212	ANN COLLINS	(330) 555-1212	(330) 555-121;
4	GOMEZ, JENNIFER	292 Main Street	South Bend	IN	46556	(330) 555-1212	JEAN GOMEZ	(330) 555-1212	(330) 555-121;
5	HUNT, NANCY	141 Main Street	South Bend	IN	46556	(330) 555-1212	THERESA HUNT	(330) 555-1212	(330) 555-121;
6	JAMES, ANN	1271 Main Street	South Bend	IN	46556	(330) 555-1212	JANICE JAMES	(330) 555-1212	(330) 555-121;
7	JORDAN, STEPHEN	1354 Main Street	South Bend	IN	46556	(330) 555-1212	TERESA JORDAN	(330) 555-1212	(330) 555-121;

10

This basic database is fine for contact information. However, once you want to start keeping track of incidents, it would be better to keep one entire worksheet for each student.

You will set up one basic worksheet for the first student and then copy this worksheet for each student. Thus, it makes sense to think about the fields and information that you will want to track for each student. In this example, you will copy the headings already in the database, and then add a table with date, event, and comments. In your case, you may want to add additional sections.

Building the First Student Worksheet

From the menu, select Insert – Worksheet. This will add a new worksheet before the Class worksheet. If you like things to be neat and organized, you might want the Class worksheet to be the first worksheet. It is easy to move worksheets around. Click on the worksheet tab for Class and drag it to the left of the worksheet tab for Sheet2.

Figure 173	
Moving a worksheet tab by clicking and dragging	

1. The first step is to copy the headings that go across row 1 of the Class worksheet and have them go down column A of Sheet2. This process is called transposing the data. Select the Class worksheet. Select the headings in A1:N1. Type Ctrl+C to copy. Select the Sheet2 worksheet. Select cell A1. From the menu, choose Edit – Paste Special. On the Paste Special dialog, choose the bottom option to Transpose the data.

Figure 174

Transpose headings using Copy and Paste Special

2. Double click the line between the gray A heading and the gray B heading to make column A wide enough.

Figure 175

Automatically adjusting column widths

3. Choose the Align Right icon in the Formatting toolbar to align the headings to the right.

Figure 176

Right-aligned headings

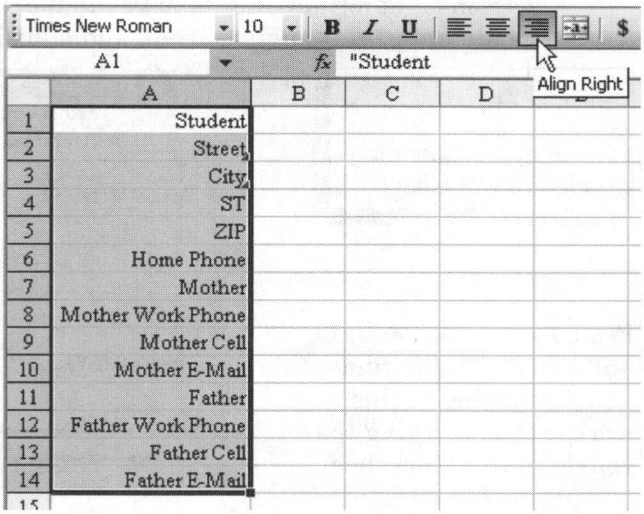

	A
1	Student
2	Street
3	City
4	ST
5	ZIP
6	Home Phone
7	Mother
8	Mother Work Phone
9	Mother Cell
10	Mother E-Mail
11	Father
12	Father Work Phone
13	Father Cell
14	Father E-Mail

4. Copy the first student name to cell B1 of the worksheet.

It would be very clever if the worksheet could look at the name in B1 and pull the rest of the contact information from the Class worksheet. It is possible to build such a formula in B2 and copy the formula down to the other rows.

5. The formula for B2 is:
   =INDEX(Class!$A$2:$N$16,MATCH(B$1,Class!$A$2:$A$16,0),ROW())

The INDEX function is used to pull a particular row and column out of a rectangular range of data. =INDEX(Class!$A$2:$N$16,2,1) would return the second row and first column from the students listed in A2:N16 on the class worksheet. By itself, the INDEX function is nearly useless. However, if you can create clever formulas to specify the row and column, INDEX will then become very useful.

You can use the MATCH function to look at the student name in B1 and return the row number within the student list. MATCH is described in more detail on page 82.

To get the column number, I used a very specific trick. Note that I made sure that the first column of data in the class worksheet was pasted to the first row of the student worksheet. This allowed me to use the ROW function. On row 14, the ROW function will return the value of 14. Thus, in the student worksheet, using ROW as the column indicator will return the 14th column from the Class worksheet to the 14th row of the student worksheet.

Figure 177

Completed formula

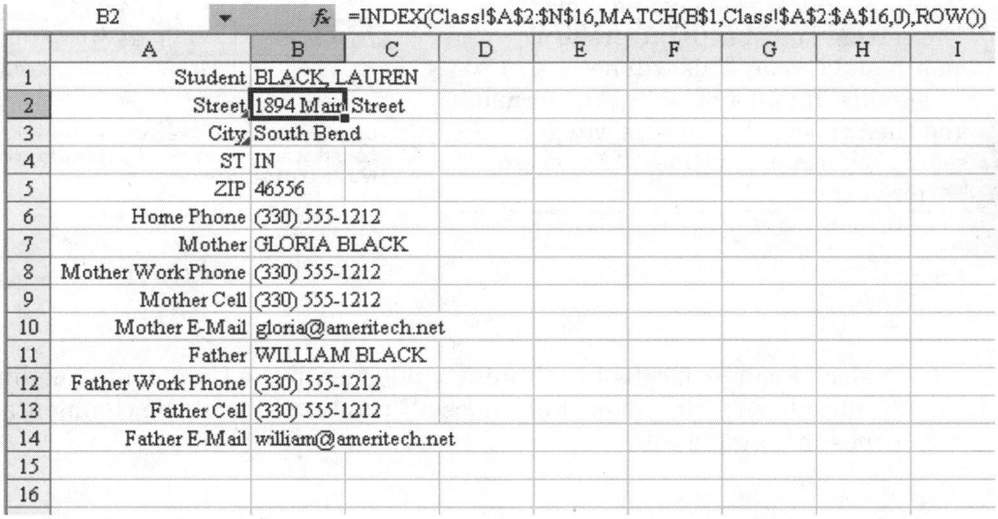

=INDEX(Class!$A$2:$N$16,MATCH(B$1,Class!$A$2:$A$16,0),ROW())

	A	B
1	Student	BLACK, LAUREN
2	Street	1894 Main Street
3	City	South Bend
4	ST	IN
5	ZIP	46556
6	Home Phone	(330) 555-1212
7	Mother	GLORIA BLACK
8	Mother Work Phone	(330) 555-1212
9	Mother Cell	(330) 555-1212
10	Mother E-Mail	gloria@ameritech.net
11	Father	WILLIAM BLACK
12	Father Work Phone	(330) 555-1212
13	Father Cell	(330) 555-1212
14	Father E-Mail	william@ameritech.net
15		
16		

This is all pretty complex stuff, so feel free to copy the formula to B2 and then copy it down without entirely understanding how it works.

6. Because this worksheet will be the template for all additional students, add more sections and formatting. In my example, I have one section for Notes, and then an incident log. You might wish to add additional sections.

Figure 178

Notes and incident log added to worksheet

	A	B	C
13	Father Cell	(330) 555-1212	
14	Father E-Mail	william@ameritech.net	
15			
16	Special Notes:		
17			
18			
19			
20			
21			
22	Events this Year		
23			
24	Date	Type	Comments
25			
26			
27			
28			

It may seem like overkill, but it is worth the time to add formatting to this worksheet. Anything that you do to this worksheet will get copied 30 times over, so it makes sense to get this worksheet correct.

7. Highlight the range of blank cells underneath the date heading. Choose however many you think that you might need for your most troublesome student – perhaps A25:A75. Select Format – Cells, and apply the date format that you would prefer.

Figure 179

Formatting a range of cells as dates

 Note:

Be careful when choosing date formats. "14-Mar" indicates a day and a month. The setting for "Mar-01" refers to a month and a year. This will not be acceptable. If in doubt, select the format and then choose the Custom category to see if the format contains "d" for day or "y" for years.

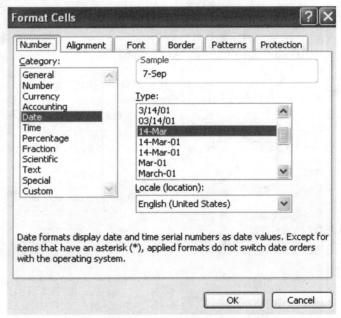

8. Select a range of cells in column C underneath the Comments heading. Select Format – Cells. On the Alignment tab, choose Wrap text so that the comments can take several lines in a single cell.

10

Figure 180

Selecting Wrap text

9. Select the range of cells from A25:C75 and format the cells. On the Alignment tab, choose a Vertical alignment of Top.

10. Do you want to standardize the types of incidents in column B? Select B25:B75. From the menu, choose Data – Validation.
    In the Allow box, select List.
    In the Source box, type a list of the popular events. The list won't be all-inclusive, but it should include the most popular ones.

Figure 181

Type the validation list in the Source field

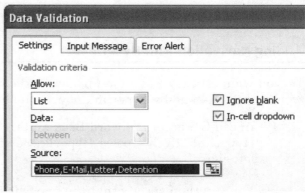

11. You want the flexibility to put something else in column B, so choose the Error Alert tab. Change the Error Alert from Stop to Information. Even better, uncheck the "Show Error Alert" option and Excel will not hassle you at all.

Figure 182

Turn off error alerts to allow other values

12. Setting up the validation will allow you to easily choose a type for each incident. You are free to type a different value in column B if you choose.

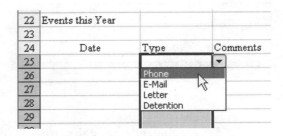

Figure 183

Drop-down to select validation criteria

13. You will want to set up the print settings for this sheet before making 30 copies of it. Select File – Page Setup. On the Margins tab, choose margins that you prefer. On the Sheet tab, indicate that the print area is A:C and that you want to repeat rows 1:1 at the top of every page.

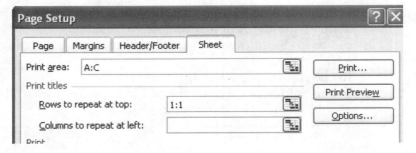

Figure 184

Selecting print area and rows to repeat

Adding Navigation with Hyperlinks

Do you want an easy way to jump back to the main Class worksheet from any student worksheet? Then add a hyperlink now to the top of the student worksheet.

1. In cell C1, enter the word Back and right-justify that cell. Select C1 and choose Insert-Hyperlink. In the Insert Hyperlink dialog, choose "Place In This Document" along the left side.

2. You can then specify that the hyperlink should go to the Class worksheet, cell A1.

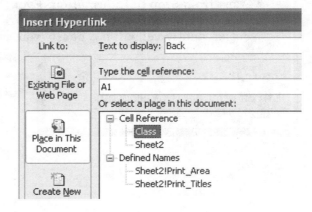

Figure 185

Setting hyperlink destination

Making the Student Name a Dropdown

As I started to use the worksheet in real life, I realized that it would be cool if the student name field on each worksheet contained a dropdown so that I could select the student. This way, I wouldn't have to copy and paste the names once for each student.

1. Technically, you are not supposed to be able to have a data validation dropdown that uses a list of cells on another worksheet. However, there is a tricky workaround. Go to the Class worksheet. Select the range of A2 down to a few cells below the last student.

Figure 186

Selecting a range

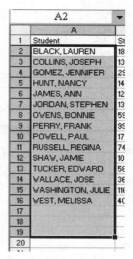

2. To the left of the formula bar, there is an area indicating that the current cell is A2. This area is known as the Name Box. Click inside the name box and type a one-word name for the range, perhaps something like ClassList. After typing the name, press Enter.

Figure 187

Naming the range

3. This shortcut sets up a named range called ClassList. (The long way of setting up a named range is to use Insert – Name – Define. If you later need to edit the range specified by the name, you would have to use that menu command to access the full dialog box.)

4. By setting up a named range, the name is available to all worksheets in the workbook. Go back to the Sheet2 worksheet. Select cell B1. Select Data Validation. On the Settings tab, choose List from the Allow dropdown. In the Source box, type an equals sign followed by the name given above.

Figure 188

Using a Named Range in the Source field

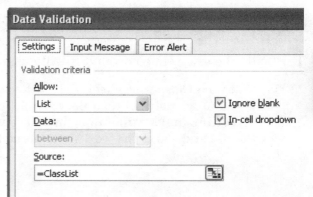

10

Replicating the Worksheet for Each Student

Once you believe that you have correctly formatted the student worksheet, it is time to make copies of the worksheet for each student.

1. The first student worksheet is complete. Double-click the Sheet tab and type a new name for the worksheet. Since this sheet is for Lauren Black, a logical name would be Black.

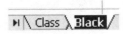

Figure 189 Naming the new worksheet

2. To copy a worksheet, hold down Ctrl while you drag the sheet tab to a new location. Ctrl+Drag Black and you will have a new worksheet called Black (2).

3. Select cell B2. From the dropdown, select the next student.

Figure 190 Using a drop-down to select the next student

4. Since this student is Joe Collins, double-click the sheet tab and rename the worksheet as Collins.

5. Ctrl+Click and Drag the Collins tab to create a new worksheet for the third student. Continue dragging, changing the name in B1, and renaming the worksheet until you have one worksheet for each student. By far, this is the most tedious part of the process. Once you get into a rhythm, you can do perhaps two per minute, so it will take you 15 minutes to rename sheets for your whole class.

6. Before you begin entering any incident data, make a copy of a blank student worksheet and name it ForNewStudents. As new students enter your class, you can Ctrl+Click ForNewStudents and drag to create a copy of the blank workbook.

Optional: Adding Hyperlinks from the Class Worksheet to the Individual Worksheets.

This will take extra time now, but it will make the worksheet easier to use later.

1. Go to the Class worksheet. Select the student in cell A2. Type Ctrl+K to add a hyperlink. If you previously set up a Back hyperlink on the student worksheet, then the Insert Hyperlink dialog will still be in "Place in this Document" mode. Scroll up to the top of the list and select the worksheet name for Black.

Figure 191

Selecting the Black worksheet

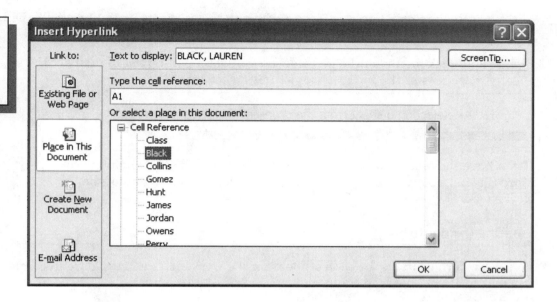

2. Click OK to dismiss the dialog. Move down to the student in A3 of the Class worksheet. Repeat the steps to add a hyperlink, pointing this student to the Collins worksheet. As you keep adding hyperlinks, you will note that the Insert Hyperlink always defaults to show you defined names such as the Print Titles names on each worksheet. You will have to continually keep scrolling up to the Cell Reference section to select the proper worksheet.

3. When you have completed adding hyperlinks to each student, you will find that you can quickly jump to any student worksheet by clicking on the underlined student name. You can return to the class list by choosing the Back link in C1 of each worksheet.

Using the Application

Assuming you have more than 10 students in the class, you will have more tabs listed than you can see. This makes it somewhat hard to navigate between the worksheets. Here are some strategies for making this easier.

The bottom of the Excel screen contains a list of worksheet tabs and a horizontal scrollbar. You can allocate more space for the sheet tabs and less space for the scrollbar. Click on this button and drag to the right.

Figure 192 Adjusting sheet tab space

To the left of the sheet tabs are four arrow buttons for tab selection. You can use these buttons to scroll to the first worksheet, back one sheet, forward one sheet, or to the last worksheet.

Figure 193 Scrolling through sheet tabs

Note that clicking on a button does not select the next sheet. It simply scrolls the tabs into view so that you can select the proper tab.

If you right-click on any of the arrows, you will get a pop-up list of many of the sheets. If the sheet you want is in the list, you can simply select that sheet.

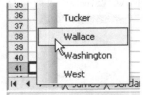

Figure 194 Selecting a sheet from the drop-down menu

If you have too many sheets, this contextual menu will offer an option for More Sheets. You will then get a scrollable dialog box listing all of the worksheets.

Entering Incidents

You can record contacts for each student on the worksheet. Enter a date in column A, type of incident in B, and notes in column C.

Figure 195

Listing events

	A	B	C
24	Date	Type	Comments
25	2-Sep	Detention	Distracting others in class
26	5-Sep	Detention	Caught stealing gum from another student's class
27	6-Sep	Phone	Talked to mom. She said she would discuss the problem with Joe. We agreed to follow up in one week.
28	7-Sep		

Excel Details

Once you have several incidents entered for a student, you might want to turn on the AutoFilter for that worksheet. Select cell A25 and choose Data – Filter – AutoFilter. This will add dropdowns to the headings in row 24. You can now easily see all of the Detentions or Phone calls at a glance.

Figure 196 View detentions using AutoFilter drop-down

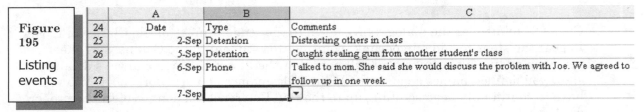

Chapter 11 – Student Mailing Lists

Opportunity

Many times during the school year, I have needed to access the school's database to find students that would benefit from offered services and different types of information. Sometimes, this need is for formal purposes as directed by the school office, such as an informational letter sent home to all third grade parents. Often, I need to find student data for my own classroom of students. An example would be a listing of my students who ride a particular bus route that will be affected by a change in schedule. Unfortunately, the school database is only available by asking the school secretary or the principal; due to their often busy and hectic schedules, the information is not easily accessible. Also, the school database does not lend itself to quick disaggregation of information. Usually, I have to use the program to find the information, going student by student, and then write out the information needed by hand.

Is there a way to use Excel to take student information, such as name, address, ethnicity, special services, language spoken at home, gender, age, grade level, and teacher, from the school-wide data base and to disaggregate needed information to quickly create data lists and mailing lists?

Solution and Overview

In my experience, the school secretary is often the key person to really keeping the school running.

You need to partner with the secretary in the first portion of this task. The benefits will be mutual, however. If you work together for 30 minutes to figure out how to make the first part work, then you will never have to bother her for student lists again this year.

Teachers, don't take this the wrong way, but if your secretary knew that in 10 minutes, she could get rid of your pain-in-the-neck requests for the rest of the year, she would gladly be willing to help.

(Note to the school secretary: Don't tell the nice teacher who bought my book, but whenever any of the other 30 teachers in the building ask for a list, you can just send them to the teacher asking you for help right now – she can start producing the mailing labels from Excel. Really – I am freeing you up from a bunch of teacher requests so that you can deal with kids and parents and school board members – as if that is any better than the teachers.)

11

Creating the Solution

Getting the Data from the School Database

Your school database has a way to export student information to a file. In rare cases, the software might offer to export to an Excel file. Most often, it will have an option to write to a special kind of file called a CSV file. CSV stands for Comma Separated Values and it is the most common way for getting data from one computer to another. Other times, the software will offer to print a report to a file. In this case, the computer writes the report out to report.txt. Working with the school secretary, figure out some way to export the database to a file. You only want to have to do this once, so make sure to get all of the fields that you think you might need. If you can get first name and last name in separate fields, that is preferred to a single field. Certainly, you will need street address, city, state, zip code, and telephone. Other fields might include bus route, parent name, language spoken at home, etc.

The school secretary will probably be able to produce a file on her hard drive. She will either have to e-mail this file or put it on a floppy, a CD, or a USB drive for you to get the data to your classroom computer.

Importing the Data into Excel

If you are fortunate, you were given an Excel file or a CSV file. These can be opened directly in Excel. It is also possible that you were given a report that was printed to a file. These can be imported into Excel, but they present their own challenges.

If you have a Windows PC, use Notepad or WordPad to take a look at the file. If the columns are nicely lined up as shown in Figure 197, then the file is called a Fixed Width file.

Figure 197

Example of a Fixed Width file

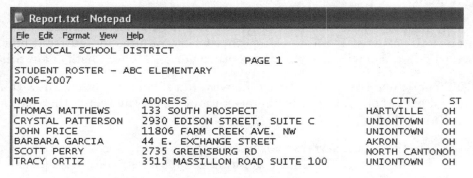

If you scroll down through the file, you might find that the data stops after a number of rows so that the program can print new titles on the next page. All of these problems are typical.

11

Figure 198

Gaps in data rows

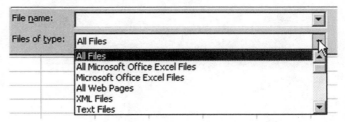

```
Report.txt - Notepad
File  Edit  Format  View  Help
KEVIN RODRIGUEZ        12992 CLEVELAND AVENUE NW        UNIONTOWN    OH
ROBERT BROOKS          650 SOUTH PROSPECT              HARTVILLE    OH
KENNETH LEE            905 WEST MAPLE STREET           HARTVILLE    OH
DONALD WILSON          PO BOX 247                      HARTVILLE    OH

XYZ LOCAL SCHOOL DISTRICT
                                            PAGE 2
STUDENT ROSTER - ABC ELEMENTARY
2006-2007

NAME                   ADDRESS                             CITY     ST
LILLIAN WAGNER         418 EAST MAPLES STREET          HARTVILLE    OH
BETTY KING             3790 EDISON STREET NE           HARTVILLE    OH
LORI WALLACE           864 WEST MAPLE STREET           HARTVILLE    OH
MARJORIE MARSHALL      9260 PLEASENTWOOD AVE NW        NORTH CANTONOH
CHARLES ALEXANDER      3874 HIGHLAND PARK NW           NORTH CANTONOH
```

 Note:

The above examples will work because the data takes up only one row per student. Some systems will produce a report where each student takes several rows. These reports are significantly harder to deal with. I spent several chapters in ""Learn Excel from Mr Excel" teaching how to deal with these reports. Because they only happen perhaps 5% in real life, I will not fill up a bunch of pages describing them here. If you have such a file, you can download the example from "Learn Excel from Mr Excel" at this secret page: http://www.mrexcel.com/manyrows.html

Otherwise, follow these steps:

1. In Excel, open Report.txt. You will use the File – Open menu. Once in the Open dialog, change the Files of Type setting to All Files. You can then select Report.txt.

Figure 199

Selecting all file types

File name:		▼
Files of type:	All Files	▼
	All Files	▲
	All Microsoft Office Excel Files	
	Microsoft Office Excel Files	
	All Web Pages	
	XML Files	
	Text Files	▼

1a. Excel will launch the Text Import Wizard, Step 1 of 3. If your secretary provided a file where each field is separated by commas, you will want to choose Delimited on this screen. Otherwise, choose Fixed Width and click Next.

11

Figure 200

Selecting Fixed Width

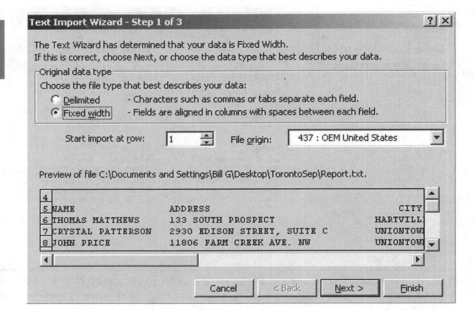

In Step 2 of 3 of the Wizard, Excel guesses at the column divisions. The data preview window probably is just showing you the title rows and headings. This is not entirely useful.

Figure 201

Wizard suggests column divisions

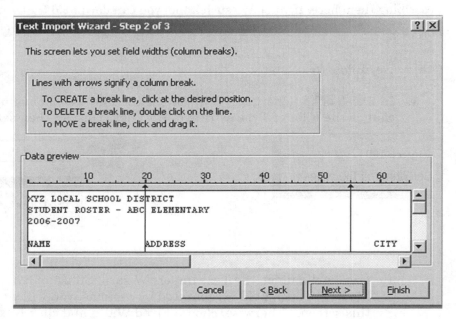

2. Use the vertical scroll bar to move down so that you can see the headings and the first few data records. In this particular data set, there are spaces between each column, and Excel does a fairly good job of guessing the first few columns.

11

Figure 202

Scroll down to see more data

2a. Use the scroll bar to scroll right to check more columns.

In Figure 203, notice that Excel decided to break between the City and State column at character position 65. Excel may scan the first 50 rows looking for patterns. It seems that there might be a student from a city with a longer name (why else would the program have left spaces before the state?).

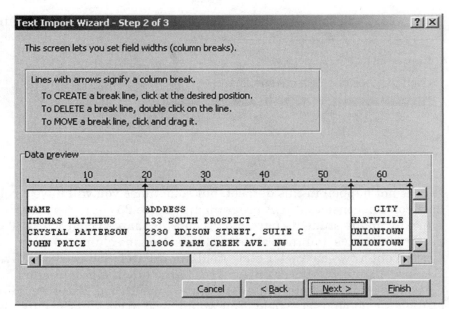

Figure 203

Watch for extra spaces before a column

2b. If you scroll down a few more records, you will see that the original selection would have cut off part of the longer North Canton city name.

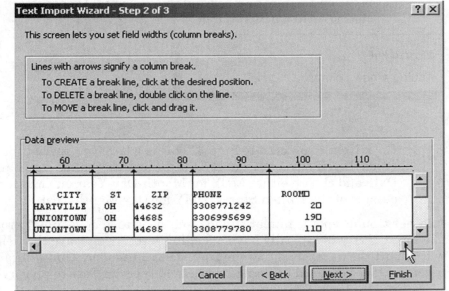

Figure 204

Column line cutting off part of an entry

2c. Drag that line over so that it is adjacent to the state column.

Figure 205

Changing position of a column line

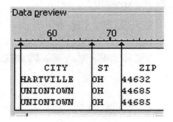

It does not happen in this dataset, but sometimes you will have a column that runs into the next column consistently. A program may leave 25 characters for the Student Name but, typically, many students have names shorter than 25 characters. This allows Excel to see a pattern of spaces and then a new field starting in column 26. Now, imagine if the program had written out a two-character state field immediately followed by a five-digit zip code field. Because a state will never have three characters, the program might have started writing the zip code field immediately after the state. In this case, Excel would have predicted that this was a single seven-character field. You would need to click in the data preview to add a new line to the dataset.

2d. Another trouble spot comes at the end of the record. You will see that Excel has put the rectangle indicating a non-printable character after every row number. Click between the row number and the unprintable character to move that garbage character to a new column.

Figure 206

Adding a new column

3. Click Next to proceed to Step 3. This is where you specify the field type for incoming fields. If you have dates in the file, be sure to change the column type from General to Date and choose either MDY for Month-Day-Year or YMD for Year-Month-Day (or outside of the United States, DMY for Day-Month-Year.)

Another trouble spot is numeric fields that need to keep leading zeroes. Zip codes in the northeast U.S. will typically have a leading zero. If you leave the field type as General, Excel will import the data, changing the zip code to a number. This will cause a zip code of 04256 to become 4256. You need to change these field types to Text to preserve leading zeroes.

3a. First, click the word General above the field heading in the Data Preview window. Then, click Text in the Column Data Format.

11

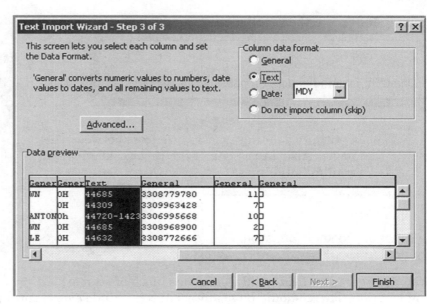

Figure 207

Changing column format

3b. If there are any columns that you don't need to import – in this case, the funny character at the end of the row is a candidate – choose the column header and select Do Not Import. The heading changes to Skip.

Figure 208

Skipping a column

3c. Click Finish and the data will be imported into columns that are the default Excel width. In this case, few of the columns are wide enough to hold the data. Live with this for a few minutes; you will be able to fix it easily after deleting titles.

Figure 209

Importing data

	A	B	C	D	E	F	G
1	XYZ LOCA	TRICT					
2	STUDENT	ELEMENTARY					
3	2006-2007						
4							
5	NAME	ADDRESS	CITY	ST	ZIP	PHONE	ROOM
6	THOMAS I	133 SOUT	HARTVILL	OH	44632	3.31E+09	2
7	CRYSTAL	2930 EDIS	UNIONTO\	OH	44685	3.31E+09	19
8	JOHN PRI	11806 FAF	UNIONTO\	OH	44685	3.31E+09	11
9	BARBARA	44 E. EXC	AKRON	OH	44309	3.31E+09	7
10	SCOTT PE	2735 GRE	NORTH C/	Oh	44720-142	3.31E+09	10

4. You will want to keep the headings that say Name, Address, and so forth, but there is no reason to keep the page titles.

Click and drag on the row numbers one through four to select them. Right-click and choose Delete to delete those rows.

Figure 210

Deleting unnecessary rows

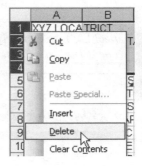

4a. Use the PgDn or PageDown key to scroll through the worksheet. When you get to the break between pages one and two, delete the title rows, any blank rows, and the heading row for page two. Since you've already kept the heading from the first page, there is no need to keep headings from subsequent pages.

4b. Delete the highlighted rows as shown in Figure 211.

Figure 211

Delete titles and headers on subsequent pages

4c. Continue deleting excess rows from between the pages. Also, at the end of the report, delete any trailing total lines.

Figure 212

Delete any footer information

You are now left with a solid contiguous block of student information. There should be headings in row 1 and several rows of student data.

Now that the long titles are gone from the worksheet, you can use the AutoFit command to make the columns fit your data. If you tried to use AutoFit before this point, column A would have resized to accommodate the title rows. There is no need to have column A wide enough to hold "Wapakoneta Local School District" when your longest student name is "Jennifer Smith".

5. Select all cells by clicking in the gray box above and to the left of cell A1.

Figure 213

Format column widths

5a. From the menu, select Format – Column – AutoFit Selection. This will make each column wide enough for the longest value in that column.

 Tip:

If the columns do not resize enough and if some of the cells appear on two lines, then those cells have the Wrap text property checked. To undo the Wrap text, follow these steps. Select all of the cells. From the menu, choose Format – Cells. On the Alignment tab, the Wrap text checkbox probably has a square in it. This means that in your selection, some cells have this turned on and some cells have it turned off.

You will want to turn it off in all cells. Click the checkbox once to turn it on in all cells (indicated by a checkbox), then click again to turn it off in all cells. Click OK to close the Format Cells dialog, then repeat the AutoFit selection command.

Figure 214

Click Wrap text twice

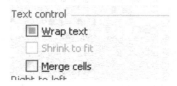

6. In Figure 209, the telephone numbers were actually displayed in scientific notation. After adjusting the column widths, the phone numbers are numeric, but they are hard to read.

Figure 215

These phone numbers are difficult to read

F
PHONE
3308771242
3306995699
3308779780

6a. Click on the "F" heading above the phone column to select the entire column. Select Format – Cells from the menu. On the Numeric tab, choose the category for Special and then select Telephone. Excel will not change the values, but will display them in a different format that is easier to read.

Figure 216

Phone numbers formatted as Telephone

F
PHONE
(330) 877-1242
(330) 699-5699
(330) 877-9780

7. When you use the application, you will want to be able to select only certain students based on room number or some other field in your dataset. Turn on the AutoFilter. Select a single cell in the dataset. From the menu, select Data – Filter – AutoFilter. This will add a dropdown to the heading above each row.

Figure 217

Adding AutoFilter dropdowns

E	F	G
ZIP ▾	PHONE ▾	ROO ▾
44632	(330) 877-1242	2

Using the Application

The process of producing mailing labels will involve three basic steps.

First, you will use the AutoFilter to isolate the particular addresses needed for this mailing

Next, you will copy the filtered records to a new workbook and save them.

Finally, you will use the Mail Merge tools in Microsoft Word to produce the labels.

Selecting Records with AutoFilter

To isolate a particular group of students, select an attribute from the dropdown next to each heading. To isolate just the students in Room 7, select the Room dropdown and select 7 from the list.

11

Figure 218

Selecting filter criteria

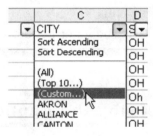

Excel will hide all of the students who are not in Room 7. Although you cannot tell from the pages of this black and white book, Excel changes the color of the dropdown arrow next to Room from black to blue to alert you that a filter is applied to that column.

Figure 219

Dropdown arrow indicates which column is filtered

	C	D	E	F	G
1	CITY	S	ZIP	PHONE	ROO
5	AKRON	OH	44309	(330) 996-3428	7
8	HARTVILLE	OH	44632	(330) 877-2666	7
9	HARTVILLE	OH	44632	(330) 877-8507	7
16	HARTVILLE	OH	44632	(330) 877-7997	7

1. To return to showing all students in all rooms, select the Room dropdown again and choose the (All) selection from the top of the list.

2. If you need to find all students in Akron or Canton, select the City dropdown and choose Custom.

Figure 220

Selecting filter criteria

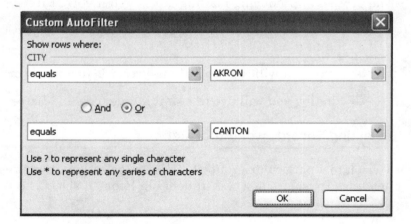

2a. In the Custom AutoFilter dialog, choose both cities and choose the OR option button.

Figure 221

Combining filter criteria

Tip:

The Custom AutoFilter will allow you to combine only two conditions. There is no built-in way to combine three or more conditions for the same column.

Copying Filtered Records

Once you've filtered the list to see just selected students, you need to copy those students to a new workbook. However, if you try to copy the records, you will find that Excel copies the hidden rows as well. This is very frustrating. Follow these steps to handle this.

1. In Figure 222, click on the last visible cell with data in G123. Hold down the mouse button and drag upwards to cell A1 in order to select all of the rows with data.

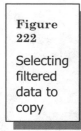

Figure 222

Selecting filtered data to copy

	B	C	D	E	F	G
1	ADDRESS	CITY	S	ZIP	PHONE	ROO
5	44 E. EXCHANGE STREET	AKRON	OH	44309	(330) 996-3428	7
10	2213 CLEVELAND AVE. NW	CANTON	OH	44709	(330) 453-0146	17
12	6551 MIDDLEBRANCH AVE. NW	CANTON	OH	44721	(330) 494-2995	20
13	2600 SIXTH STREET	CANTON	OH	44710	(330) 438-7482	1
23	300 N. CLEVELAND-MASSILLON RD	AKRON	OH	44333		16
31	646 UNIZAN BANK PLAZA	CANTON	OH	44702	(330) 452-4335	5
62	4571 STEPHEN CIRCLE NW	CANTON	OH	44718	(330) 499-1016	11
97	2515 CLEVELAND AVE. N	CANTON	OH	44709	(330) 454-5320	18
100	3976 FULTON DRIVE NW	CANTON	OH	44718	(330) 492-6063	12
123	4470 DRESSLER RD NW	CANTON	OH	44718	(330) 493-8866	12

2. You have now selected from A1:G123, including the hidden rows. To change the selection to just the visible rows, you will have to use the Go To Special dialog. Type F5 to display the Go To dialog. In the lower left corner of the dialog, choose the Special button.

2a. In the Go To Special dialog, choose the Visible Cells Only option. The option is in the second column, near the end of the list.

Figure 223

Selecting Visible cells only

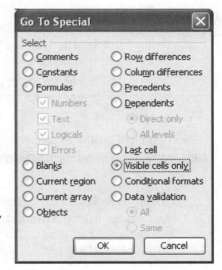

2b. Click OK to dismiss the dialog box. You will now have selected just the filtered rows.

3. Press Ctrl+C to copy. Press the New Workbook icon to create a new workbook. In the new workbook, press Ctrl+V to paste the records.

3a. The new workbook will not look great – the column widths will all be wrong. However, no one will see it, so it is OK to save it. Use File – Save As to save the file with a new name. Save the file in My Documents or somewhere that you can easily find it again.

4. You can now close the new workbook. The rest of the mail merge will happen in Microsoft Word.

Using Word to Create Mailing Labels from Excel Data

Open a blank document in Word. From the menu, select Tools – Letters and Mailing – Mail Merge.

1. In Step 1 of 6, indicate that you are creating labels.

Figure 224

Selecting document type

2. You will want to change the blank document into a page of labels. Click the Label options link.

Figure 225

Selecting label size

3. Choose the appropriate label type. If you buy Avery or off-brand labels, the labels should say that they are compatible with a particular Avery label number. 5160 is a popular choice – it is a sheet of three columns of 10 labels.

Figure 226

Selecting label product number

4. In Step 3, your Excel file counts as an existing list. Choose that option button and then click Browse.

4a. In the File Open dialog, browse to My Documents and select your file. Next, Word will ask you to identify the table to be used. Select Sheet one and indicate that the first row contains field names. (Make sure the box in the lower left is checked.)

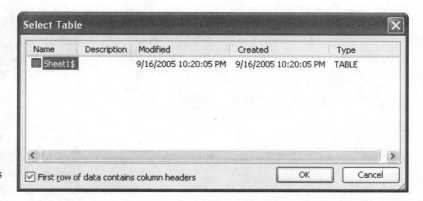

Figure 227

Selecting data source

4b. After you click OK to Figure 227, Word will display the list of students in the file. Leave all of the names selected.

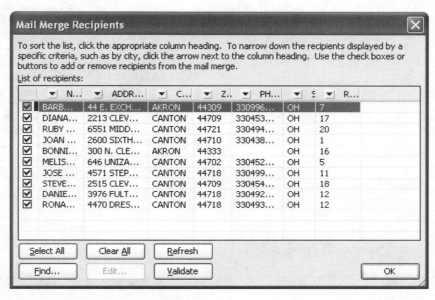

Figure 228

Selecting recipients

5. In Step 4, you will layout the first label on the sheet. Word offers various choices. Choose the top choice, Address block.

Figure 229

Choosing Address block for the label layout

Arrange your labels

If you have not already done so, lay out your label using the first label on the sheet.

To add recipient information to your label, click a location in the first label, and then click one of the items below.

📄 Address block...

📄 Greeting line...

📩 Electronic postage...

|||| Postal bar code...

📄 More items...

When you have finished arranging your label, click Next. Then you can preview each recipient's label and make any individual changes.

Replicate labels

You can copy the layout of the first label to the other labels on the page by clicking the button below.

[Update all labels]

11

5b. At the bottom of the Insert Address Block dialog, choose Match Fields.

Figure 230

Configuring the address block

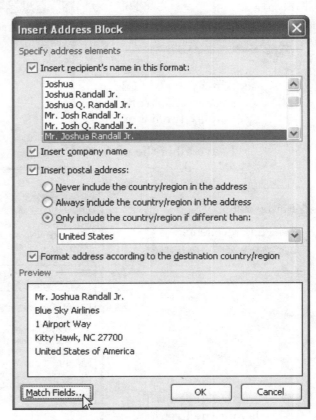

6. In the Match Fields dialog, make sure that Word understands all of your columns. In the current file, Word did not understand that the abbreviation "ST" meant "State".

Figure 231

Reconciling field matches

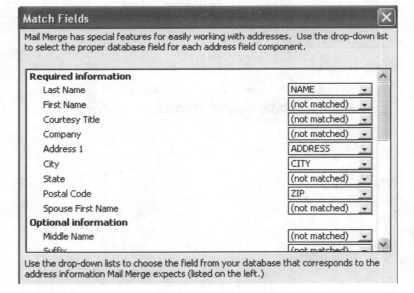

6a. Click the dropdown next to state. Choose ST as the matching field.

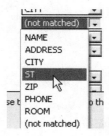

Figure 232

Reconciling ST as the State field

7. Word will update the first label with the field name of Address Block. The remaining labels have a field for Next Record. After formatting the first label, you need to copy this formatting to all additional labels. In the task pane, choose Update all Labels.

Figure 233

Copying first label's format

7a. After updating the labels, Word will add the setup from label one to each other label.

Figure 234

Applying label 1 setup

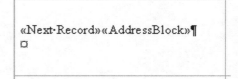

«Next·Record»«AddressBlock»¶

8. Step 5 is called Preview Your Labels. Actually, at this point, the first page of labels appears to be done. If everything looks OK, click Next to finish the labels.

9. In Step 6, you are given the option to print or edit. Even if you don't want to edit, choose Edit. This will permanently add the addresses to the current document. You can then print, print again, save, etc. I find that labels sometimes jam in the manual tray and I like knowing that I can later reprint.

9a. Word will ask you which addresses you want. Choose All. Word will create a new document with all of the addresses. You can now save or print.

Chapter 12 – Sorting Class Lists by First Name

Opportunity

I am going to be out of the classroom for a few days. The substitute teacher seems to be able to learn the students' first names more easily than their last names. Could I temporarily sort the class list by first name?

While you are at it, are there any more techniques for dealing with text – converting to upper case, lower case, proper case, joining cells, and so forth.

Solution and Overview

There are a variety of functions that you can use for calculations with text. There is also a Text to Columns wizard in case your names have a comma between the last and first names.

Creating the Solution

How can you sort this list by first name?

Figure 235

Unsorted list

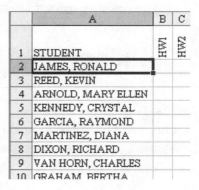

Splitting Data

There are a couple of ways to do this. In the first method, you will use the Text to Columns wizard to split a copy of column A into two columns.

Splitting a Delimited Column Using Text to Columns Wizard

1. Insert two blank columns, B and C. Copy the student names in A to column B. Select the range of names in column B. From the menu, select Data – Text to Columns. In Step 1 of the wizard, choose Delimited. This choice will work because your data has a comma between the first and last name.

12

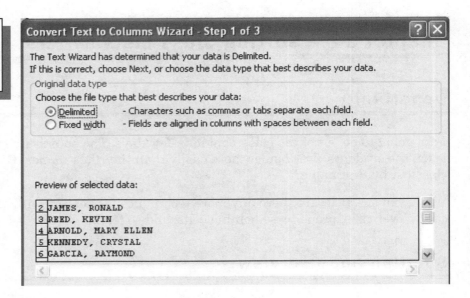

Figure 236

Selecting Delimited Data type

2. Click Next to proceed to Step 2 of the wizard.
   The default in Step 2 is for columns to be separated by a tab character.

Figure 237

Selecting the delimiter

2a. Uncheck the box for Tab and choose the box for Comma. The data preview will redraw with a line between the last and first names.

Figure 238

Choosing Comma as delimiter

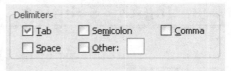

3. At this point, you can click Finish. The last names will be in column B and the first names will be in column C. Add headings in B1 and C1.

Figure 239

First and last names separated into two columns

	A	B	C
1	STUDENT	Last	First
2	JAMES, RONALD	JAMES	RONALD
3	REED, KEVIN	REED	KEVIN
4	ARNOLD, MARY ELLEN	ARNOLD	MARY ELLEN

3a. You can now select a single cell in column C and press the AZ Sort button in the Standard toolbar. The list will be sorted by first name.

Figure 240

List sorted by first name

	A	B	C
1	**STUDENT**	**Last**	**First**
2	GRAHAM, BERTHA	GRAHAM	BERTHA
3	TUCKER, BETTY	TUCKER	BETTY
4	VAN HORN, CHARLES	VAN HORN	CHARLES
5	KENNEDY, CRYSTAL	KENNEDY	CRYSTAL
6	MARTINEZ, DIANA	MARTINEZ	DIANA
7	WATSON, EMMA	WATSON	EMMA

Using Formulas to Isolate First Name with Delimited Data

Instead of using the Text to Column wizard, it is possible to use text functions to isolate the first name. Here are some common text functions:

=MID(A2,7,10)	Returns 10 characters of A2, starting at the seventh character.
=LEN(A2)	Returns the total number of characters in A2
=FIND(",",A2)	Indicates that the comma in A2 occurs as the seventh character of A2
=RIGHT(A2,10)	Return the right-most 10 characters from A2
=LEFT(A2,10)	Return the left-most 10 characters from A2
=TRIM(A2)	Removes trailing spaces from text
=PROPER(A2)	Converts A2 to proper case
=UPPER(A2)	Converts A2 to upper case
=LOWER(A2)	Converts A2 to lower case

Given this list of functions, either of the two formulas below will return the first name:

1. First, you could use: =TRIM(MID(A2,FIND(",",A2)+2,25)). This formula finds the character position of the comma in A2. Add two to this position to get the starting point for the MID function. Tell MID to return 25 characters, figuring that this will be long enough for any possible first name. The problem with using a big number is that MID will pad the right side of "TOM" with 22 additional spaces. The TRIM function will remove the spaces.

2. You could also use =RIGHT(A2,LEN(A2)-FIND(",",A2)-1). Again, this formula finds the location of the comma. You ask for the right-most characters from A2. The number of characters is the total number of characters minus the position of the comma, minus one to remove the leading space.

You can now sort by column B. Select a single cell in column B and press the AZ Sort button in the Standard toolbar.

12

		fx	=RIGHT(A2,LEN(A2)-FIND(",",A2)-1)

Figure 241

List sorted by first name

	A	B	C	D	E	F	G	H	
			HW1	HW2	HW3	Quiz 1	HW4	Test	
1	**STUDENT**	**First**							
2	ARNOLD, MARY ELLEN	MARY ELLEN							
3	BLACK, ESTHER	ESTHER							
4	DIXON, NICOLE	NICOLE							
5	DIXON, RICHARD	RICHARD							
6	FOSTER, LORI	LORI							
7	GARCIA, RAYMOND	RAYMOND							
8	GRAHAM, BERTHA	BERTHA							

Isolating a First Name When There Is No Comma

The problem of isolating the first name is more complicated when there is not a comma between the last and first name. It is possible, but you will have to manually correct a few entries.

In the following image, "Charles Van Horn" and "Mary Ellen Arnold" are going to cause problems. If you use a formula to split the names based on the first space, Charles will be correctly split, but the formula will think that Mary is the first name and "Ellen Arnold" is the last name.

Figure 242

Last names with two words

	A	B
1	**STUDENT**	**First**
2	ARNOLD MARY ELLEN	
3	VAN HORN CHARLES	
4	BLACK ESTHER	
5	DIXON NICOLE	
6	DIXON RICHARD	
7	FOSTER LORI	
8	GARCIA RAYMOND	

If you use the Text to Columns Wizard, Excel will split these names into three columns. Be sure to leave extra blank columns to handle Billy Joe Jim Bob Smith.

Joining Text from Two Columns

How do you join text from two columns into a single column? In the following figure, you would like to combine first name and last name into a single column.

Figure 243

First and last names in separate columns

	A	B	C
1	FIRST	LAST	DOB
2	ANTHONY	MATTHEWS	4/6/1999
3	CATHERINE	WOOD	7/31/1999
4	CHARLOTTE	BRYANT	12/9/1998
5	DENNIS	PARKER	2/27/2000
6	DENNIS	RICE	3/22/1999

While the plus sign is used to add numbers, you need to use the ampersand (&) character to join text. The official Microsoft name for the ampersand is the concatenation operator. However, I don't know many people who use the term "concatenation" at the dinner table!

1. You might try a formula such as =A2&B2. This will join the text but it will not have a space between the names. Edit the formula to show =A2&" "&B2.

Figure 244

No space between names

		fx	=A2&B2		
	A	B	C	D	E	F
1	FIRST	LAST	DOB	NAME		
2	ANTHONY	MATTHEWS	4/6/1999	ANTHONYMATTHEWS		

Caution!

While you need to hold down the Shift key to enter the quotation marks, do not hold down the Shift key while typing the space. Shift+Spacebar is an obscure Excel shortcut for selecting the current row. You might end up with something like 2:2 inserted into your formula.

2. Double-click the fill handle in D2 to copy the formula down to all cells. You now have new column with the first and last name joined together.

Figure 245

First and last names joined with a space

	A	B	C	D
1	FIRST	LAST	DOB	NAME
2	ANTHONY	MATTHEWS	4/6/1999	ANTHONY MATTHEWS
3	CATHERINE	WOOD	7/31/1999	CATHERINE WOOD
4	CHARLOTTE	BRYANT	12/9/1998	CHARLOTTE BRYANT
5	DENNIS	PARKER	2/27/2000	DENNIS PARKER

D2 =A2&" "&B2

3. What if you want to convert the name to proper case?
    Edit the formula to put the entire formula as an argument to the PROPER function.

Figure 246

Converting to proper case

	A	B	C	D
1	FIRST	LAST	DOB	NAME
2	ANTHONY	MATTHEWS	4/6/1999	Anthony Matthews
3	CATHERINE	WOOD	7/31/1999	Catherine Wood

D2 =PROPER(A2&" "&B2)

Joining Text with Dates or Numbers

Now that you know the concatenation operator, you might be tempted to join some text with a date field. You will initially be disappointed.

Figure 247

Joining text and a date initially produces undesired results

	A	B	C	D
1	FIRST	LAST	DOB	NAME
2	ANTHONY	MATTHEWS	4/6/1999	Anthony Matthews was born on 36256
3	CATHERINE	WOOD	7/31/1999	Catherine Wood was born on 36372

D2 =PROPER(A2&" "&B2)&" was born on "&C2

Although column C is formatted to display the date in m/d/yyyy format, Excel actually stores the date as the number of days elapsed since 1900 (or 1904 on a Mac). To get the correct result, you have to use the TEXT(D2,format) function to correctly format the date. This requires a bit of knowledge about some arcane date codes. The formula TEXT(C2,"m/d/yyyy") will give the expected result.

Figure 248

Use TEXT function to format dates

	A	B	C	D	E
1	FIRST	LAST	DOB	NAME	
2	ANTHONY	MATTHEWS	4/6/1999	Anthony Matthews was born on 4/6/1999	
3	CATHERINE	WOOD	7/31/1999	Catherine Wood was born on 7/31/1999	

D2 =PROPER(A2&" "&B2)&" was born on "&TEXT(C2,"m/d/yyyy")

If you know the codes, you can also make Excel do some date magic. TEXT(C2,"dddd") will reveal the day of the week on which the student was born.

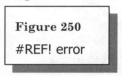

Figure 249

Showing day of the week

	A	B	C	D	E
				=PROPER(A2&" "&B2)&" was born on "&TEXT(C2,"dddd")	
1	FIRST	LAST	DOB	NAME	
2	ANTHONY	MATTHEWS	4/6/1999	Anthony Matthews was born on Tuesday	
3	CATHERINE	WOOD	7/31/1999	Catherine Wood was born on Saturday	
4	CHARLOTTE	BRYANT	12/9/1998	Charlotte Bryant was born on Wednesday	

Freezing the Results of a Formula as Values

The last few techniques showed you how to combine data from columns A, B, and C into a single column. You might then be tempted to delete columns A, B, and C. If you do this, the wonderful formula in column D will change to an error, indicating that it is based on cells that are no longer there!

Figure 250

#REF! error

	A	B	C	D	E	F	G
	=PROPER(#REF!&" "&#REF!)&" was born on "&TEXT(#REF!,"dddd")						
1	NAME						
2	#REF!						
3	#REF!						

Before you can delete those columns, you need to convert the live formulas to their current values. Highlight the range of data in column D. Type Ctrl+C to copy. From the menu, select Edit – Paste Special. In the Paste Special dialog, choose Values and then OK. If you look in the formula bar, you will see that the formula has been replaced by a static value. It is now safe to delete the other columns.

Figure 251

Copying and pasting values avoids the #REF! error

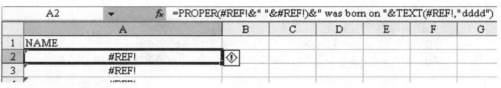

'Anthony Matthews was born on Tuesday

C	D
DOB	NAME
4/6/1999	Anthony Matthews was born on Tuesday
7/31/1999	Catherine Wood was born on Saturday
12/9/1998	Charlotte Bryant was born on Wednesday

12

Chapter 13 – Reporting Long Term Testing Results

Opportunity

This is an opportunity to set up a workbook that could store testing data on a long-term basis. This would not be particularly useful to individual teachers, but it could be very important to someone in a position (such as a principal or literacy/curriculum coordinator) required to look at testing information for an entire grade level or for a whole school over a long period of time. This type of workbook would allow a teacher or administrator to look at educational programs, curriculum, or teacher effectiveness over a period of time. It could give insightful information on whether programs and teaching methods were helping students to meet educational goals and objectives and if improvements were being made over time. Our state government now requires schools to show proof of student improvement (proof being in the form of test scores). This would be an easy and efficient way to store and retrieve student testing data.

The teacher/administrator would need to enter the data in the workbook and find a way to use the workbook's cells to manipulate the data. Student testing information would need to be entered. Possibly, students could have an ID number if this would help with the manipulation of the information. The ID number could be from the school-wide database or some other identification method. Besides name and ID number, other information could be included in the workbook such as: teacher name, current grade level, testing results from a variety of different testing methods. (My school uses writing prompts, Rigby Benchmark reading assessments, Indiana mandated tests (ISTEP, Indiana Reading Assessment), Gates-McGinitie, TOPAS, and G-Made (standardized tests), and STAR Reading (a computerized standardized test).)

Once the testing information for each student is entered, the workbook could provide information about scores for individual students. The workbook would be like a cumulative record keeper and would be able to rank students by particular test scores to find students who score above or below a specific score on a particular test. For example, I could generate a list of students who would require remediation efforts because they scored below 75% on a particular reading test. I could also gather class averages on a specific test or find the average score on a test for an entire grade level.

I would also like to be able to compare student results from year to year, class to class, and grade to grade. Examples of such results might include:

➢ Finding that 80% of second graders passed the G-Made math test with an 80% proficiency while 92% of the third graders passed the G-Made math test with an 80% proficiency.

➢ In 2004, 72% of first graders passed the TOPAS test with a score of 80% or better while in 2005, 81% of first graders passed the TOPAS test with a score of 80% or better.

13

Solution and Overview

Way back in 1985, a man named Pito Salas was working in the Advanced Technologies Group at Lotus Development Center and was trying to develop a brand new way of thinking about spreadsheets. He developed technology that was released by Lotus as Lotus Improv. The main idea of this technology was later included in Excel as a Pivot Table. By far, Pito Salas' concept became the most powerful feature in all of Excel.

The sample workbook contains six years of state testing data for a fictitious school. This school has 150 students per grade; it is mandated to take Reading tests in third and fifth grades and then proficiency tests in Reading, Writing, Math, Science and Citizenship during fourth and sixth grades.

Someone in the curriculum office has been downloading and compiling the state data year after year. There are now almost 10,000 rows of data in this format. The workbook recorded that during her sixth grade year, Sylvia Nelson scored a 190 on the Reading proficiency. She is a member of the class of 2007 and had Mrs. Colon that year.

Figure 252 Workbook with sample data for six years of proficiency tests

	A	B	C	D	E	F	G	H	I	J
1	Student ID	Student Name	ClassOf	DateTaken	Teacher	GradeLevel	Test	Score	Level	Passed
2	56754811	NELSON, SYLVIA	2007	3/31/2001	TATE	6	READING	199	Basic	FALSE
3	19448727	WALKER, STEPHEN	2007	3/31/2001	NORTON	6	READING	197	Basic	FALSE
4	25562171	STONE, LEAH	2007	3/31/2001	VANCE	6	READING	208	Proficient	TRUE

In past chapters, you learned how to use the AutoFilter. If you used AutoFilter to just look at one student's records, you might be able to spot some trends. Here is the progress of a fictional Caroline Blair, who was a third grader in 2001.

Figure 253 Using AutoFilter to look for trends in one student's records

	A	B	C	D	E	F	G	H	I	J
1	Student	Student Name	ClassO	DateTak	Teacher	GradeLev	Test	Sco	Level	Passed
534	26337645	BLAIR, CAROLINE	2010	3/31/2001	DRAKE	3	READING	202	Proficient	TRUE
2195	26337645	BLAIR, CAROLINE	2010	3/31/2002	RAYMOND	4	READING	199	Basic	FALSE
2648	26337645	BLAIR, CAROLINE	2010	3/31/2002	RAYMOND	4	MATH	200	Proficient	TRUE
2950	26337645	BLAIR, CAROLINE	2010	3/31/2002	RAYMOND	4	SCIENCE	192	Basic	FALSE
3252	26337645	BLAIR, CAROLINE	2010	3/31/2002	RAYMOND	4	WRITING	193	Basic	FALSE
3554	26337645	BLAIR, CAROLINE	2010	3/31/2002	RAYMOND	4	CITIZENSHIP	192	Basic	FALSE
3856	26337645	BLAIR, CAROLINE	2010	3/31/2003	STONE	5	READING	203	Proficient	TRUE
5517	26337645	BLAIR, CAROLINE	2010	3/31/2004	TATE	6	READING	208	Proficient	TRUE
6121	26337645	BLAIR, CAROLINE	2010	3/31/2004	TATE	6	MATH	210	Proficient	TRUE
6423	26337645	BLAIR, CAROLINE	2010	3/31/2004	TATE	6	SCIENCE	198	Basic	FALSE
6725	26337645	BLAIR, CAROLINE	2010	3/31/2004	TATE	6	WRITING	200	Proficient	TRUE
7027	26337645	BLAIR, CAROLINE	2010	3/31/2004	TATE	6	CITIZENSHIP	200	Proficient	TRUE

Using AutoFilter would be a very slow way to look at each student or grade or year. Pivot Tables are far superior.

Creating the Solution

1. Start with a dataset such as the LongTermResults.xls workbook. It is important that the data have a unique one-row heading above every column. Leave no blank rows and no blank columns in the data. Select a single cell in the data. From the menu, select Data – Pivot Table and Pivot Chart Report.

2. Assuming that your testing data contains less than 65,535 rows of data, you can use Excel. If you are tracking 10 years of data for an entire school district, it is possible that the data could exceed 65,536 rows, so you would have to store it in an Access database. You can analyze Access databases with a pivot table as well, using the External data source option in Step 1. For the purposes of this book, we will use the data in Excel. Click Next.

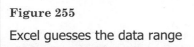

Figure 254

Selecting Excel as the data source for a pivot table

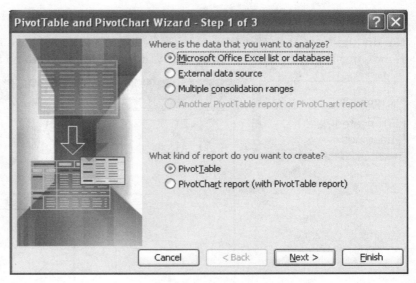

3. If your data is set up properly in list format (see first step), Step 2 of the Wizard will accurately predict the location of your dataset. Click Next to proceed to Step 3.

Figure 255

Excel guesses the data range

 Note:

If you are using Excel 97 or older, the Pivot Table Wizard includes four steps. In newer versions of Excel, the third step of the Wizard was relegated to a button. If you get this version of Step 3, press the Layout button in the lower left corner.

13

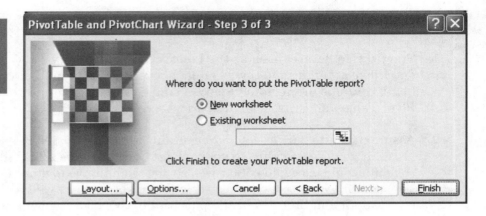

Figure 256

Choose the Layout button

The Layout dialog appears below. Your field names from the worksheet are on the right side of the dialog. Note that this is not perfect – long field names are truncated. You will have to remember that Student I is probably Student ID and Student N is probably student name.

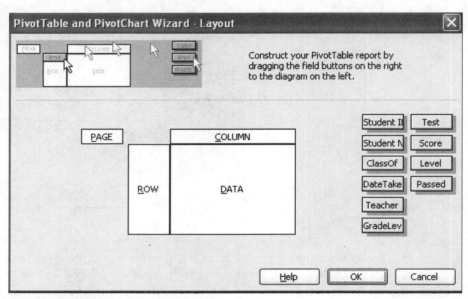

Figure 257

Truncated field headings

Notice also on the Layout dialog that there are four white sections of a pivot table report. The Data area is the heart of the report. You will either count students in this area or average their scores.

The Row and Column areas allow you to summarize the data by several fields. For example, you might want to see a count of students by Test, Grade, and Level. These fields would go in the Row or Column area. The Page area is a place to put criteria fields. Right now, the report contains data from six years of testing. If you want to just see 2003 results, you might put the DateTaken field in the Page section of the report.

This is all hard to visualize, so go ahead and build your first report – it is very easy to change the report after it is built.

4. Drag the DateTaken field and drop it on the Page section of the dialog. Take the Passed field and drop it in the Column area of the dialog. Take first the GradeLevel field and then the Test field and drop each in the Row area of the dialog.

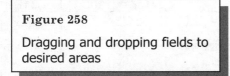

Figure 258

Dragging and dropping fields to desired areas

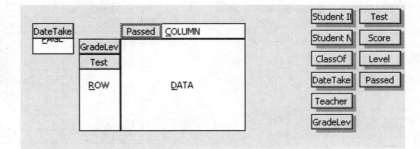

Choosing a field for the Data section presents an interesting choice. If you moved the Score field to the data section, you could ask Excel to give you an average score. However, we don't really care about average scores – we really care about the number of students who passed.

5. Thus, even though it may be counter-intuitive, drag the Student Name to the Data section of the report. Because Student Name contains text instead of numbers, Excel will automatically decide to Count the number of students who scored at each level.

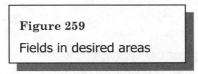

Figure 259

Fields in desired areas

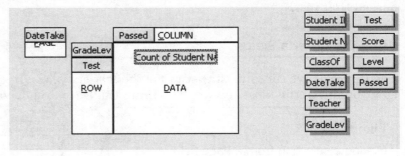

Notice that the field name changes to Count of Student Name when you drop it in the Data section

6. Click OK to return to the Pivot Table Wizard. In the final step of the wizard, Excel offers to put the pivot table on a new worksheet. This is fine. Click Finish.

Very quickly, Excel will calculate and draw the pivot table.

13

Figure 260

New pivot table

	A	B	C	D	E
1	DateTaken	(All) ▾			
2					
3	Count of Student Name		Passed ▾		
4	GradeLevel ▾	Test ▾	FALSE	TRUE	Grand Total
5	3	READING	519	378	897
6	3 Total		519	378	897
7	4	CITIZENSHIP	477	429	906
8		MATH	480	426	906
9		READING	481	425	906
10		SCIENCE	473	433	906
11		WRITING	474	432	906
12	4 Total		2385	2145	4530
13	5	READING	350	556	906
14	5 Total		350	556	906
15	6	CITIZENSHIP	249	657	906
16		MATH	241	665	906
17		READING	241	665	906
18		SCIENCE	242	664	906
19		WRITING	239	667	906
20	6 Total		1212	3318	4530
21	Grand Total		4466	6397	10863

This report shows the number of students who scored at each level on the various subject tests. Because cell B1 contains (All), it is a composite result of students for the last six years. This fictional school's third grade reading test scores are not very good – only 378 of 897 students passed that test.

Using the Criteria Fields

The figure above contains statistics for the last six years. It would be more interesting to see how you did in the most recent year. From the Date dropdown, choose 2006.

Figure 261

Making a selection from a Page field

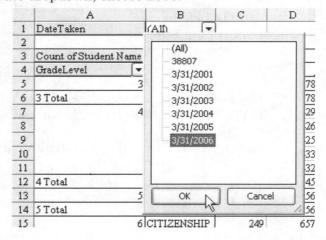

Instantly, the pivot table will redraw with only results from 2006.

Figure 262

Pivot table redrawn according to selected criteria

	A	B	C	D	E
1	DateTaken	3/31/2006 ▼			
2					
3	Count of Student Name		Passed ▼		
4	GradeLevel ▼	Test ▼	FALSE	TRUE	Grand Total
5	3	READING	51	91	142
6	3 Total		51	91	142
7	4	CITIZENSHIP	90	61	151
8		MATH	97	54	151
9		READING	94	57	151
10		SCIENCE	88	63	151
11		WRITING	89	62	151
12	4 Total		458	297	755
13	5	READING	54	97	151
14	5 Total		54	97	151
15	6	CITIZENSHIP	54	97	151
16		MATH	48	98	146
17		READING	50	101	151
18		SCIENCE	58	93	151
19		WRITING	47	104	151
20	6 Total		257	493	750
21	Grand Total		820	978	1798
22					

Adding Fields to the Pivot Table

When you select any cell in the pivot table, a pivot table field list will appear. In Excel 2002 and 2003, the pivot table field list appears as a separate floating list. In earlier versions, the pivot table field list appeared as an extension of the pivot table toolbar. Here is how it appears in Excel 2003.

Figure 263

Excel 2003 floating pivot table list

 Tip:

In the Excel 2002/2003 version of the field list, you can add a field by selecting the field, selecting the area, and then clicking Add To. In all versions, you can also drag and drop the field right on the pivot table. The key to being able to drag and drop is to watch the mouse cursor. The mouse cursor will change to an outline of a pivot table. Three sections of the pivot table will be white. The section in blue indicates where you are ready to drop the field.

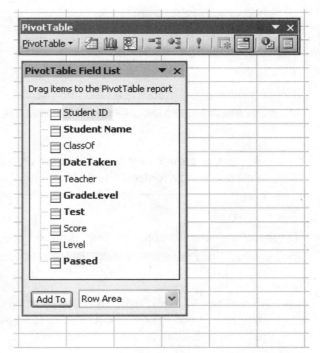

13

Let's say that you want to see how one particular class has fared on the tests. You would want to reset the Date Taken selection to (All).

1. With the Mouse, grab the ClassOf field and start to drag it to the pivot table. As you hover over various areas, the mouse cursor will change. Figure 264 shows the mouse pointer as you drag the field over the Data area. The large section of the pivot table outline is blue.

Figure 264

Mousepointer changes to indicate area in which field will be dropped

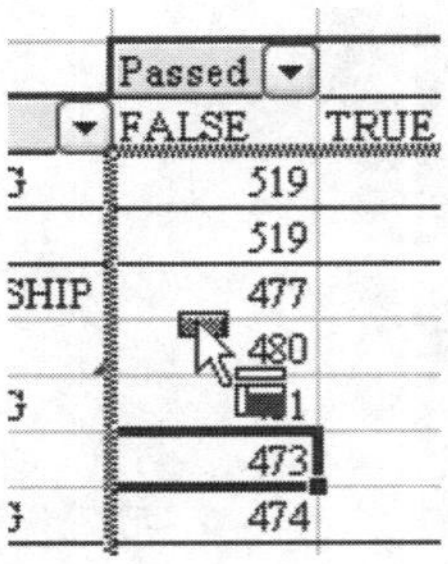

1a. Keep moving the mouse to the left. Once you cross into column B, the mouse pointer changes so that the Row area of the pivot table is highlighted in blue. If you dropped the field here, you would see results for all of the classes broken out.

Figure 265

Mousepointer when dropping a field into the Row area

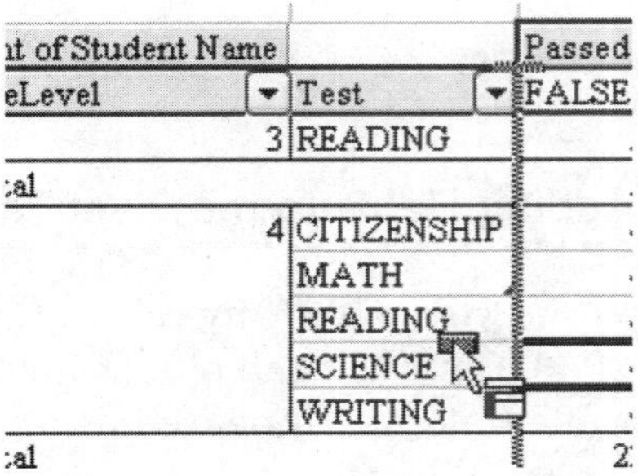

1b. As you move the mouse up above row 5, the mouse pointer changes to highlight the Column area.

Figure 266

Mousepointer when dropping a field into the Column area

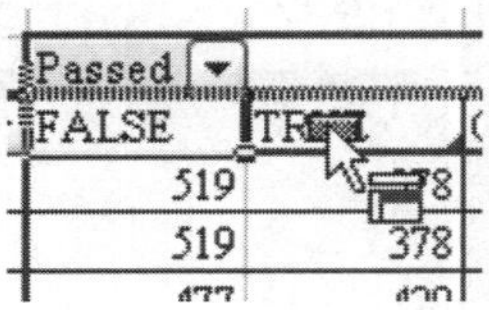

2. Move the mouse pointer all the way up to row 1 or 2; the pointer changes to indicate that you are ready to drop the field in the Page area of the pivot table. Drop the field here.

Figure 267

Mousepointer when dropping a field into the Page area

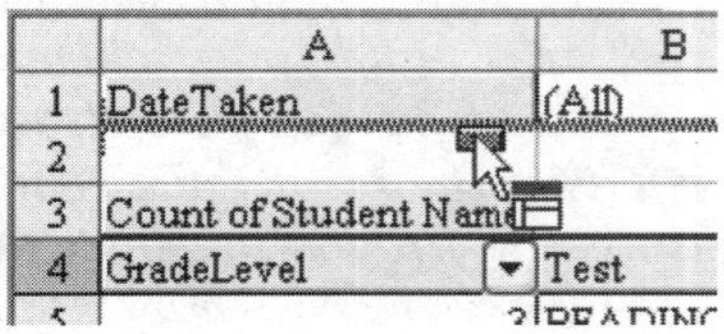

3. From the ClassOf dropdown, select the class of 2012. The report redraws showing only the results of from the class of 2012. You can see that this class did poorly in the third and fourth grades but is doing better in sixth grade.

Figure 268

Selecting a specific class

	A	B	C	D	E
1	DateTaken	(All) ▼			
2	ClassOf	2012 ▼			
3					
4	Count of Student Name		Passed ▼		
5	GradeLevel ▼	Test ▼	FALSE	TRUE	Grand Total
6	3	READING	104	47	151
7	3 Total		104	47	151
8	4	CITIZENSHIP	98	53	151
9		MATH	100	51	151
10		READING	99	52	151
11		SCIENCE	99	52	151
12		WRITING	100	51	151
13	4 Total		496	259	755
14	5	READING	83	68	151
15	5 Total		83	68	151
16	6	CITIZENSHIP	54	97	151
17		MATH	50	101	151
18		READING	50	101	151
19		SCIENCE	58	93	151
20		WRITING	47	104	151
21	6 Total		259	496	755
22	Grand Total		942	870	1812
23					

Formatting a Data Field

Right now, the Data area shows a count of students who passed the test. You might instead want to see the percentage of students who passed the test.

1. Double-click the gray Count of Student Name button in cell A4. Initially, the shortened PivotTable Field dialog displays.

Figure 269

PivotTable Field dialog before pressing Options button

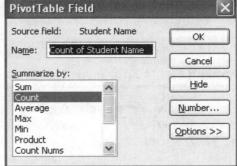

2. Click the Options>> button to display additional options available for Data fields.

   2a. In the Show Data As field, Excel shows the data as Normal. Choose this dropdown and choose Percentage of Row.

Figure 270

Selecting % of row

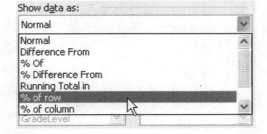

3. Choose OK to close the dialog. The pivot table redraws to show the percentage of students who passed each test.

13

Figure 271

Chart changes to display percentage of students who passed each test

	A	B	C	D	E
1	DateTaken	(All)			
2	ClassOf	2012			
3					
4	Count of Student Name		Passed		
5	GradeLevel	Test	FALSE	TRUE	Grand Total
6	3	READING	68.87%	31.13%	100.00%
7	3 Total		68.87%	31.13%	100.00%
8	4	CITIZENSHIP	64.90%	35.10%	100.00%
9		MATH	66.23%	33.77%	100.00%
10		READING	65.56%	34.44%	100.00%
11		SCIENCE	65.56%	34.44%	100.00%
12		WRITING	66.23%	33.77%	100.00%
13	4 Total		65.70%	34.30%	100.00%
14	5	READING	54.97%	45.03%	100.00%
15	5 Total		54.97%	45.03%	100.00%
16	6	CITIZENSHIP	35.76%	64.24%	100.00%
17		MATH	33.11%	66.89%	100.00%
18		READING	33.11%	66.89%	100.00%
19		SCIENCE	38.41%	61.59%	100.00%
20		WRITING	31.13%	68.87%	100.00%
21	6 Total		34.30%	65.70%	100.00%
22	Grand Total		51.99%	48.01%	100.00%

You might find it somewhat annoying to see two decimal places displayed everywhere. It is important *not* to format these cells using the Formatting toolbar.

4. Instead, double-click on the Count of Student Name button in A4 and choose the Number... button. Change the number of decimals on this special version of the Format Cells dialog.

Figure 272

Formatting number of decimal places in percentage cells

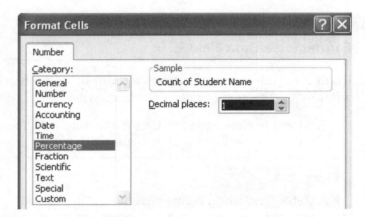

Moving Fields on a Pivot Table

Once you see some summary data, it inevitably makes you start thinking about other ways to summarize the data. This school has a problem with fourth grade reading scores. How have the scores trended over time? Are they improving?

You can move gray field names around an existing report.

Figure 273

Moving gray field names

	A	B	C	D
1	DateTaken	(All)		
2	ClassOf	2012		
3	GradeLevel	(All)		
4				
5	Count of Student Name	Passed		
6	Test	FALSE	TRUE	Grand Total
7	CITIZENSHIP	50.3%	49.7%	100.0%
8	MATH	49.7%	50.3%	100.0%
9	READING	55.6%	44.4%	100.0%
10	SCIENCE	52.0%	48.0%	100.0%
11	WRITING	48.7%	51.3%	100.0%
12	Grand Total	52.0%	48.0%	100.0%

1. Grab the GradeLevel button from A5 and drag it up to just below A2 to make the GradeLevel field a criteria field.

2. Take the Test button from A6 and drag it to just below GradeLevel in A4.

	A	B		C	D
1	DateTaken	(All)	▼		
2	ClassOf	2012	▼		
3	GradeLevel	(All)	▼		
4	Test	(All)	▼		
5					
6	Count of Student Name	Passed	▼		
7		FALSE		TRUE	Grand Total
8	Total	52.0%		48.0%	100.0%
9					

Figure 274

Moving the Test button

3. In B2, change the ClassOf dropdown from 2012 back to (All). Change the GradeLevel dropdown in B3 to 4 and the Test dropdown in B4 to Reading.

4. Grab the ClassOf field from A2 and drag it to A7. The cursor will confirm that you are adding the field to the Column area of the pivot table.

Figure 275

Changing dropdowns and moving ClassOf field to Column area

	A	B	
1	DateTaken	(All)	▼
2	ClassOf	(All)	▼
3	GradeLevel	4	▼
4	Test	READING	▼
5			
6	Count of Student Name	Passed	▼
7		FALSE	TR
8	Total	53.1%	
9			

After you drop the field, you will have an analysis of fourth grade reading scores over time.

Figure 276

Analysis based on changes in Step 4

	A	B		C	D
1					
2	DateTaken	(All)	▼		
3	GradeLevel	4	▼		
4	Test	READING	▼		
5					
6	Count of Student Name	Passed	▼		
7	ClassOf	▼ FALSE		TRUE	Grand Total
8	2009	28.5%		71.5%	100.0%
9	2010	47.0%		53.0%	100.0%
10	2011	62.3%		37.7%	100.0%
11	2012	65.6%		34.4%	100.0%
12	2013	53.0%		47.0%	100.0%
13	2014	62.3%		37.7%	100.0%
14	Grand Total	53.1%		46.9%	100.0%
15					

For some reason, the class of 2009 had excellent test scores in Reading in fourth grade. Did they always do better? Are they a "smarter" class? Or was there a flaw in the state test that year?

5. Change the Test dropdown in B4 back to "(All)". Drag the Test button and drop it in the Column area.

13

Figure 277

Test button moved to right side of Column area

	A	
1		
2	DateTaken	(Al
3	GradeLevel	4
4	Test	(Al
5		
6	Count of Student Name	Pas
7	ClassOf ▼	FA
8	2009	
9	2010	
10	2011	
11	12	
12	2013	
13	2014	
14	Grand Total	
15		

Note that there is a very subtle difference about where you can drop the field. If you drop the field towards the *right* side of column A, a gray fuzzy line will draw between columns A and B. This indicates that the new field will be added to the right of Class. Within each Class, you will see their subject scores

Figure 278 shows the result of dropping the field as shown in Figure 277. This is not exactly what you wanted.

Figure 278

Analysis with undesired results

	A	B	C	D	E
1					
2					
3	DateTaken	(All) ▼			
4	GradeLevel	4 ▼			
5					
6	Count of Student Name		Passed ▼		
7	ClassOf ▼	Test ▼	FALSE	TRUE	Grand Total
8	2009	CITIZENSHIP	29.1%	70.9%	100.0%
9		MATH	28.5%	71.5%	100.0%
10		READING	28.5%	71.5%	100.0%
11		SCIENCE	29.1%	70.9%	100.0%
12		WRITING	29.8%	70.2%	100.0%
13	2009 Total		29.0%	71.0%	100.0%
14	2010	CITIZENSHIP	45.0%	55.0%	100.0%
15		MATH	43.0%	57.0%	100.0%
16		READING	47.0%	53.0%	100.0%
17		SCIENCE	45.7%	54.3%	100.0%
18		WRITING	44.4%	55.6%	100.0%
19	2010 Total		45.0%	55.0%	100.0%
20	2011	CITIZENSHIP	66.9%	33.1%	100.0%

6. Instead, if you drag the class button and drop it on the *left* side of column A, the gray fuzzy line will appear to the left of the Class. Because it is to the left of column A, you can barely see the gray line.

Figure 279

Moving test button to left side of Column area

	A	
1		
2	DateTaken	
3	GradeLevel	
4	Test	
5		
6	Count of Studer	
7	ClassOf	
8		
9		
10		
11		
12		
13		
14	Grand Total	
15		

When you drop the field here, you see an analysis of Class scores within each subject area for the fourth grade test. The class of 2009 did better on their fourth grade tests than any other class. Maybe the test was easier that year.

Figure 280

Analysis with desired results

DateTaken	(All) ▼			
GradeLevel	4 ▼			
Count of Student Name		Passed ▼		
Test ▼	ClassOf ▼	FALSE	TRUE	Grand Total
CITIZENSHIP	2009	29.1%	70.9%	100.0%
	2010	45.0%	55.0%	100.0%
	2011	66.9%	33.1%	100.0%
	2012	64.9%	35.1%	100.0%
	2013	50.3%	49.7%	100.0%
	2014	59.6%	40.4%	100.0%
CITIZENSHIP Total		52.6%	47.4%	100.0%
MATH	2009	28.5%	71.5%	100.0%
	2010	43.0%	57.0%	100.0%
	2011	62.3%	37.7%	100.0%
	2012	66.2%	33.8%	100.0%
	2013	53.6%	46.4%	100.0%
	2014	64.2%	35.8%	100.0%
MATH Total		53.0%	47.0%	100.0%
READING	2009	28.5%	71.5%	100.0%
	2010	47.0%	53.0%	100.0%
	2011	62.3%	37.7%	100.0%
	2012	65.6%	34.4%	100.0%
	2013	53.0%	47.0%	100.0%
	2014	62.3%	37.7%	100.0%
READING Total		53.1%	46.9%	100.0%
SCIENCE	2009	29.1%	70.9%	100.0%
	2010	45.7%	54.3%	100.0%

7. Change the GradeLevel dropdown in B4 from 4 to 6. The whole school is doing better in sixth grade, but you can still see that the class of 2009 had the highest passing ratio in each subject area.

Figure 281

Using dropdown to change analysis

DateTaken	(All) ▼			
GradeLevel	6 ▼			
Count of Student Name		Passed ▼		
Test ▼	ClassOf ▼	FALSE	TRUE	Grand Total
CITIZENSHIP	2007	34.4%	65.6%	100.0%
	2008	25.8%	74.2%	100.0%
	2009	15.2%	84.8%	100.0%
	2010	17.9%	82.1%	100.0%
	2011	35.8%	64.2%	100.0%
	2012	35.8%	64.2%	100.0%
CITIZENSHIP Total		27.5%	72.5%	100.0%
MATH	2007	37.7%	62.3%	100.0%
	2008	23.8%	76.2%	100.0%
	2009	10.6%	89.4%	100.0%
	2010	19.2%	80.8%	100.0%
	2011	35.1%	64.9%	100.0%
	2012	33.1%	66.9%	100.0%
MATH Total		26.6%	73.4%	100.0%
READING	2007	37.1%	62.9%	100.0%
	2008	26.5%	73.5%	100.0%
	2009	9.9%	90.1%	100.0%
	2010	17.9%	82.1%	100.0%
	2011	35.1%	64.9%	100.0%
	2012	33.1%	66.9%	100.0%
READING Total		26.6%	73.4%	100.0%
SCIENCE	2007	29.1%	70.9%	100.0%
	2008	26.5%	73.5%	100.0%
	2009	11.3%	88.7%	100.0%

You can continue dragging fields around the report to do analyses by teacher, by year, by grade level, and by subject.

As you start to get down to the student level, it may not make sense anymore to show the count of students. After all – there is only one student per row.

13

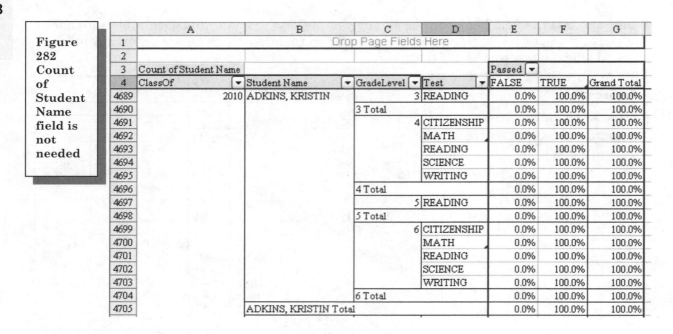

Figure 282
Count of Student Name field is not needed

		A	B	C	D	E	F	G
	1			Drop Page Fields Here				
	2							
	3	Count of Student Name				Passed ▼		
	4	ClassOf ▼	Student Name ▼	GradeLevel ▼	Test ▼	FALSE	TRUE	Grand Total
	4689	2010	ADKINS, KRISTIN	3	READING	0.0%	100.0%	100.0%
	4690			3 Total		0.0%	100.0%	100.0%
	4691			4	CITIZENSHIP	0.0%	100.0%	100.0%
	4692				MATH	0.0%	100.0%	100.0%
	4693				READING	0.0%	100.0%	100.0%
	4694				SCIENCE	0.0%	100.0%	100.0%
	4695				WRITING	0.0%	100.0%	100.0%
	4696			4 Total		0.0%	100.0%	100.0%
	4697			5	READING	0.0%	100.0%	100.0%
	4698			5 Total		0.0%	100.0%	100.0%
	4699			6	CITIZENSHIP	0.0%	100.0%	100.0%
	4700				MATH	0.0%	100.0%	100.0%
	4701				READING	0.0%	100.0%	100.0%
	4702				SCIENCE	0.0%	100.0%	100.0%
	4703				WRITING	0.0%	100.0%	100.0%
	4704			6 Total		0.0%	100.0%	100.0%
	4705		ADKINS, KRISTIN Total			0.0%	100.0%	100.0%

8. Drag the Count of Student Name button past the right side of the pivot table. The mouse pointer will change to a red X to indicate that you are removing the field from the report.

Figure 283

Removing Count of Student Name field

9. Take the Score field and drop it in the Data area of the report.

Figure 284

Moving Score field to Data area

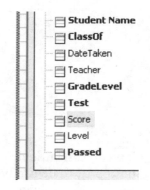

The report now shows the score for each student for each test.

Figure 285 Analysis showing score for each student for each test

3	Sum of Score				Passed ▼		
4	ClassOf ▼	Student Name ▼	GradeLevel ▼	Test ▼	FALSE	TRUE	Grand Total
4706		ALEXANDER, BARBARA	3	READING	193		193
4707			3 Total		193		193
4708			4	CITIZENSHIP	185		185
4709				MATH	192		192
4710				READING	192		192
4711				SCIENCE	183		183
4712				WRITING	184		184
4713			4 Total		936		936
4714			5	READING		202	202
4715			5 Total			202	202
4716			6	CITIZENSHIP	191		191
4717				MATH		200	200
4718				READING		201	201
4719				SCIENCE	194		194
4720				WRITING	192		192
4721			6 Total		577	401	978
4722		ALEXANDER, BARBARA Total			1706	603	2309
4723		ANDERSON, CLAIRE	3	READING	193		193

The report above is accurate because each cell in the Data area includes only one test. You can see in row 3, however, that the report is actually totaling the scores. If you had a student who repeated fourth grade, this pivot table would show that they remarkably scored a 301 – 147 in fourth grade one year and 155 the next year.

10. To solve this problem, double click the Sum of Score button and change the function from Sum to Average.

Figure 286

Changing the function from Sum to Average

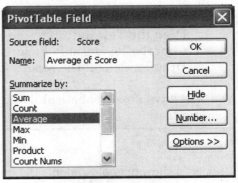

You can now see the Average score by subject and class. Again, that class of 2009 was a smarter than average class.

13

Figure 287

Analysis shows Average score by subject and class

	A	B	C	D	E
1			Drop Page Fields Here		
2					
3	Average of Score		Passed ▼		
4	ClassOf ▼	Test ▼	FALSE	TRUE	Grand Total
5	2007	CITIZENSHIP	194.0	209.1	203.9
6		MATH	193.5	209.5	203.5
7		READING	193.5	209.5	203.6
8		SCIENCE	193.1	208.6	204.1
9		WRITING	193.7	209.0	204.0
10	2007 Total		193.6	209.1	203.8
11	2008	CITIZENSHIP	194.2	208.9	205.1
12		MATH	193.8	209.4	205.7
13		READING	193.3	209.2	203.8
14		SCIENCE	194.5	209.1	205.2
15		WRITING	194.2	208.9	205.2
16	2008 Total		193.8	209.1	204.8
17	2009	CITIZENSHIP	194.8	211.6	207.9
18		MATH	194.3	211.2	207.9
19		READING	194.3	211.1	207.8
20		SCIENCE	194.2	211.2	207.8
21		WRITING	194.5	211.3	207.7
22	2009 Total		194.4	211.3	207.8
23	2010	CITIZENSHIP	193.0	209.2	204.1
24		MATH	193.1	208.9	204.0
25		READING	193.2	208.7	202.9
26		SCIENCE	193.4	209.3	204.0
27		WRITING	193.0	209.1	204.0
28	2010 Total		193.2	209.0	203.6

Finding Top or Bottom Students

You need to identify students for a summer reading program. Which students scored the worst on the test?

1. Drag the Test button to the Page area and choose Reading. Drag the DateTaken field from the Pivot Table Field List to the Page area and choose this most recent school year. Drag Passed off the report. Drag Student Name to the Column area of the report.

You will have an alphabetical listing of how everyone in the school did this year on their Reading test.

Figure 288

Analysis show how all students did on the Reading test

	A	B
1	Test	READING ▼
2	DateTaken	3/31/2006 ▼
3		
4	Average of Score	
5	Student Name ▼	Total
6	ABBOTT, RUBY	208.0
7	ADKINS, THOMAS	187.0
8	AGUIRRE, EUNICE	199.0
9	ALBERT, DANNY	197.0
10	ALLEN, GEORGE	194.0
11	ALLISON, RUSSELL	212.0
12	ALSTON, JAMES	204.0
13	ALVARADO, VELMA	203.0

By default, Excel orders the pivot tables in an alphabetical sequence. The settings to override this are a bit hidden.

2. Double-click on the Student Name button in cell A5. In the PivotTable Field dialog, choose the Advanced... button.

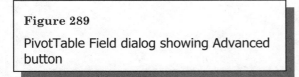

Figure 289

PivotTable Field dialog showing Advanced button

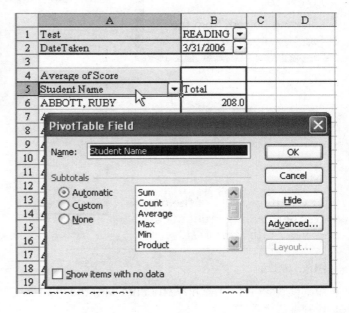

3. In the PivotTable Field Advanced Options dialog, choose the Ascending AutoSort option. From the dropdown, indicate that you want the field sorted ascending by Average of Score.

Figure 290

Selecting Ascending AutoSort option using Average of Score field

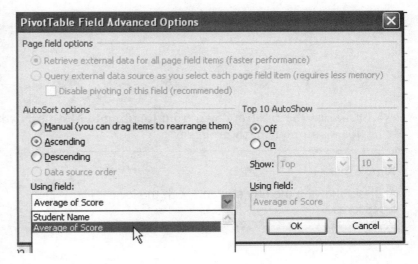

13

4. Perhaps budget constraints will only allow 50 students to take the summer reading program. On the right side of this dialog, you can use the Top 10 Autoshow features to show the Bottom 50 students.

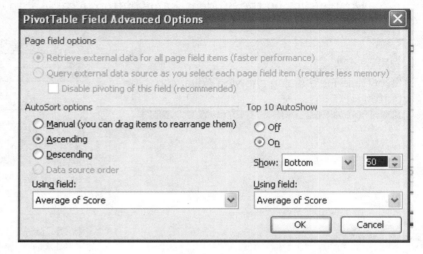

Figure 291

Selecting Bottom from the Top 10 AutoShow feature

You will have a list of the 50 worst performing students on this year's Reading test.

Figure 292

Analysis showing the fifty students with the lowest Reading test scores

	A	B
1	Test	READING ▾
2	DateTaken	3/31/2006 ▾
3		
4	Average of Score	
5	Student Name ▾	Total
6	NIELSEN, JACQUELINE	173.0
7	CALHOUN, ALLISON	175.0
8	PORTER, SANDY	177.0
9	TANNER, JOSE	177.0
10	FERNANDEZ, RYAN	178.0
11	BLEVINS, VIVIAN	178.0
12	BRIGHT, JEFF	179.0
13	GRAVES, JEFF	180.0
14	HICKS, KENNETH	180.0
15	BURGESS, CARL	181.0

5. Change the B1 dropdown from Reading to Math and you will have a list of candidates for a summer math program.

Figure 293

Analysis showing the fifty students with the lowest Math test scores

	A	B
1	Test	MATH ▾
2	DateTaken	3/31/2006 ▾
3		
4	Average of Score	
5	Student Name ▾	Total
6	NIELSEN, JACQUELINE	173.0
7	CALHOUN, ALLISON	175.0
8	TANNER, JOSE	177.0
9	PORTER, SANDY	179.0
10	GLOVER, SARA	181.0
11	BRIGHT, JEFF	181.0
12	FARMER, HARRY	182.0
13	FERNANDEZ, RYAN	182.0
14	TERRELL, BRANDON	182.0
15	MCCLAIN, KAYLA	183.0
16	BURGESS, CARL	183.0

Using the Application

Once you get the hang of dragging the fields, you will find pivot tables to be very flexible and powerful. You can run into trouble when you try to drop a field into the wrong place. If you drop a field somewhere and get a bizarre result, remember to type Ctrl+Z to undo the drop and try again.

Figure 294

When you get unexpected results, immediately type Ctrl+Z to undo your last

	A	B	C
1	Test	MATH ▼	
2	DateTaken	3/31/2006 ▼	
3			
4	**Student Name** ▼	Data ▼	Total
5	NIELSEN, JACQUELINE	Average of Score	173.0
6		Count of DateTaken	1
7	CALHOUN, ALLISON	Average of Score	175.0
8		Count of DateTaken	1
9	TANNER, JOSE	Average of Score	177.0
10		Count of DateTaken	1

Excel Details

There is one bizarre feature of pivot tables that is very counter-intuitive. The following pivot table shows the number of students passing a sixth grade reading test.

Figure 295

Analysis showing number of students who passed a Reading test

	A	B	C	D	E
1	Test	READING ▼			
2	GradeLevel	6 ▼			
3					
4	Count of Student Name	Level ▼			
5	ClassOf ▼	Advanced	Basic	Proficient	Grand Total
6	2007	19	56	76	151
7	2008	32	40	79	151
8	2009	59	15	77	151
9	2010	35	27	89	151
10	2011	15	53	83	151
11	2012	21	50	80	151
12	Grand Total	181	241	484	906

The state awards scores of Basic, Proficient, and Advanced. Because of the alphabetical sort, the pivot table shows Advanced first, Basic second, and Proficient third. It would make more sense to have Proficient appear next to Advanced.

It is unbelievable that this trick works. Click into cell D5. Type the word Basic and press Enter. Amazingly, Excel understands that you are trying to manually re-sequence the Levels and will redraw the report appropriately.

13

Figure 296

Using Excel to automatically re-sequence fields

	A	B	C	D	E
1	Test	READING ▼			
2	GradeLevel	6 ▼			
3					
4	Count of Student Name	Level ▼			
5	ClassOf ▼	Advanced	Proficient	Basic	Grand Total
6	2007	19	76	56	151
7	2008	32	79	40	151
8	2009	59	77	15	151
9	2010	35	89	27	151
10	2011	15	83	53	151
11	2012	21	80	50	151
12	Grand Total	181	484	241	906
13					
14					

Chapter 14 – Reading Grade Level Test Results

Opportunity

This type of test looks for a student's instructional reading level. I need a way to record the results of each test given. We give the test in the fall, winter, and spring. Students should "grow" in their reading levels along a specific development path (stipulated by research data). I'd like a way to determine which students are progressing at accelerated speeds, which are moving steadily along, and which are at risk for failure.

Solution and Overview

The solution will produce a Column chart showing progress from one test to the next. Further, the solution can be used during parent teacher-conference time to show each parent their student's individual results.

Creating the Solution

Start with a blank Excel worksheet. On the keyboard, type the PageDown key to move below the first screen full of rows. Go down one more row and type headings for Student, Fall, Winter, and Spring in columns A:D.

<table>
<tr><td>

Figure 297

Worksheet with seasonal headings

</td><td>

	Student	Fall	Winter	Spring
33	Student	Fall	Winter	Spring
34	Allison Hupp			
35	Amanda Detwiler			
36	Ashley Mullen			
37	Austin Boxler			
38	Brittany Poling			
39	Courtney Mcginnis			
40	Courtney Robert			

</td></tr>
</table>

As the students take the tests, you will record their scores in the appropriate cells.

Building the Chart for Parent-Teacher Conferences

1. Type the PageUp key to return to the first rows in the worksheet. Add a title to cell A1. Copy the Fall, Winter, and Spring headings to cells B3:D3.

   1a. Select cell A4. From the menu, choose Data – Validation. Initially, the validation for all cells say that the cell is allowed to select Any value.

14

Figure 298

Data Validation dialog box

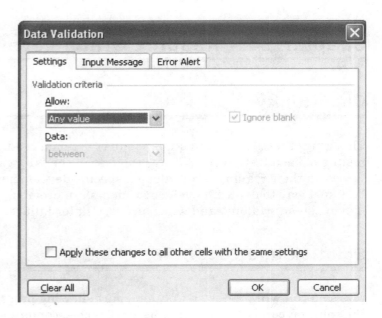

1b. There are a number of ways to add validation to a cell. In this case, you would like cell A4 to be limited to the list of students in your class. Choose the Allow dropdown and choose the value for List.

Figure 299

Selecting Validation criteria

2. After choosing List, the dialog box changes to include a checkbox for In-cell dropdown plus a Source box. On the right side of the Source box is a spreadsheet icon with some blue cells and a red arrow. Click on this icon to collapse the dialog box and to be able to specify a range on the worksheet.

Figure 300

Finding the Source icon

2b. With the dialog box collapsed, highlight the list of students with your mouse. Excel fills in the range for you.

Figure 301

Selecting the range

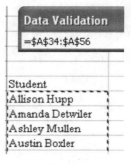

3. To return to the full-size version of the Data Validation dialog, click this icon at the right end of the collapsed box: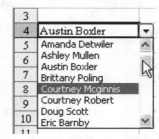

3a. Click OK to close the Data Validation dialog. When you make cell A4 the active cell, it will have a dropdown arrow. Choose the dropdown arrow in order to display a list of students. You can select a student from the list.

14

Figure 302

Selecting a student from the dropdown

3	
4	Austin Boxler ▼
5	Amanda Detwiler
6	Ashley Mullen
7	Austin Boxler
8	Brittany Poling
9	Courtney Mcginnis
10	Courtney Robert
	Doug Scott
	Eric Barnby

In cells B4:D4, you will want a formula to retrieve the values from the data table shown below. A VLOOKUP formula can find the student selected in A4 and return the proper values.

4. Enter this formula in cell B4: =VLOOKUP($A4,$A$34:$I$56,2,FALSE)

Figure 303

Using a VLOOKUP formula

B4   *fx* =VLOOKUP($A4,$A$34:$I$56,2,FALSE)

	A	B	C	D	E	F
1	Reading Levels					
2						
3		Fall	Winter	Spring		
4	Courtney Mcginnis	4.1	4.4	4.3		
5						
6						

There are four arguments to this version of the VLOOKUP formula. The first argument tells Excel to should try to find the student name specified in cell A4. The second argument tells Excel that the student name will be found in the first column of the table in A34:I56. The third argument tells Excel that you want to return the second column from the lookup table. The fourth argument is FALSE to indicate that you will only accept exact matches instead of close matches. Previously, in the grade book example, you used VLOOKUP without the FALSE argument. This allowed you to say that an A was every score from 95% on up. You don't want Excel to return the reading scores from a student with a name close to the chosen name, so you have to specify FALSE as the last argument to the function.

Note that the formula has some judicious use of dollar signs. The "A" in the first argument is locked so that you can copy the formula from B4 to C4 and D4 while always looking at the student name in A. The lookup range argument has dollar signs throughout to keep it fixed.

5. After you copy the formula from B4 to C4:D4, you will have to edit those two formulas. The third argument in C4 needs to change from 2 to 3 in order to return the third column of the lookup table. Similarly, the fourth argument in D4 needs to change from 2 to 4 in order to return the fourth column of the lookup table.

14

6. Select cells A3:D4. From the menu, choose Insert – Chart. In Step 1 of the Chart Wizard, choose a Column chart.

Figure 304

Selecting a Column chart in the Chart Wizard

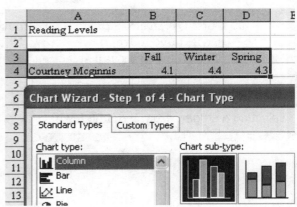

7. Click Next two times to move to Step 3 of the wizard. In Step 3, choose the Titles tab and give the chart a title of Reading Scores. Also in Step 3, choose the Data Labels tab and check the box for Value. Click Finish to embed the chart in the current worksheet.

7a. The chart will be inserted in the middle of the screen with some default size. Using the mouse, click on a white section of the area outside of the plot area and drag the chart up to cell A5.

 Tip:

When the chart is selected, there are eight black square dots around the edge of the chart. You can click and drag any of these dots to resize the chart, thus making the chart larger or smaller.

Using the Application

As you are preparing for the parent-teacher conference, select the student name from the dropdown in cell A4. The student's scores will automatically be copied to B4:D4. Because the chart is based on the scores shown in B4:D4, the chart will instantly update to show that student's reading progress.

Chapter 15 – Tracking Proficiency

Opportunity

Many schools require tracking proficiency for skill testing (focused instruction). Our school has a program called focused instruction where, for 30 minutes a day, students "focus" on one particular skill in either math or language arts. Students are put in specific groups by a pretest score. At the end of a two-week instruction period, students are given a posttest. I need a way to record each student's pretest and posttest scores and to determine if they reached a mastery level of 80% or higher. I also need to determine what percentage of each class and grade reached the mastery level for each math and reading skill. I know that this specialized way of teaching skills (focused instruction) may only be pertinent to a small number of teachers, but I know that all teachers are concerned about having their students reach proficiency levels of state standards. This way of tracking information could be related to a means of making sure not only that the state standards are taught (a record could be made of when/how each standard is taught) but also of tracking student progress of state standard mastery.

Solution and Overview

Recording the scores and the improvement is basic Excel math. This chapter introduces the concept of the IF function to determine if the student has met the 80% level and also the SUMIF function to count how many students met the 80% level.

Creating the Solution

Start with a blank Excel workbook. Set up columns for Name, Subject, Pretest Score, PostTest Score, Points Improved, and Mastery. Enter the student names (copy and paste from your grade book application). Enter the student's assigned area of focused instruction and his or her pretest score. Save the file for use after the focused instruction.

Figure 305

Worksheet showing student's Pretest scores in a particular subject

	A	B	C	D	E	F
1	Student	Subject	Pretest	PostTest	Change	Mastery
2	Wood, Rebecca	Math	77			
3	Matthews, Irene	LangArts	66			
4	Alexander, Alicia	LangArts	70			
5	Taylor, Larry	Math	65			
6	Harris, Judith	Math	79			
7	Watson, Anthony	Math	77			
8	Price, Mark	LangArts	78			
9	Fisher, Joan	LangArts	65			
10	Phillips, Gloria	Math	69			
11	Campbell, Michele	Math	75			
12	Smith, Gloria	LangArts	70			
13	White, Joann	Math	75			
14	Shaw, Jose	LangArts	71			
15	Ward, Rosa	Math	67			
16	Young, Amy	Math	72			
17						

Using the Application

1. After the two weeks, administer a posttest and enter the posttest scores in column D.

2. The formula in E2 is =D2-C2. Enter this formula. Move the cellpointer back to E2. Double-click the fill handle to copy the formula down to the other students.

Figure 306

Using the fill handle to copy down a formula

	E2		▼	*fx*	=D2-C2	
	A	B	C	D	E	M
1	Student	Subject	Pretest	PostTest	Change	
2	Wood, Rebecca	Math	77	88	11	
3	Matthews, Irene	LangArts	66	73		

Using the IF Function

In column F, you want to display whether the student scored 80 percent or higher on the posttest. The Excel IF function can put one value in a cell if a condition is met and another value in a cell if the condition is not met.

There are three arguments used in the IF function.

> First, indicate the condition that you want to test. In this case, you want to test to see if D2 is greater than or equal to 80. This would be specified as D2>=80.

> Second, indicate the value (or formula) that should be used if the condition is met. If you indicate a value, enter that value inside quotation marks. In this case, the second argument would be "Mastered".

> For the final condition, indicate the value or formula that should be used if the condition is not met. In this case, the third argument would be "Not Mastered".

The complete formula in F2 would be =IF(D2>=80,"Mastered","Not Mastered").

Figure 307

Completed IF formula

	F2		▼	*fx*	=IF(D2>=80,"Mastered","Not Mastered")	
	A	B	C	D	E	F
1	Student	Subject	Pretest	PostTest	Change	Mastery
2	Wood, Rebecca	Math	77	88	11	Mastered
3	Matthews, Irene	LangArts	66	73	7	Not Mastered
4	Alexander, Alicia	LangArts	70	75	5	Not Mastered

Adding Summary Statistics for the Entire Class

1. Leave a blank row between your data and the summary line. Type "Class Average" in column A. Move the cellpointer to columns C, D, and E in the total row. Look for the AutoSum button (Greek letter Sigma) in the Standard Toolbar. Next to the icon is a dropdown. Select the dropdown and choose Average from the list.

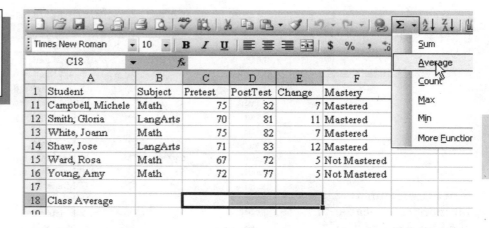

Figure 308

Configuring the AutoSum button to calculate an average

2. Excel will propose average formulas for C, D, and E. Press Enter to accept the proposed formulas. Excel will calculate an average. There is a good chance that the average will include a lot of decimal places.

Figure 309

Averages calculated for each test score and the difference between them show too many decimal places

=AVERAGE(C2:C17)

C	D	E	
Pretest	PostTest	Change	]
75	82	7	]
70	81	11	]
75	82	7	]
71	83	12	]
67	72	5	]
72	77	5	]
71.73333	79.73333	8	

3. There are icons in the Formatting toolbar to decrease or increase the number of decimal places. Press the Decrease Decimal icon four times to change the format to display only one decimal place.

Figure 310

Using the Decrease Decimal button

Decrease Decimal

Using COUNTIF and SUMIF for Totals

You are probably familiar with the functions to sum and count. SUM adds numbers in a range. COUNT counts the numeric cells in a range. COUNTA counts all non-blank cells in a range. Back in Excel 97, Microsoft added two specialized functions that can sum or count based on a single condition.

In the total line for column F, the COUNTIF function counts how many students have the value of Mastered. The COUNTIF function needs a range of values and then the criteria to be used. In this case, the formula is =COUNTIF(F2:F16,"Mastered"). In this particular group of students, eight students have met the 80% mastery level.

15

Figure 311

Using COUNTIF

	B	C	D	E	F	G	H	I
					F18 ▼ fx =COUNTIF(F2:F16,"Mastered")			
1	Subject	Pretest	PostTest	Change	Mastery			
2	Math	77	88	11	Mastered			
3	LangArts	66	73	7	Not Mastered			
4	LangArts	70	75	5	Not Mastered			
5	Math	65	77	12	Not Mastered			
6	Math	79	84	5	Mastered			
7	Math	77	89	12	Mastered			
8	LangArts	78	83	5	Mastered			
9	LangArts	65	75	10	Not Mastered			
10	Math	69	75	6	Not Mastered			
11	Math	75	82	7	Mastered			
12	LangArts	70	81	11	Mastered			
13	Math	75	82	7	Mastered			
14	LangArts	71	83	12	Mastered			
15	Math	67	72	5	Not Mastered			
16	Math	72	77	5	Not Mastered			
17								
18		71.7	79.7	8.0	8	<--Number of Students Mastered		

The SUMIF function is a bit more complicated. In the figure below, the formula tells Excel to look at each subject in B2:B16. If it matches the entry in B19, then total the corresponding value in C2:C16.

Figure 312

Using SUMIF

	A	B	C	D	E	F
1	Student	Subject	Pretest	PostTest	Change	Mastery
2	Wood, Rebecca	Math	77	88	11	Mastered
3	Matthews, Irene	LangArts	66	73	7	Not Mast
4	Alexander, Alicia	LangArts	70	75	5	Not Mast
5	Taylor, Larry	Math	65	77	12	Not Mast
6	Harris, Judith	Math	79	84	5	Mastered
7	Watson, Anthony	Math	77	89	12	Mastered
8	Price, Mark	LangArts	78	83	5	Mastered
9	Fisher, Joan	LangArts	65	75	10	Not Mast
10	Phillips, Gloria	Math	69	75	6	Not Mast
11	Campbell, Michele	Math	75	82	7	Mastered
12	Smith, Gloria	LangArts	70	81	11	Mastered
13	White, Joann	Math	75	82	7	Mastered
14	Shaw, Jose	LangArts	71	83	12	Mastered
15	Ward, Rosa	Math	67	72	5	Not Mast
16	Young, Amy	Math	72	77	5	Not Mast
17						
18	Class Average		71.7	79.7	8.0	
19		Math	=SUMIF($B$2:$B$16,$B19,C$2:C$16)			
20		LangArts	SUMIF(range, criteria, **[sum_range]**)			

The formula here would total all of the Pretest scores for math. To actually calculate an average, you would have to divide that total by the students in the Math program. Thus, the formula becomes a SUMIF divided by a COUNTIF.

Figure 313 Dividing a SUMIF by a COUNTIF

	71.7	79.7	8.0	8 <--Number of Studer
Math	=SUMIF($B$2:$B$16,$B19,C$2:C$16)/COUNTIF($B$2:$B$16,$B19)			
LangArts				

Note that the formula makes careful use of the dollar signs in several references to that the formula can easily be copied to the five adjacent cells. The dollar signs everywhere make the range of B2:B16 absolute. This is because no matter where the formula is copied, we need to look in B2:B16 to figure if the student's subject was math or language arts.

The range of C2:C16 has dollar signs to make the rows always be 2:16, but the reference to C will be allowed to change if the formula is copied to columns D and E. The reference to the subject in B19 is locked to column B but will be allowed to change to B20 if the formula is copied to row 20.

Copy the formula in C19 to C19:E20. You will see that math students improved from an average of 72.9 on the pretest to 80.7 on the posttest. Language arts students improve from an average of 70.0 to 78.3.

Figure 314

Results showing average improvement

Class Average		71.7	79.7	8.0
	Math	72.9	80.7	7.8
	LangArts	70.0	78.3	8.3

Note that all of the calculations in the preceding example worked because there was only one criterion.

Excel has had special array formulas that could perform calculations based on several criteria. They realized that array formulas were scaring a lot of people away. Microsoft added SUMIF and COUNTIF to handle the special situation where there is only one criterion.

Once someone has mastered the concept of SUMIF and COUNTIF, that person naturally wants to create a COUNTIF that handles two criteria. For example, at this point, we want to count the math students who have mastered the material. The SUMIF and COUNTIF functions cannot do this.

Array formulas are a fairly advanced concept. For an introduction to using the Conditional Sum Wizard to create array formulas, read: http://www.mrexcel.com/tip083.shtml

15

Chapter 16 – Creating Checklists

Opportunity

A big part of a teacher's job is to manage and organize all types of information. This information could vary from testing and assignment grades to project completion data to a listing of bus numbers and drivers. The key to successful organization is being able to easily and efficiently retrieve the data. Checklists, charts, and forms help a teacher organize all types of assessment, student measurement, and organizational data. There are numerous books devoted to blank checklists and forms for classroom use; however, they often do not fit my specific needs. I want a way to create my own forms to fit any given situation.

Can Excel be used to help make customized checklists for varying classroom use? Often I need these checklists, charts, and forms to include boxes to record checkmarks and/or other types of data. These types of charts can help me visually keep track of information and student data and, depending on the data, I may or may not transfer the information to my grade book. The checklists need to have a column of student names and a row of values (of varying natures) across the top. Boxes under each "value" need to be part of the printing. I like to print off the checklist, attach it to a clipboard, and I'm ready to record, evaluate, and assess.

These checklists and forms would not need to calculate the information/data. The information gathered is often informal in nature and may or may not be transferred to a grade book. Excel allows for the creation of neat and organized forms and charts. I know that Word does allow the user to draw boxes and lines but I am forever fighting with the program and it takes me too much time. I have found that Excel draws precise lines and boxes easily and quickly!

Some application examples:
- ➢ Who has returned permissions slips and money
- ➢ Assignment/Project completion checklist

Solution and Overview

Excel is perfect for this type of application. It is easy to quickly format the worksheet to handle any type of checklist. Without needing any calculation, you can create the worksheet using mostly commands on the Formatting toolbar.

Creating the Solution

1. Start with a blank worksheet. Save the worksheet as Checklist.xls. Type a heading of "Student" in cell A1.

    1a. You will want to enter the student's names in column A. However, by this time, it is very likely that you already have the student names in another Excel workbook. Open your Grade book workbook or your Attendance workbook. Select a range containing the student names. Type Ctrl+C to copy the names to the clipboard.

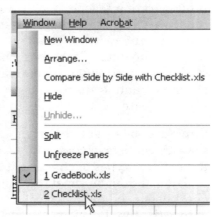

Tip:

Although you can use Alt+Tab to switch from one open workbook to another workbook, you can also use the Window menu. At the bottom of the Window menu, there is a list of all of the open workbooks. In the image below, GradeBook is the active workbook. Only one other workbook – Checklist – is open.

1b. Using the mouse, select the Checklist.xls entry to switch back to the checklist.

Figure 315

Using the Window menu to switch between workbooks

2. Once in the checklist, select cell B2. From the menu, select Edit – Paste Special. In the Paste Special dialog choose Values and then OK. This will copy the student names, without any formatting, to the workbook.

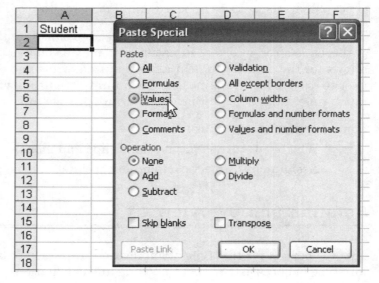

Figure 316

Using Paste Special Values to copy data without any formatting

2a. You can now use the Window command to switch back to the grade book and close it. Once you close the grade book, the checklist workbook should again be the active workbook.

3. In cell B1, type one of the steps for your checklist. Perhaps it would be "Permission Slip" and cell C1 would be "Money". Of course, the Excel columns are not wide enough for long headings like these.

Figure 317

Headings wider than their columns

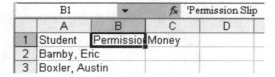

4. Select cells B1:J1. Type Ctrl+1 to display the Format Cells dialog. On the Alignment tab, change the Orientation to 90 degrees.

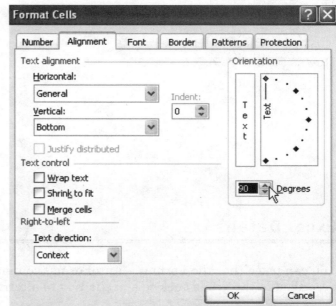

Figure 318

Changing the cell orientation

4a. Choose OK to close the Format Cells dialog. From the menu, select Format – Column – Width and change the column width to 4 for the checkbox column headings.

5. Select column A by clicking on the gray "A" heading above cell A1. From the menu, choose Format – Column – AutoFit Selection to make the column wide enough for the longest student name.

16

6. Finally, you will want to add borders around all of the cells. Select the range from A1:J22 (include enough rows to include the last student). In the Formatting toolbar, there is a Borders icon that looks like an underline. Next to this Borders icon is a dropdown arrow. Touch the dropdown arrow with the mouse and choose the icon with the four boxes. This will fill in borders on the inside and outside of the selected area.

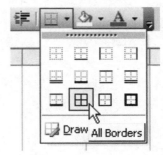

Figure 319

Using the Borders icon to select all borders

Using the Application

You now have an easy-to-use checklist worksheet. Feel free to save the original workbook with a name like Checklist Template. As you come up with the need for a new checklist, open the Checklist Template; use File – Save As to save the file with a new name, and type new tasks going across row 1.

Figure 320

Using the Checklist template

	A	B	C	D	E
		Permission Slip	Money	Thank you Note	
1	Student				
2	Barnby, Eric				
3	Boxler, Austin				
4	Boyes, Julie				
5	Cairns, Mike				
6	Coerver, Nate				
7	Dutton, Meredith				

Excel Details

You can use either the Format – AutoFormat command or the Conditional Formatting trick described in the grade book to add shading to alternating rows of the worksheet.

Figure 321

Shading alternate rows

	A	B	C	D	E	F
1	**Student**	Lunch		Field Trip	Money	
2	Barnby, Eric					
3	Boxler, Austin					
4	Boyes, Julie					
5	Cairns, Mike					
6	Coerver, Nate					

Chapter 17 – Requisition Forms

Opportunity

Over the summer, I was given a grant to spend on books for my school's reading library. These books are to be used by teachers to supplement their reading instruction. Once I decided on which books to order, I had to itemize my catalog orders with catalog name, page numbers, product numbers, quantity, and prices so that the school's business manager could order the books via purchase order. I didn't have a way to get the order information down on paper so I used Word (of all things!) and, in a very time consuming way, typed out all the information. I then had to add the prices by hand with a calculator. I knew Excel had a way of calculating numbers easily and quickly and was kicking myself all through the ordering process for not knowing how to set up a workbook to help me meet my goal of spending lots of money!

Solution and Overview

You will create a requisition form that automatically totals your expenses for orders from one or more vendors on separate forms. Additionally, you will be able to compare the total amount spent with a budget amount and compute how much over or under budget you are.

Creating the Solution

1. Start with a blank worksheet. From the File menu at the top, select Page Setup. Click on the Margins tab at the top. Change the top, bottom, and right margins to 0.5 by clicking on the up or down arrow next to each current margin. Change the left margin to 0.8. To do this, you will need to click on either the up or down arrow that blackens the number that is already there and then type in "0.8". This will maximize the printing area of the requisition form while allowing a left margin large enough to three-hole punch the edge.

Figure 322

Setting margin to allow for three-hole punching

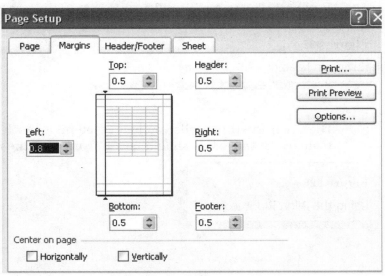

2. Look on the toolbar at the top where the font style and size are listed. If you do not have both Arial and 10, do the following: Click your mouse cursor in the empty gray box to the left of the Column A header.

2a. This will highlight the entire spreadsheet. Right click on any cell and select Format Cells, then click on the Font tab. Select Arial from Font, and 10 from Size, and click OK.

Figure 323

Formatting cells to be 10-point Arial

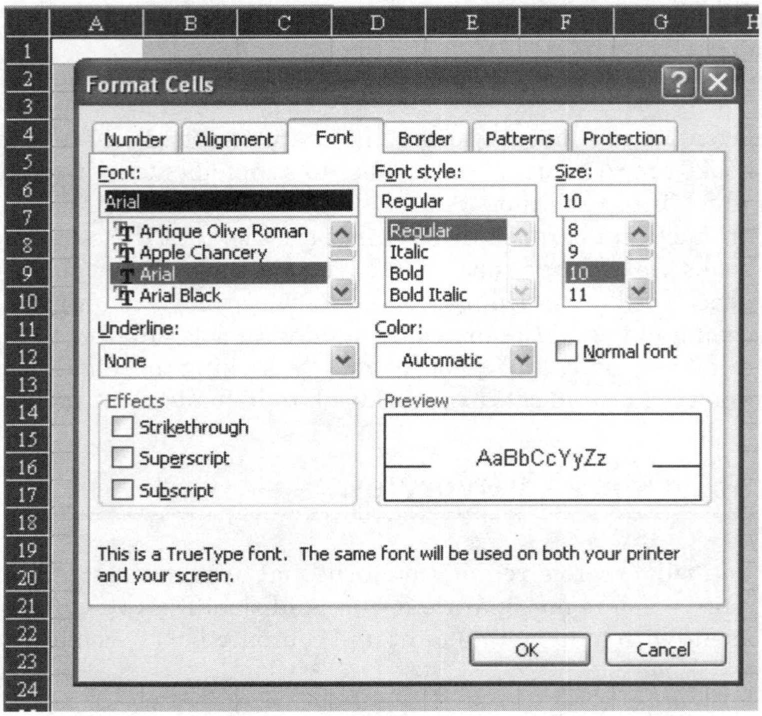

2b. Even if you did not do the previous step, do this one. Place your mouse cursor over cell A1 and slowly move to the left. When the cursor changes to an arrow, click on the 1 in the first row, which should highlight the entire row. Drag down to row 19 and release. Right-click anywhere in the selected rows and select Format Cells. Now click on the Font tab at the top. Select 12 from Size, and click OK.

Figure 324

Selecting entire first row

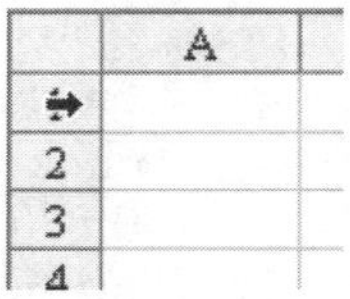

3. In E1, type in "Budget Amount:"; in E2 type in "Total Spent:"; and in E3 type in "Under Budget:". The text will spill over into the adjacent cells, but that's OK.

Figure 325

Keying in headings

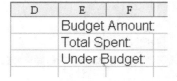

4. Highlight the three cells you just typed in, and select the Align Right icon from the toolbar. All the words should now line up with the right margin of column E.

Figure 326

Using the Align Right icon

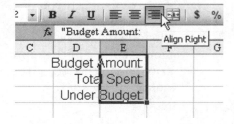

5. Highlight cells F1, F2, and F3; right-click and select Format Cells and then click the Number tab. Under Category, select Currency and make sure that the Decimal places box has a 2. (Change it if it doesn't.) Click OK. We will come back to these later and enter some formulas for keeping track of your spending.

Figure 327

Formatting cells as Currency

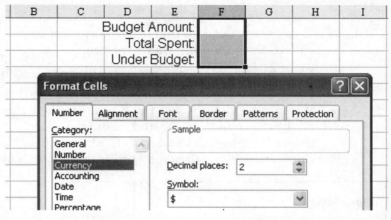

6. In C6, type in [name of your school] Requisition Form. In C7, type in your name; in C8, type in your classroom number and/or grade or subject. This is entirely up to you and any standards that your school may use in referring to the staff. Again, the text will spill over, but we will fix it later.

Figure 328

Entering text that spills over into adjacent cells

	A	B	C	D	E	F	G
1				Budget Amount:			
2				Total Spent:			
3				Under Budget:			
4							
5							
6			XYZ City Schools Requisition Form				
7			Mrs. Smith				
8			Classroom 14				
9							
10							

7. In D6, type in "Date:". Move to cell E6. There is a Borders icon in the Formatting toolbar. The usual operation of this toolbar is to add a border to the bottom edge of the selected cell. Provided your Borders icon looks like the one shown in Figure 329, click the icon.

Figure 329

Adding a bottom edge border

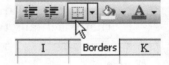

| I | Borders | K |

8. Type these labels into column A as follows:
   - A10: Company Name
   - A11: Contact Person
   - A12: Address
   - A14: City, St, Zip (Note that we skipped a row!)
   - A15: Phone Number

As before, the text will spill over into adjacent cells, but we will leave it as is.

	A	B
10	Company Name	
11	Contact Person	
12	Address	
13		
14	City, State, Zip	
15	Phone Number	

Figure 330

Keying in labels

9. Next, you want to add a line to the bottom of each cell in C10 through C15. There are two methods.

  ➤ You can select each cell individually and click the Borders icon in the Formatting toolbar. With six cells to format, this would be a total of 12 clicks.

  ➤ It might be faster to use the Format Cells dialog to add borders to the entire range. Highlight cells C10:C15 and right click.
  Select Format Cells and click the Border tab. The third icon on the left side of the Borders section will add a border to the bottommost cell of the selection - cell C15.

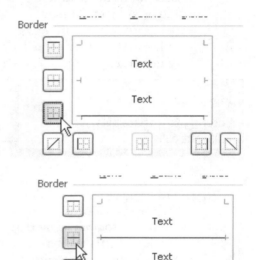

Figure 331

Adding a bottom edge border to the bottom of a range

9a. You also have to select the second icon down to add a border to the bottom of each cell in the range – C10 through C14.

Figure 332

Adding a bottom edge border to all selected cells

10. Highlight cells A18 and A19. Right click, select Format Cells, and click on the Alignment tab. In the Text control section, click on the boxes next to Wrap text and Merge cells and then click OK. This creates a single cell that is actually two rows tall. Text will be able to flow and wrap in this larger cell.

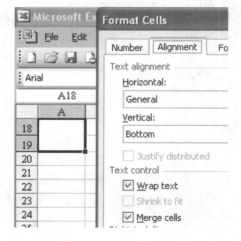

Figure 333

Selecting Wrap text and Merge cells to handle text that spills over into adjacent cells

Note that when you select this super A18/A19 cell, the address bar shows that you are in cell A18. Technically, cell A19 does not exist anymore in this worksheet.

10a. Now highlight B18 and B19, and do exactly the same thing. Repeat again for C18 and C19, D18 and D19 and E18 and E19, except under Text control, only click the box next to Wrap text.

11. Starting at Cell A18/19 (now merged) and moving to the right, type in the following labels:

   ➢ A18/19   Catalog or Part No.
   ➢ B18/19   How Many
   ➢ C18/19   Description
   ➢ D18/19   Unit Cost
   ➢ E18/19   Total

Figure 334

Keying in text that spills over into adjacent cells

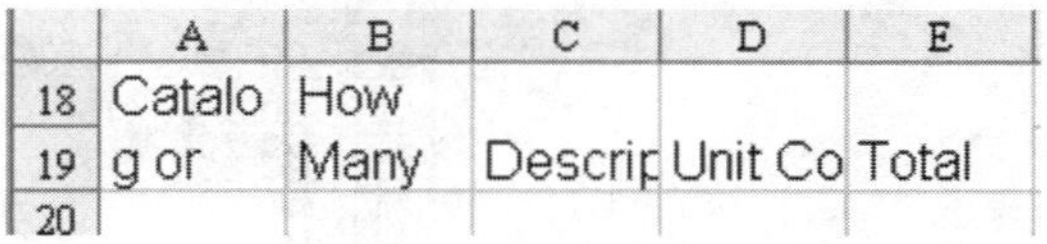

	A	B	C	D	E
18	Catalo	How			
19	g or	Many	Descrip	Unit Co	Total
20					

Again, there will be serious problems with text overflowing into the next cells. Now let's fix it!

12. You want column A to be wide enough to allow the words "Catalog or" to be above the words "Part No.". You will need to make column A wider. Move your mouse cursor to the top of column A in the column heading area until it turns into an arrow and move slowly towards the B. Stop when it looks like a plus sign with arrow heads on the horizontal part.

Figure 335

Adjusting column width by dragging the mouse cursor

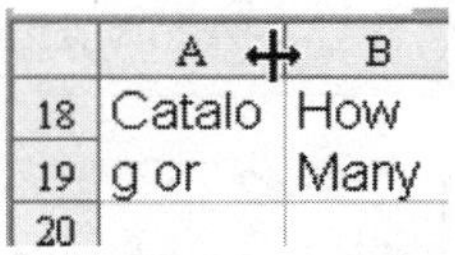

	A	B
18	Catalo	How
19	g or	Many
20		

When the mouse pointer is in this shape, clicking your mouse button and holding shows you how wide the column is, with the pixel count in parenthesis. Also, clicking and holding and moving left or right will adjust the column width.

12a. You want to make the column just wide enough so that there are two lines of readable text in the two combined cells. On my computer, that's about a width of 12. Adjust all the other columns D through E the same way, using these values as starting points.

   ➢ Column A: 12
   ➢ Column B: 7
   ➢ Column C: 49
   ➢ Column D: 11
   ➢ Column E: 11

12b. Now highlight all the text in combined rows 18 and 19 and click on the Bold icon (B) in the toolbar. After making the cells bold, you might have to adjust the column widths again.

At this point, the requisition form is starting to take shape.

Figure 336

Requisition form with column widths adjusted

	A	B	C		D	E
1					Budget Amount:	
2					Total Spent:	
3					Under Budget:	
4						
5						
6			XYZ City Schools Requisition Form		Date:	
7			Mrs. Smith			
8			Classroom 14			
9						
10	Company Name					
11	Contact Person					
12	Address					
13						
14	City, State, Zip					
15	Phone Number					
16						
17						
18	**Catalog or**	**How**				
19	**Part No.**	**Many**	**Description**		**Unit Cost**	**Total**
20						

13. You will want to add boxes to the order detail block. You can easily add boxes around every cell in the selection. Drag from A18 through E52 to select that range. Next to the Borders icon in the Formatting toolbar is a dropdown arrow. Select this arrow and choose the icon that looks like a four-pane window to apply All Borders.

Figure 337

Applying all borders to a range

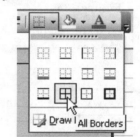

13a. You also want boxes around E53 and E54. Highlight just cells E53 and E54. If you look at the Borders icon in the toolbar, it remembers your last applied border. Just click the icon to apply the All Borders selection to these two cells.

Figure 338

Borders icon retains last selected format

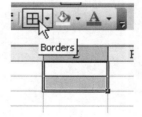

14. In cell D53, type in "Shipping and Handling". Highlight the cell, and type Ctrl-B, which is another way to apply boldface type. On the toolbar, click on the Align Right icon.

Figure 339

Making text bold and right-aligned

15. In cell D54, type in Total Order. Bold Face and Right Align as before. Now, select cells D54 and D55, and change the font size to 12.

Figure 340

Changing font size

16. Now we will "fine tune" the column widths and the number of rows to make sure your requisition form will actually fit on one page. Starting at cell A6, click and drag to highlight all cells down to and including E54. From the File dropdown menu, select Print Area, move to the right, and click on Set Print Area.

After setting the print area, Excel will draw a broken border around the print area. Excel might also draw a dashed line inside your print area to indicate page breaks. In Figure 341, the line to the right of column E is the edge of the print area. The line between columns D and E indicates that with the current column widths, Excel will have to print column E on a new page.

Figure 341

Column E will fall on a new page

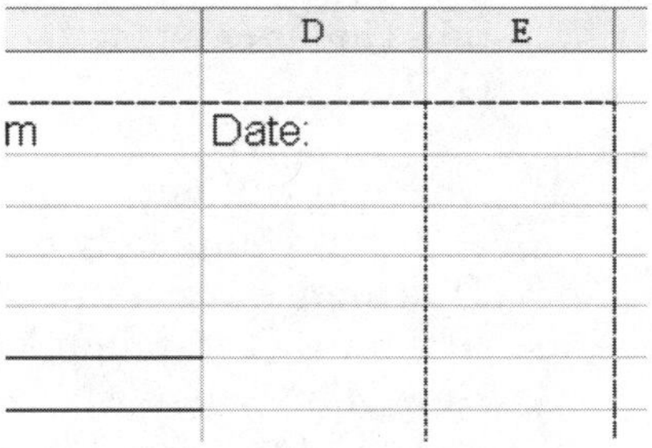

If you do not have a dashed line inside the print area, you can skip this step. Otherwise, you will have to tweak column widths a little at a time until the page break disappears. You will be surprised to find out that a very small change can make a big difference, so work slowly with trial and error. In my case, adjusting column C to be just 6 points less wide allowed column E to fit on the page.

17. You also might have too many rows on the form to fit on the page. Scroll down so you can see rows 50 and higher. Figure 342 shows that the print area extends to row 54, but there is a page break after row 53.

Figure 342

Row 54 will fall on a new page

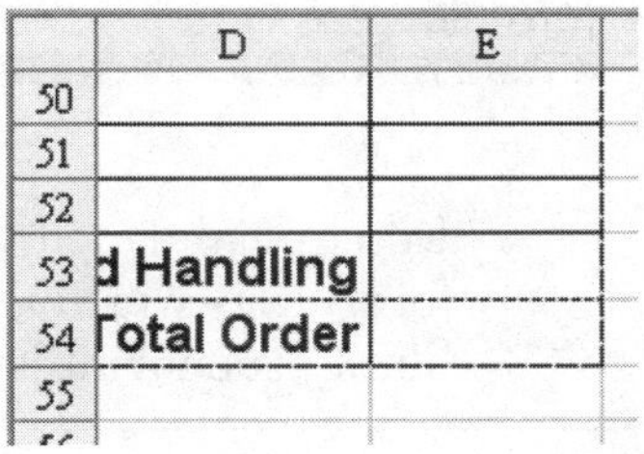

This is easier to fix. Since the form apparently has one too many rows, you can select one row from the ordering block and delete it. You will delete the same number of rows that are currently outside the print area.

17a. Highlight a row or rows by clicking on the row number. When you have the row highlighted, right click and select Delete. When you are done, double check to make sure your form fits on one page by choosing the Print Preview icon from the Standard Toolbar.

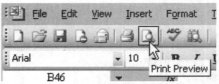

Figure 343

Using Print Preview

17b.The page count will appear in the lower left corner of the Print Preview. If you are still printing to more than one page, go back and tweak some more.

Figure 344 Page count in lower left corner of Print Preview

Preview: Page 1 of 1

 Note:

From this point on, the text assumes that the last row of your form is Row 54. If it is not, you will need to change every reference to E54 or E53 to reflect the last two rows of your form.

18. To make the numbers on your form look like dollars and cents, do the following: Highlight cells D20 through E54. Right-click; select Format Cells and then the Number tab. Under category, select Currency and make sure that Decimal Places has a 2. Click OK.

19. Now you will put a formula in the Total column on the requisition form. In order to keep each row completely blank when there is no item ordered, we will use an IF function. This allows Excel to make a decision based on criteria you provide. We want to keep column E (Total) blank if nothing has been ordered but to multiply the Unit Cost by How Many when we do order. Select cell E20; type in =IF(D20="","",D20*B20) and then press Enter.

Notice that after the second equals sign, there are two sets of quotes, a comma, two more sets of quotes, and another comma. If you don't have that, select E20 again, press F2 to edit the formula, and make your changes.

Figure 345 Editing the formula

	B	C	D	E
19	**Many**	**Description**	**Unit Cost**	**Total**
20				
21				

E20   fx =IF(D20="","",D20*B20)

Don't be alarmed that nothing appears in cell E20. A blank result actually shows that the formula is working correctly. Type some test numbers in B20 and D20. Once D20 is not blank, the formula portion of the IF statement will cause a total to appear in column E.

Figure 346

Total appears when data is in reference cells

	B	C	D	E
19	**Many**	**Description**	**Unit Cost**	**Total**
20	5		$8.99	$44.95
21				
22				

20. The great thing about Excel formulas is that you can enter a formula once and copy it to similar cells. The formula in E20 can be copied to all of the detail rows of the order form. Here are four methods for copying the formula. Choose your favorite.

Select cell C20. Type Ctrl+C to copy. Highlight cells C21:E52. Type Ctrl+V to paste.

Select cell C20. Choose the Copy icon in the Standard toolbar. Highlight cells C21:E52. Choose the Paste icon in the Standard toolbar to paste.

Select cell C20. Right-click and choose Copy. Highlight cells C21:E52. Right-click and choose Paste.

Select cell C20. In the lower right corner of the selected cell is a square dot. This is called the fill handle. When the mouse pointer is over the fill handle, it changes to a plus sign. Drag the fill handle down to cell E52. When you release, the formula will be copied to the range.

After doing any of these methods, you will not see any visible change to the worksheet on your screen. This is because the formula is calculating a blank for all of those rows. However, if you select a cell in the middle of E21:E52, you will see that the formula bar does indeed have the formula.

Figure 347

Formula for blank cell displays in formula bar

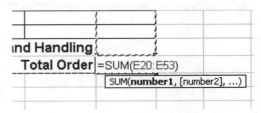

	E32	▼		f_x =IF(D32="","",D32*B32)		
		C			D	E
30						
31						
32						
33						

21. You will want to add a formula at the bottom of the form to total all of the values in column E. Select cell E54, and click on the AutoSum icon (Greek letter sigma) on the toolbar: **Σ ▾**

    21a. Excel starts to enter a SUM formula, but then waits for you to specify the range of cells to include in the total. Click on E53; it becomes surrounded by "marching ants". Click again and drag upward to E20; release the mouse button. Excel suggests a formula of =SUM(E20:E53). Press Enter to accept the formula.

Figure 348 Accepting suggested SUM formula

The form is now essentially done, but we will make some changes that will allow you to order from several vendors while keeping track of the total amount spent and how much you have left from your budget.

nd Handling		
Total Order	=SUM(E20:E53)	
	SUM(**number1**, [number2], ...)	

22. This would be a good time to save the workbook. If your Excel workbooks typically have three worksheets, you will want to delete the blank extra worksheets. At the bottom of the page, select the tab that says Sheet2 and then right click. Choose Delete from the right-click menu. Do the same for the Sheet3 tab. (If you happen to be using the old version of Excel that puts 16 blank worksheets in the workbook, you should delete these tabs as well.

 Note:

You can actually control the number of blank worksheets in each new workbook. Select Tools – Options. On the General tab, change the Sheets in New Workbook setting to 1.

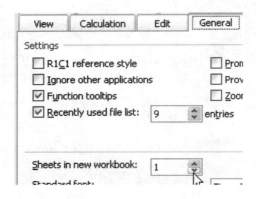

Figure 349

Changing default number of sheets in a new workbook

After spending the time to build the first requisition form, you want to make exact copies of this sheet. Many people try to use Copy and Paste to do this, but it leads to unsatisfactory results. Copy and Paste does not copy column widths or print range settings. Instead, if you use the Move or Copy dialog, Excel will copy the entire sheet, including column widths and the print range settings.

There are two ways to access the Move or Copy command. For the first method, start by right-clicking the Sheet1 tab. Select Move or Copy from the right-click menu.

Figure 350

Selecting Move or Copy

On the Move or Copy dialog, check the box for Create a Copy. Select (move to end) and click OK.

Figure 351

Using Move or Copy to move sheets

23. There is an even faster method to copy a worksheet. Ctrl+Click on the sheet tab and drag it to the right. Drop the new sheet icon and Excel will create a copy of the worksheet.

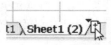

Figure 352 New sheet created by copying using Ctrl+Click

23a. There will now be a tab that says Sheet1 (2). Do this one more time to create a third tab.

The Move or Copy dialog produces perfect copies of the sheets, but uses the silly names of Sheet1(2) and Sheet1 (3).

	Shipping and Handling	
	Total Order	$0.00

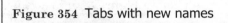
\ Sheet1 / Sheet1 (2) \ **Sheet1 (3)** /

Figure 353

Format for names of copied sheets

24. You can rename the worksheets. One at a time, select each tab and double click the tab. Its name will become highlighted. Change the names of the tabs to Form 1, Form 2, and Form 3.

Figure 354 Tabs with new names

\ Form 1 / Form 2 \ **Form 3** /

 Tip:

With earlier versions of Excel, you have to right-click the sheet tab and choose Rename to change the sheet name.

25. Now, on the Form 1 sheet, select cell F2. You will enter a formula that will add all the totals from the three sheets. Start by entering an equals sign, and then type in E54+. Then click on the Form 2 tab, and click on cell E54 and type another +. Click on the Form 3 tab, click E54 and press Enter. The formula in F2 should now read as follows: =E54+'Form 2'!E54+'Form 3'!E54.

Figure 355 Entering formula in Form 2

=E54+'Form 2'!E54+'Form 3'!E54

D	E	F
Budget Amount:		
Total Spent:		$0.00
Under Budget:		

26. Back on Form 1, select F3.
    Type in =F1-F2 and press Enter.

    You will want to carry this budget information to the other two worksheets. Basically, you want the numbers in F1:F3 to show in the same cells on Form 2 and Form 3.

    26a. Move to Form 2, and select cell F1. Type =, then click on the Form 1 tab, select cell F1 and press Enter. Copy that formula down to F2 and F3. Move to Form 3, and do the exact same thing, starting with the formula in cell F1.

27. Save your file as Requsition.xls.

Using the Application

To use your form, start by entering the amount of money you have to spend in cell F1 on Form 1. Fill out each form with the name of the company you will be ordering from and start entering your items. As you complete each row, the total spent and under budget cells will constantly update. If you are ordering from other companies, fill out Form 2 and Form 3 as needed. At the top of each sheet, your budget amount will be shown, along with the total spent and the amount under budget. If you need to order from more than three vendors, make additional sheets as we did in Steps 23 and 24.

 Note:

If you add more sheets, you will need to change the formula in cell F2 on Form 1 to add up the totals from all the sheets. Refer back to Step 25 on page 163 (the paragraph before Figure 355) to do this.

When you are finished, and have printed out a copy to send off to your building principal or other administrator, you may want to print out another copy for your own records, or use the Save As command to save the workbook with a name that reflects what type of order you made. If you don't want to keep an electronic copy, be sure to click NO when you close the workbook and Excel asks if you want to save your changes. That way, you will start with a clean requisition form when you are ready to make your next orders.

Chapter 18 – Printing Grid Paper

Opportunity

You need some grid paper for math class or for mapping or for art class. You realize that you have run out of grid paper in your supply cabinet. The school doesn't have any. Or – you have grid paper with five squares per inch, but you need grid paper with two squares per inch for your young students.

Solution and Overview

By its nature, Excel is the world's largest sheet of grid paper. With 256 columns and 65,536 rows, it is fairly easy to convert a blank Excel spreadsheet into a printed sheet of grid paper.

Creating The Solution

The main problem is that Excel's cells are rectangular instead of square. This is fairly easy to resolve.

1. Open a blank Excel worksheet. To the left of cell A1 is a gray box with the row number 1 in it. Below the number for row 1 is another gray box with the number 2 in it. Take your mouse pointer and hover it on the line between the gray 1 and the gray 2. When your mouse is in the right position, the mouse pointer will change to a horizontal line with arrows pointing up and down as shown below.

Figure 356

Mousepointer indicates that you are ready to change the row height

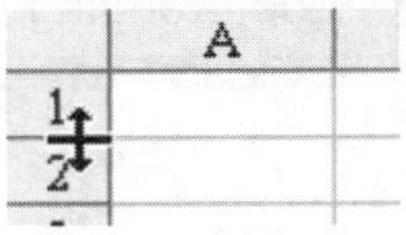

1a. When the mouse pointer looks like the one in the figure above, left-click the mouse without moving it up or down. A tooltip appear showing that your rows have a height of 12.75, which corresponds to 17 pixels. You will want to remember the 17 pixels figure. (This will be different on each computer, based on your default font).

Figure 357

Finding row height in pixels

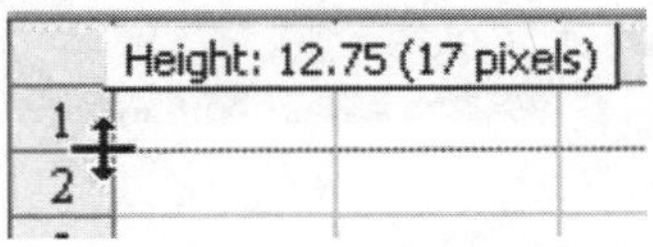

2. Next, you will want to adjust all of the columns to be 17 pixels wide. There is an easy way to do this. To select all of the cells on the worksheet, click the gray box above and to the left of cell A1. This will highlight the entire spreadsheet.

Figure 358

Selecting the entire spreadsheet

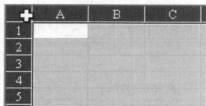

2a. Next, position the mouse between the gray A column header and the gray B column header. When the mouse is resting just on the line between the A header and the B header, the cursor will change to a vertical line with arrows pointing left and right.

Figure 359

Mousepointer indicates that you are ready to change the column width

2b. When the mouse pointer looks like the figure above, left-click the mouse and slowly drag to the left. The tooltip will show that you are starting at 56 pixels.

18

Figure 360

Starting to change column width

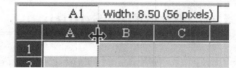

2c. As you drag to the left, the width of the column will narrow. When you have reached 17 pixels, release the mouse button.

Figure 361

Stop dragging when column width is equal to row height

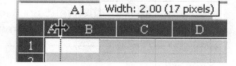

Because you selected all of the cells, changing the width of column A will change the width of all columns. You have now created cells that are perfectly square.

Figure 362

Spreadsheet filled with square cells, 17 pixels on a side

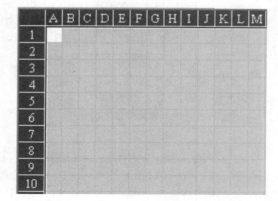

Using the Application

Even though you will be drawing gridlines, Excel expects there to be something inside of the cells. When you later try to print or use Print Preview, Excel will complain that there is nothing to print.

Figure 363

Nothing to print prompt

To prevent this objection from Excel, enter a single spacebar character in cell A1 of the spreadsheet.

Adding Gridlines

In order to print the grid paper, you will have to either turn on gridlines or add borders to the cells. It is easiest to turn on gridlines, but you have more control when you use borders.

Formatting with Cell Borders

1. While you have all cells selected, type Ctrl+1 (in case it is hard to read in this font, that is the numeric "one" key while you are holding down the Ctrl key). Ctrl+1 is the shortcut to display the Format Cells dialog box.

2. The Format Cells dialog has six tabs across the top. Choose the Border tab.

Figure 364

Formatting cell borders

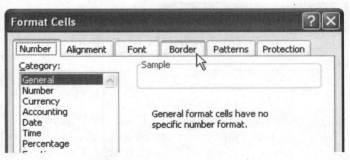

As shown in the next figure, the Border tab of the Format Cells dialog contains three sections. Be sure to make selections in the Line section on the right before touching anything in the Presets and Borders section.

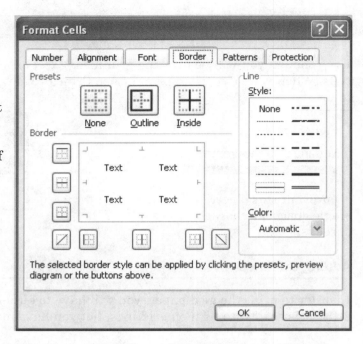

Figure 365

Border tab options

3. The Line section offers 15 different line styles. You can choose to use the default thin solid line (the last choice in the left column), or any of the dotted line styles. You choice will depend on the project. If your students are drawing a floor plan of their room, you might want the gridlines to be barely visible. A thin dotted line might be the most appropriate. If the students are plotting points on an XY coordinate, you might want solid lines throughout.

4. The Color dropdown offers 56 colors. If your classroom has a laser printer capable of printing only black, then one of the three gray options might be appropriate for printing lighter lines.

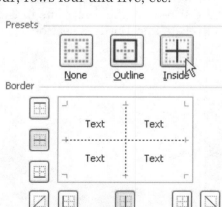

Figure 366

Color dropdown menu

Once you have selected a color and a line weight, it is time to draw the lines. Although the Border section would let you draw any combination of lines, in this case it is easiest to use the Presets section.

5. Clicking the preset for Inside will draw borders between all cells in your selection. It will draw a vertical border between column A and column B. It will draw vertical borders between B and C, C and D, D and E, and so on. Similarly, it will draw horizontal borders between rows one and two, rows two and three, rows three and four, rows four and five, etc.

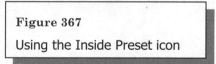

Figure 367

Using the Inside Preset icon

6. The Inside preset will not draw the border around the outside of the selection. So, you will not have a vertical border to the left of A or a horizontal border above row 1. To draw the border around the outside of the selection, choose the Outline preset icon. This will complete the grid paper.

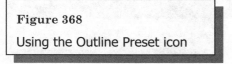

Figure 368

Using the Outline Preset icon

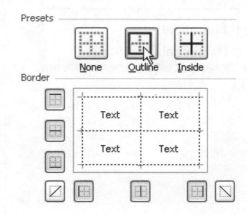

7. Choose OK to close the Format Cells dialog.

Formatting with Gridlines

While the Border method offers control over the line weight and color of the lines, for basic grid paper, the Gridlines method will be simpler.

1. From the File menu, select Page Setup. In the Page Setup dialog, there are four tabs across the top. Select the right-most tab called Sheet. On the Sheet tab, in the second section under Print, click the checkbox for Gridlines.

Figure 369

Use gridlines in Page Setup

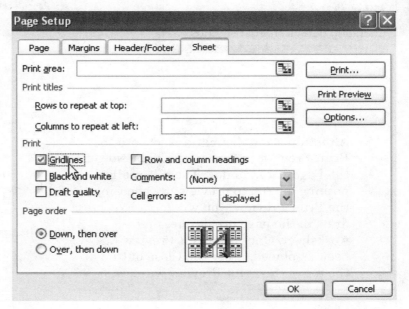

Configuring Print Settings

Whether you used the Gridlines option or Borders, you will want to make some settings to the Page Setup to maximize the printed area on the page.

1. From the menu, select File – Page Setup. On the Page Setup dialog, choose the Margins tab. The default margins on the page might be one inch at the top and bottom, three-fourths of an inch on the left and right.

Figure 370

Margins tab

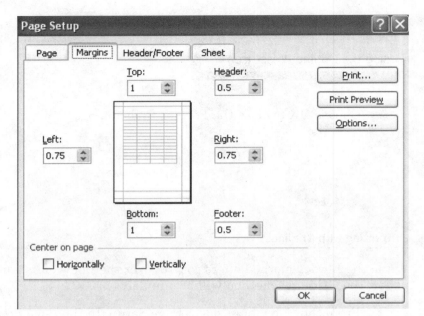

1a. Click the down arrow
on the spin buttons to
change the top,
bottom, left, and right margins to 0.25.

18

Figure 371

Changing default margin settings

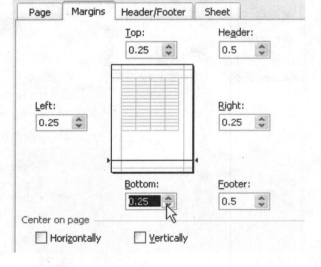

2. After adjusting the margins, choose the
Print Preview button on the right side of
the Page Setup dialog. There is really
nothing for you to preview. By choosing
the Print Preview, you will force Excel to
draw in the page break lines on the
worksheet. Once the Print Preview has
been displayed, press the Close button at
the top of the Print Preview window.

Figure 372

Closing Print Preview

Don't be concerned that the Print Preview only shows one box. This will be corrected
soon.

2a. In the midst of the gridlines on your worksheet, you will see one vertical line that
represents the right edge of the first printed page. On my computer, this line occurs
around cell AN.

Tip:

Depending on your border settings, it may be impossible to distinguish the darker line marking the edge of the page. In this case, select View – Page Break Preview to display these lines in blue. After you have determined the edge of the page, choose View – Normal to return to Normal mode.

Figure 373

Dotted vertical line shows right border of page

2b. If you scroll down several rows, you will eventually see a darker horizontal line around row 59. This is the bottom of the printed page.

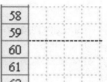

Figure 374

Dotted horizontal line shows bottom border of page

3. As mentioned previously, Excel looks at all of these seemingly empty cells and is not sure why you would want to print them. You need to explicitly tell Excel to print the entire page of borders.

3a. In the preceding images, the last cell on the first page would be AN59. Earlier in this section, you entered a single spacebar character in cell A1. Now, you need to select cell AN59 and enter a single spacebar in that cell.

3b. Finally, you will want to make sure that you don't print more than one page. Click in cell AN59 and drag up to cell A1 to select the range of A1:AN59. With this range selected, go to the File menu and select Print Area – Set Print Area.

Figure 375

Setting Print Area according to selected range of cells

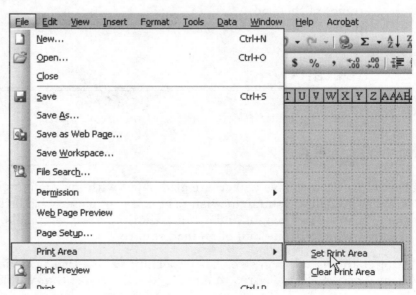

Saving the Document

It would make sense to use File – Save As to save the document as Gridpaper.xls. You will certainly need to use grid paper again throughout the year or next year and you wouldn't want to have to repeat these steps again.

Printing the Grid Paper

You probably know that you can print a single copy of the worksheet by using the Printer icon in the Standard toolbar. However, rather than clicking the Printer icon 25 times, it would be easier to print 25 copies at once.

1. From the menu, select File – Print to display the Print dialog.

2. Click and hold the upward-pointing part of the spin button near the Copies setting until you have specified the correct number of copies.

18

> **Figure 376**
>
> Selecting desired number of copies

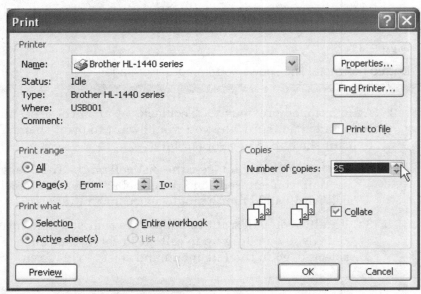

3. Click OK to print 25 copies of the grid paper.

Excel Details

Use the following instructions to modify your grid paper.

Making Larger Grids

The instructions above will create grid paper with approximately five squares per inch. For younger students, you might wish to create grid paper with larger grids. Select all of the cells and adjust the row height and column width to about 48 pixels. This will produce squares that are approximately one-half of an inch square.

After changing the grid size, it is important to do a Print Preview, and then adjust the File – Print Area – Set Print Area to include just the range that will fit on page 1.

Producing Cartesian Coordinates

Perhaps your older students need to have grid paper with a dark X-Y-axis drawn in the center of the page. This is easy to do.

1. First, you need to determine the midpoint of the printed page. With 59 rows, the vertical midpoint will be around row 29. But – how many columns are represented by A:AN? If you happen to know that N is the 14th letter of the alphabet, you can add the 26 columns from A:Z to the 14 columns from AA:AN. However, there is an easier way. Using the mouse, click in any cell in column A and start dragging to the right to select additional cells. Keep selecting more cells until you have reached column AN. Keep the mouse button down and look in the Name box just above cell A1. While you have the mouse button down, the name box will show that your selection includes one row x 40 columns.

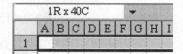

Figure 377

While you are selecting cells, the Name box shows the range size

1a. Half of 40 is 20. Again, if you have some strange command of the alphabet, you might know off the top of your head that T is the 20th letter of the alphabet. However, you can use the above trick again. Click in cell A1 and start dragging to the right to select more cells. Watch the Name box. When it displays 1R x 20C, look over to see the last column selected. This will confirm that the 20th column is indeed the T column.

2. Select the range of T1:T59. There are several ways to make this selection. You might click once in T1, scroll down so you can see row 59, and then shift-click in T59. Alternatively, you might click in T1 and drag down until you reach T59. Or, you might decide to apply the border to all of the rows and just touch the gray T heading above T1.

3. With this range of column T selected, you will want to draw a thick black border to the right of the selection. Type Ctrl+1 to display the Format Cells dialog. Choose the Borders tab.

3a. In the Color dropdown, choose black. In the Style box, choose a thick line. Then, in the border drawing, click on the right edge to indicate that this line style should be applied to the right edge of the selection.

Figure 378

Selecting line style for right border

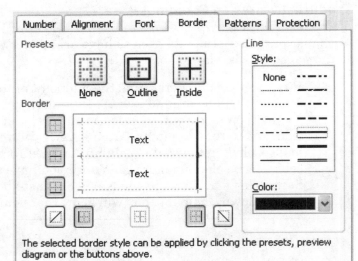

3b. Alternatively, you could click the tiny icon for the right-edge border. This icon is shown below. Click OK to dismiss the dialog box and you will have a thick black line between columns T and U.

18

Figure 379

Using icon to apply line formatting to right border

4. Next, draw a thick line underneath row 29. Select the range of A29:AN29. Type Ctrl+1 to display the Format Cells dialog. You have to again choose the black color and the thick line style. This time, apply the setting to the bottom edge of the border style. Click OK to close the dialog.

Figure 380

Cartesian axis appears

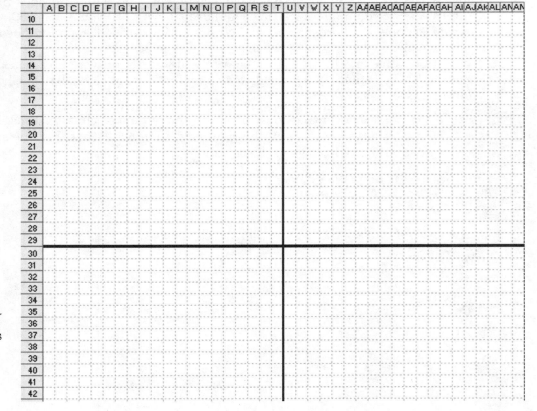

The result will be a sheet of grid paper with thicker X and Y coordinate lines drawn in.

Chapter 19 – Math Exercise Sheets

Opportunity

You've been using the same math exercise sheets for years. Some of the kids are starting to memorize the answers. Can you use Excel to create new drill sheets for math facts?

Solution and Overview

Excel has a couple of functions to generate random numbers. Using a combination of these functions will produce a fresh exercise sheet every time. You can even create different sheets for each student in the class, avoiding the urge for cheating.

Creating the Solution

Excel offers several hundred different functions ready for use. The program also ships with another 150 obscure functions that you can make available to Excel. As it turns out, this chapter will use the RANDBETWEEN function, which is in that collection of 150 functions. This is how to make the Analysis ToolPak available for use on your computer.

1. Open Excel.

2. From the Tools menu, select Add-Ins.

3. In the Add-Ins dialog, click the checkbox to enable the Analysis ToolPak add-in.

Figure 381

Accessing the Analysis Toolpack

Once you have enabled the Analysis ToolPak, you will be able to use any of the 150 extra functions on that computer.

Basic Math Facts: Adding Two Terms with an Answer Under 10

Say that you want to create a worksheet of addition problems. You want the problems to appear in a large font so that your first graders will have space to write the answer. You would like perhaps 15 different problems on the paper.

You will use the RANDBETWEEN function. To use this function, specify two numbers as arguments in the function and separate the two arguments with a comma. For example, =RANDBETWEEN(1,20) would return a random whole number between 1 and 20, inclusive.

1. In cell B2, enter the formula =RANDBETWEEN(1,8).

Figure 382

Finding a random number from 1-8

1a. In cell B3, you want to find a random number such that the answer will not exceed 9. Luckily, either argument in the function can be a reference to another cell instead of a number. You need to generate a random number between 0 and (9-B2) in cell B3. To handle any case, enter the formula =RANDBETWEEN(0,9-B2) in cell B3.

Figure 383

Finding a random number between 1 and 6

 Note:

Every time that you enter a new value or every time that you press the F9 key, Excel will recalculate all of the formulas on the worksheet. This includes generating new random numbers. Thus, as you enter the formula in B3, the value in B2 will probably change. To test that the logic is working, press the F9 key several times and you will see that you continually get new problems that total to less than 10.

2. Before making a whole sheet of these problems, take some time to get the first problem correctly formatted. With the cellpointer in B3, choose the bottom border button in the Formatting toolbar.

Figure 384

Adding a line below the second number in an equation

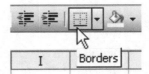

This will add a line across the entire length of the bottom of cell B3. I think using the Borders icon for a bottom border is better than using the Underline icon, which would only extend the underline as far as the digits in the cell.

3. In cell A3, enter a quotation mark and a plus sign. The quotation mark will not appear in the cell, but serves as an indicator to Excel that this is a text entry and that you want the entry to be right justified.

 Tip:

When you wish to enter numbers or mathematical operators in a cell, you need to either prefix them with an apostrophe for left justification, a quotation mark for right-justification, or a carat for centered.

4. Select all of the cells in the worksheet by clicking the gray box to the left of the "A" heading above column A.

Figure 385

Adding a plus sign to a problem

4a. While all of the cells are selected, choose a large font size such as 24 from the font size selector on the Formatting toolbar.

Figure 386

Increasing the font size

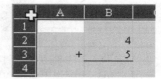

This should make the font large enough for your young students to be able to write an answer below the problem.

5. Now that you have one problem set up, you will want to copy those formulas. Select cells A2 through B3. Type Ctrl+C to copy the cells to the clipboard.

    5a. Click in cell D2 and type Ctrl+V to paste the cells from the clipboard.

Figure 387

Copying the problem formula

    5b. Click in G2 and type Ctrl+V to paste a third column of problems.

6. Now that you have one complete row of problems set up, select cells A2:H3 and type Ctrl+C to copy the formulas for all three problems. Click the mouse in A6 and type Ctrl+C to paste three more problems on the worksheet.

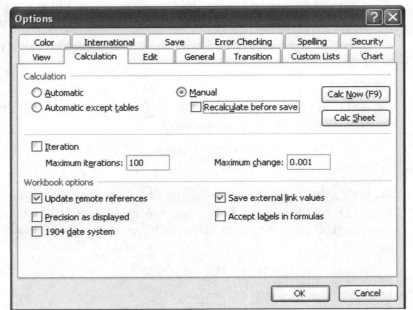

Figure 388

Copying a complete row of formulas

6a. Click in A10 and type Ctrl+V to paste a third row. Click in A14 and type Ctrl+V to paste a fourth row. Click in A18 to paste a fifth row of problems.

7. In cell A1, type NAME: followed by a long series of underline characters. This will allow the students to write their names on the paper.

Using the Application

Every time that you type the F9 key, you will generate a new set of problems. If you wish to give every student a different problem sheet, you can repeat these steps:

1. Press the F9 key to generate new problems.

2. Choose the Printer icon in the Standard Toolbar.

Although it may seem tedious, you can quickly generate 25 different worksheets in about a minute.

Keeping the Worksheet from Changing

What if you have the perfect set of problems and you want to use these same problems again for a pretest/posttest situation? In this case, you will want to turn off the automatic Excel calculation. From the menu, select Tools – Options. The Options dialog is one of the busiest in Excel, with 13 different tabs. Choose the Calculation tab, usually the second tab along the bottom row. In the Calculation tab, choose the option button for Manual and uncheck the box for Recalculate Before Save.

Figure 389

Clearing Recalculate Before Save checkbox

With these calculation settings, the current set of problems will stay constant until you press the F9 key again.

Adapting for Multiplication

Your older students need a sheet of two-digit multiplication problems.

Figure 390

Adapting the worksheet for multiplication problems

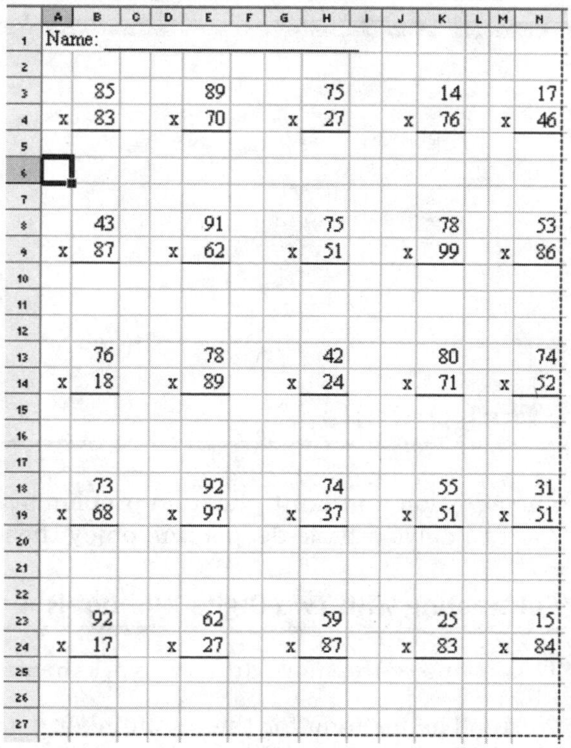

The formula for both terms can be =RANDBETWEEN(10,99). For the older students, you might not need a 24 point font; Adjust the font to 18. If you make columns A, C, D, F, G, I, J, L, and M narrower, you can fit five problems across the sheet. The students will need more space between each problem in order to show their work. Put the cellpointer in row 6 and choose Insert – Row from the menu to insert an extra blank row between the problems. You can fit 25 problems on a single page.

19

Creating an Answer Key

It would be helpful to have an answer key for the preceding multiplication example. As you enter the first problem, set up a formula to produce the answer for the problem.

1. Enter the formula =B3*B4 in cell B5.

Figure 391

Calculating the answer to a multiplication problem

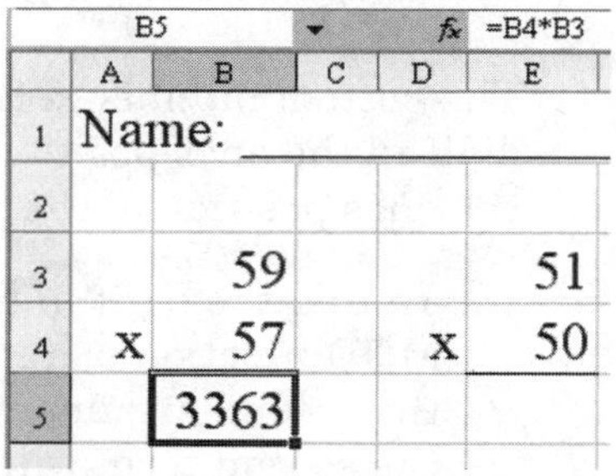

2. Select the cell containing the answer. Look on the right side of the Formatting toolbar. There is a blue A above a red rectangle. This is the font color tool. To the right of the tool is a small down arrow. Click on the down arrow to access a pallet of colors. Choose white from the pallet. This will make the answer disappear on the screen and from the printed page.

However, when you select all of the cells, Excel highlights the cells in a blue color, allowing the white answers to appear on your screen.

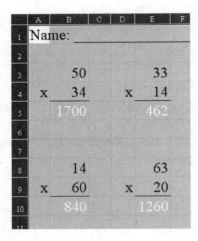

Figure 392

Hidden answers display only on your screen

Excel Details

The addition and multiplication problems above are fairly straightforward. Those of you who want to delve a little deeper will enjoy these exercises to create more complex worksheets.

Subtracting with Two-Digits Without Regrouping

This is one of the more difficult worksheets to create.

1. The formula for the top number is fairly straightforward. You want a two-digit number between 10 and 99 so use the formula of =RANDBETWEEN(10,99). Enter this formula in cell B2 as shown.

Figure 393

Using RANDBETWEEN to determine the first Term in a subtraction problem

The bottom number is far more complex. You need the digit in the ones position to be between 0 and the digit in the ones position of the number in B2.

1a. To find the digit in the ones position, you would use the formula =MOD(B2,10). The MOD function is a Modulo function. It basically returns the Remainder after dividing the second argument into the first argument. Thus, the formula to find the first digit of the second term will be =RANDBETWEEN(0,MOD(B2,10)).

1b. Next, you have to figure out a formula for the tens position of the second number. You want this number to be between 1 and the digit in the tens position of the first number. To find the number in the tens position of B2, use =INT(B2/10). For example, the INT function will calculate 77 divided by 10, drop the fractional portion, and just return the whole integer. The formula for the tens position is =RANDBETWEEN(1,INT(B2/10)).

1c. To put these two formulas together, you have to multiply the second formula by 10 and add it to the first formula. The resulting formula is shown on the following page.

2. Enter this formula in B3:
   =10*RANDBETWEEN(1,INT(B2/10))+RANDBETWEEN(0,MOD(B2,10))

Figure 394 shows a portion of a page full of these problems.

Figure 394

Worksheet with randomized subtraction problems

	A	B	C	D	E
1					
2		22			89
3		- 21			- 63
4					
5					
6		82			65
7		- 31			- 43

Expressing Problems That Go Across the Page

For variety, you might sometimes wish to build problems that read across the page. This is possible with Excel but requires a bit of trickery.

Figure 395 shows a worksheet with several pairs of =RANDBETWEEN(1,20) formulas in columns A and B.

Figure 395

Worksheet with pairs of random numbers between 1 and 20

B2   fx =RANDBETWEEN(1,20)

	A	B	C	D	E	F
1						
2	16	11				
3	7	20				
4	20	15				

Figure 396 shows a formula that concatenates the value in A with a plus sign, then the value in B, then an equals sign and several underscore characters to provide a place for the student to write the answer.

Figure 396

Adding plus signs and underscores for student's answers

C2   fx =" "&A2&" + "&B2&" = _____ "

	A	B	C	D	E	F
1						
2	4	3	4 + 3 =			
3	14	19	14 + 19 = ____			
4	19	9	19 + 9 = ____			

To join a value with text, use the concatenation operator – the ampersand. If you want to join a value with a literal such as the equals or plus sign, you have to include the literal in double quotes.

 Caution!

There is one annoying "bug" that shows up as you enter this formula. Notice that there is a space on either side of the plus sign. You generally have to hold down the Shift key to type the plus sign. You may accidentally continue to hold down the Shift key when you type the spacebar after the plus sign. Unfortunately, Shift+Spacebar is an Excel shortcut to select the entire row. If you suddenly see your formula change to Figure 397, you inadvertently typed Shift+SpaceBar instead of just the Spacebar. Simply type the Backspace to get rid of the 3:3 entry.

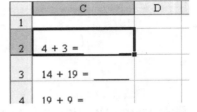

Figure 397 Result of holding down Shift key while pressing Spacebar

=" "&A3&" +3:3|

Before printing the worksheet, you will want to hide columns A and B. Select any range of cells such as A1:B1. From the menu, select Format – Columns – Hide. Excel will hide columns A and B from view.

Figure 398 Hiding columns A and B

	C	D
1		
2	4 + 3 =	
3	14 + 19 = _____	
4	19 + 9 =	

Tip:

To unhide all columns, select the gray box above row 1 and select Format – Columns – Unhide.

Avoiding Duplicate Problems

In the worksheets described so far in this chapter, it is likely that the same problem may randomly appear on the worksheet. If you absolutely want to ensure no duplicates, use the No Duplication worksheet in the downloadable worksheets. (Sample files can be downloaded from this secret page: http://www.MrExcel.com/teacherfiles.html.)

This worksheet accepts 10 possible first numbers and 10 possible second numbers. Formulas down column C and D build all possible pairs of these numbers. A RAND function in A assigns random numbers to the 100 possible problems. A RANK function in B finds the top 15 problems. Then, VLOOKUP formulas in the printable area of the worksheet pull out the numbers for the top 15 problems.

Figure 399

No Duplication worksheet

	A	B	C	D	E	F	G	H	I	J	K	L
1	Enter 10 Numbers for the top figure here:											
2		1	2	3	4	5	6	7	8	9	10	
3												
4	Enter 10 Numbers for the bottom figure here:											
5		1	2	3	4	5	6	7	8	9	10	
6												
7	Rand	Rank	The formulas here will generate the possible problems									
8	0.40318	61	1	1			NAME:					
9	0.04235	95	1	2								
10	0.65172	38	1	3			9				6	
11	0.5363	47	1	4		+	4		+		8	
12	0.38897	62	1	5								
13	0.70347	32	1	6								
14	0.19712	88	1	7			3				2	
15	0.82707	21	1	8		+	1		+		2	
16	0.95949	7	1	9								

Chapter 20 – Homework Checker

Opportunity

Do you allow your students to check their math papers with a calculator? Excel can offer a fun way to check the students' papers. You can either build a worksheet where they can plug in the problems and get the answer, or where they can plug in the problem, their answer, and Excel will indicate if the answer is correct or not.

Solution and Overview

The beauty of the visible calculator invention is that you can scroll back in time, change any previous cells, and then all future calculations will automatically re-calculate. It is fairly simple to set up a formula that multiplies two cells. Your students could plug in the terms from a sheet of math problems and the spreadsheet would show them the correct answer.

If you want to be less direct about the process, you could set up a logical formula to test if the student's answer to the problem matches the real answer. In this case, rather than seeing the right answer, they simply know that they got the problem wrong and it is up to them to work through the problem again.

Creating the Solution

1. Start with a blank spreadsheet. Select all cells by typing Ctrl+A. On the Formatting toolbar, set the font size to 24 points. Use Format – Column – Width and set the columns to a width of 15.

2. In cell A1, type a title such as "Room 4 Magic Homework Checker". In cells A3 and A4, enter directions such as, "Enter the terms of your multiplication problem in the yellow boxes below."

3. Move the cellpointer to cell B6. On the Formatting toolbar, you will see a paint bucket above a colored rectangle. This is the Fill Color tool. Next to the tool is a dropdown arrow. Select the dropdown arrow to see a pallet of colors. Choose a light yellow color.

Figure 400

Locating Fill Color dropdown

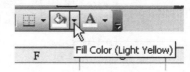

4. Near the Fill Color icon is a Borders icon. Again, there is a dropdown next to this icon.

Figure 401

Locating Borders icon dropdown

4a. Choose the dropdown arrow and then select the thick border to draw a box around cell B6.

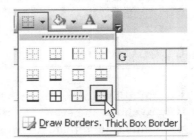

Figure 402

Selecting a thick box border

 Tip:

Note that after you select a color from the Fill icon or a border from the Border dropdown, the tool on the Formatting toolbar will change to the selected border style. You can then apply the same border to other cells with a single click.

5. In cell C6, type a carat (^) and a capital X. This will center a multiplication sign in cell C6.

6. You will want to put a yellow box in D6. There is an easy way to copy formatting from one cell to another. Select cell B6. Type Ctrl+C to copy. Select cell D6. From the menu, choose – Edit – Paste Special. In the Paste Special dialog, choose Values and click OK.

Figure 403

Using Paste Special to copy cell formatting

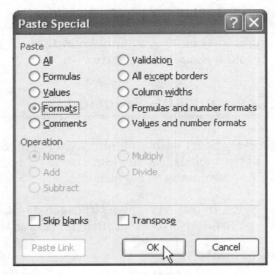

7. In cell E6, type ^= to center an equals sign in the cell. With the cellpointer in E6, type the B icon in the Formatting toolbar to make the equals sign bold.

8. In cell F6, you will want to put in a formula to multiply B6 by D6. Type the formula =B6*D6. If your answers will likely exceed 1000, then you might want to format cell F6 to include commas. Select cell F6. Select Format – Cells from the menu. On the Number tab, you will have to make three adjustments.

➢ First, in the Category list, change from General to Number. This will cause options for decimal places and the 1000 separator to appear.

➢ Check the box for Use 1000 Separator(,).

➢ In the Decimal Places field, type the down arrow on the spin button to switch to 0 decimal places.

Using the Application

After your students have completed their math worksheets, allow them to use Excel to check their answers. If they type in the terms from their math problem in the yellow cells, the answer will appear in F6.

The problem with allowing the student to check their answer with a calculator or with this Excel solution is that the student is directly given the answer. In the Excel details section, you will learn how to modify the worksheet to guide the students without giving them the answers.

Excel Details

1. You can modify the worksheet used above to be less direct. In the figure below, the students are presented with new directions. They are to enter the terms of the multiplication problem in the yellow boxes and their answer in the green box. Set up a green box in cell F6. Remove the formula in F6 by typing a number in the cell.

Figure 404

Replacing a formula with a number

A	B	C	D	E	F	G
Room 4 Magic Homework Checker						
Enter the terms of your multiplication problem						
in the yellow boxes below. Enter your answer						
in the green box.						
	42	X	56	=	252	

The goal now is to build a formula in B8 that will check to see if the answer is wrong or correct. Excel offers the IF function. There are three arguments to the IF function. The first argument is some logical test. In this case, you will check to see if B6*D6 is equal to the answer typed in F6. The second argument is the text or formula to use if the logical test is true. The third argument is the text or formula to use if the logical test is false. If the second or third argument contains a formula, you can leave off the opening equals sign. If these arguments contain text, the text must be in double quotes.

2. Enter the resulting formula as shown in Figure 405.

Figure 405

IF formula will inform students whether or not their answer is correct

B	C	D	E	F
42	X	56	=	252
=IF(B6*D6=F6,"Right!","Try Again")				

If the students enter a wrong answer, cell B8 will advise them to try again.

Figure 406

"Try Again" response to an incorrect answer

42	X	56	=	252
Try Again				

If they enter the correct answer, cell B8 will advise them that it is correct.

Figure 407

"Right!" response to a correct answer

42	X	56	=	2352
Right!				

Adding Color Based on a Result

1. You can jazz up the worksheet a little bit. Back in Excel 97, Microsoft added something called Conditional Formatting. This feature allows you to change the color of a cell depending on the value in the cell. Select cell B8. From the menu, choose Format – Conditional Formatting.

   The Conditional Formatting dialog initially looks like Figure 408. There are a couple of adjustments required to set up the formatting.

Figure 408

Conditional Formatting dialog

2. There is a dropdown that contains the word "between". Select the arrow on the right side of this dropdown to see your other choices. Choose "equal to" from the dropdown.

Figure 409

Selecting Cell Value condition to be "equal to"

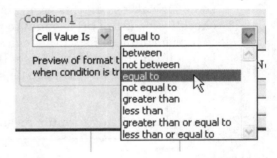

20

3. After you choose equal to, the two boxes on the right side of the dropdown change to a single box. Type the word "Right!" in that box as shown in Figure 410.

Figure 410

Setting "equal to" value

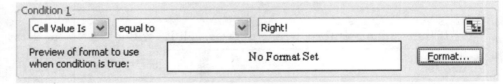

4. Click the Format… button in the lower right area of the dialog. There are three tabs on the Format Cells dialog, one each for Font, Border and Patterns. Choose a green color on the Patterns tab and change the font color to blue on the Font tab.

Figure 411

Selecting color and pattern formats for correct answers

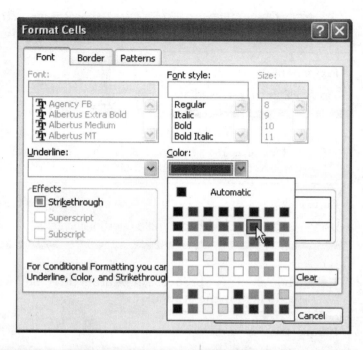

5. You have now set up a format for when the answer is correct. You can add a second condition to handle the answer if it is not correct. On the Conditional Formatting dialog, choose the Add… button to add a second condition.

Figure 412

Adding a second condition

 Note:

You can only add second and third conditions. Although many people would like this feature to handle four or more conditions, Microsoft has not yet accommodated this need.

Figure 413

Formatting the second condition

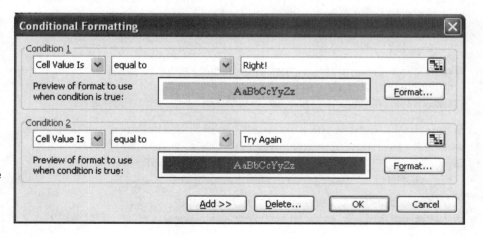

5a. Set up the second condition similar to the first. Choose a yellow font on a red background.

20

5b. Click OK to close the Conditional Formatting dialog. Cell B8 looks great when the answer is Right!, but the text in Try Again is too long.

Figure 414

Text spilling over into adjacent cell

6. Select cells B8 through F8. In the Formatting toolbar is an icon for Merge and Center. Choose this icon to extend the text and formatting in B8 to the entire range of five cells.

Figure 415

Using Merge and Center to handle overflowing text

The resulting spreadsheet offers a large box with either green positive or red negative feedback for the student.

Figure 416

Spreadsheet with text and formatting dependent upon student's answer

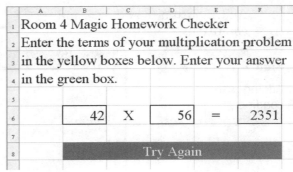

Where Did They Go Wrong?

The final example in this chapter is a worksheet to help the students figure out where they went wrong. To multiply two three-digit numbers, the students will actually perform three multiplications and one addition problem. The worksheet below identifies the correct answer for each step of the problem. Your students can compare this with their work to figure out why they had the wrong answer.

Figure 417

Worksheet showing the correct intermediate steps to answer a multiplication problem

	321
x	456
	1926
	16050
	128400
	146376

When the students type new numbers into the original problem, the worksheet recalculates to show them the new intermediate results.

Figure 418

Worksheet showing revised intermediate steps

	789
x	654
	3156
	39450
	473400
	516006

The following screen shot is taken in Excel's Show Formulas mode. Look on your keyboard. On the upper left side, just above the Tab key and to the left of the 1 key is a key with a tilde (the squiggly thing above an "n" in some Spanish words) and a reverse apostrophe. To turn on Show Formulas mode, hold down the Ctrl key while pressing the Reverse Apostrophe key (Ctrl+`).

Figure 419

Worksheet in Show Formulas mode

	C
2	789
3	654
4	=C2*RIGHT(C3,1)
5	=C2*MID(C3,2,1)*10
6	=C2*LEFT(C3,1)*100
7	=SUM(C4:C6)
8	

 Tip:

Ctrl+` toggles in and out of Show Formulas mode. To return to a normal spreadsheet, press Ctrl+` again.

Note that these formulas only work if cell C3 contains a three-digit number.

1. Enter the following formula in cell C4: =C2*RIGHT(C3,1)
   This formula multiplies 789 by the rightmost digit in C3.

2. Enter the following formula in cell C5: =C2* MID(C3,2,1)*10
   This formula uses the MID function. MID(C3,2,1) starts at the second position in C3 for a length of one character. This will multiply the 5 in 654 by 789. You have to multiply this result by 10 to properly line up the answer with C5.

3. Enter the following formula in cell C6: =C2*LEFT(C3,1)*100
   This formula uses the LEFT function to take the first character from the left of the 654. It multiplies the 6 in 684 by 789 and then multiplies that product by 100.

4. Enter the following formula in cell C7: =SUM(C4:C6)
   This formula sums the results of the formulas in C4 through C6.

The trick will be to make sure that your students complete the work first before they use the homework checker! This last version has the added benefit of letting them figure out where they went wrong.

The homework checker can be adapted to check addition, subtraction, and various other problems.

20

20

Chapter 21 – Recording Rubric Data

Opportunity

Rubrics allow students and teachers to both know the categories and requirements used for evaluation. Rubrics are extremely flexible and an important assessment tool when dealing with student work that is not easily transmitted into a percentage score.

Last year, I helped to direct all grade levels at my school into using a writing rubric based on the book The Simple Six written by Kay Davidson. In a nutshell, Davidson evaluated the grading system used for the writing portion of Indiana's state-mandated test. She came up with six different categories to help students create writings that would earn top scores (or at least pass the writing portion of the test!). Davidson then wrote a book about her findings, giving teachers ideas and lessons to teach the six different categories to students. My school has had great success in the area of writing since adopting Davidson's rubric. Teachers teach the six categories as part of the writing curriculum. Students are formally evaluated on their writing skills twice a year using school-wide writing prompts in the fall and in the spring. Teams of teachers grade the school-wide writing prompt writings and then report the findings to the principal and to me. (We are using the writing prompt as part of our informal assessment process.) My need is to find a way to record student data, report the findings to the state, and compare classes of students. I would also like to be able to show the prompt results using a graph or chart (I'm a visual learner and I love seeing data in a visual mode!)

Here is what my school's writing rubric looks like. All grades use the same categories and requirements (grades K and 1 are slightly modified due to ability levels).

It would be nice to be able to use Excel to set up a template to show the rubric's categories using rows and columns to create nice, neat boxes. Teachers could then print out a rubric form to record scores.

Second Grade Writing Rubric

The Simple 6

_____ Stick to the Topic

_____ Logical Order

_____ Interesting Words

_____ Different Sentence Patterns

_____ Descriptive Sentences

_____ Audience

_____ TOTAL POINTS

To score: Give student either a 0 or a 1 for each category (0 for not fulfilling category; 1 for meeting category requirements). Total possible score is 6.

Solution and Overview

The solution will create a database to score the student name, the testing date, their scores in the six categories, and a total.

After entering a few rubrics, we will combine AutoFilter with a chart to create a chart showing progress throughout the year by student.

The finished application is shown below.

Figure 420

Writing rubric that combines AutoFilter with a bar chart

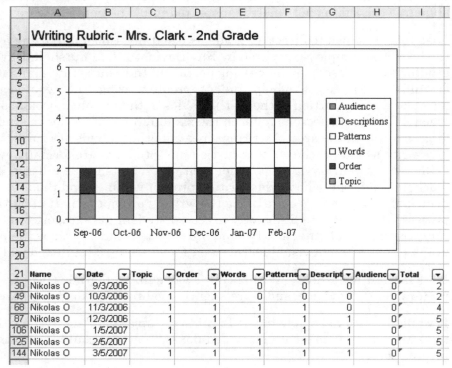

		A	B	C	D	E	F	G	H	I

Writing Rubric - Mrs. Clark - 2nd Grade

When you select a new name from the Name dropdown in A21, the chart and report update to show the scores for the selected student.

	Name	Date	Topic	Order	Words	Patterns	Descript	Audienc	Total
30	Nikolas O	9/3/2006	1	1	0	0	0	0	2
49	Nikolas O	10/3/2006	1	1	0	0	0	0	2
68	Nikolas O	11/3/2006	1	1	1	1	0	0	4
87	Nikolas O	12/3/2006	1	1	1	1	1	0	5
106	Nikolas O	1/5/2007	1	1	1	1	1	0	5
125	Nikolas O	2/5/2007	1	1	1	1	1	0	5
144	Nikolas O	3/5/2007	1	1	1	1	1	0	5

21

Creating the Solution

1. Start with a blank worksheet. Enter the teacher name, classroom, and school year in cell A1 as a title. Change the font to 20 or 24 point type.

    1b. You will want to leave a gap for the chart to go later. Move to row 21. Enter headings going across row 21 for Name, Date, Topic, Order, Words, Patterns, Description, Audience, and Total.

2. Enter the names of your students going down column A, starting with cell A21. Enter each student once. Below the last student, enter a student named "zzz Insert Above Here". Later, when you create a chart, you can include this row in your chart ranges and know that the chart will always expand.

Figure 421

Entering headings
and student names

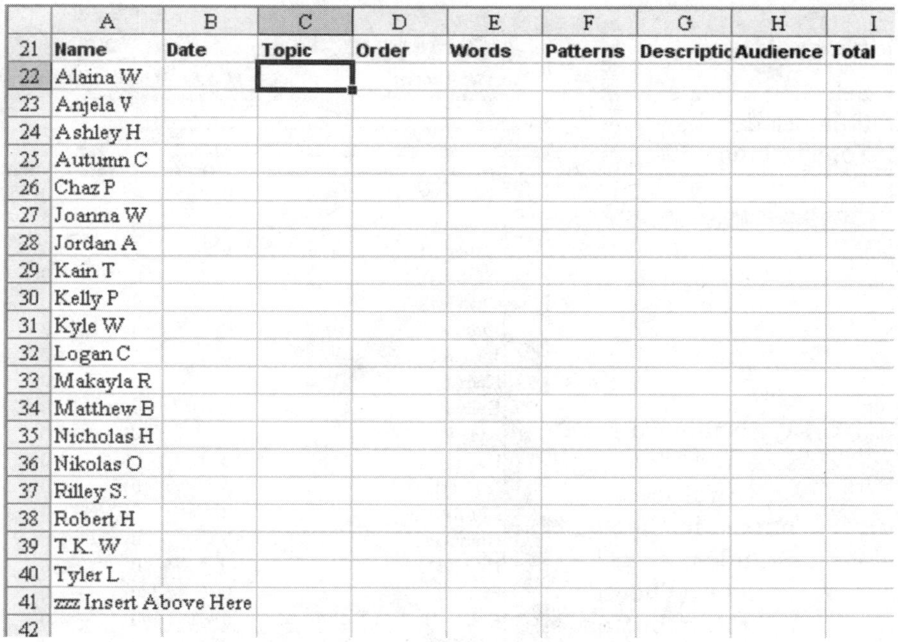

	A	B	C	D	E	F	G	H	I
21	Name	Date	Topic	Order	Words	Patterns	Descriptic	Audience	Total
22	Alaina W								
23	Anjela V								
24	Ashley H								
25	Autumn C								
26	Chaz P								
27	Joanna W								
28	Jordan A								
29	Kain T								
30	Kelly P								
31	Kyle W								
32	Logan C								
33	Makayla R								
34	Matthew B								
35	Nicholas H								
36	Nikolas O								
37	Rilley S.								
38	Robert H								
39	T.K. W								
40	Tyler L								
41	zzz Insert Above Here								
42									

Let's assume that you have given the first writing prompt of the year. You probably expect a lot of scores of one or two at this point in the year. To make your life easier, it would be faster to enter a zero in every possible cell and then simply go through entering the ones wherever the student scored a one.

3. Select the range of C22:H down to the last student. Leave the date and total columns blank for now.

Figure 422

Selecting a range
that includes the
Simple Six

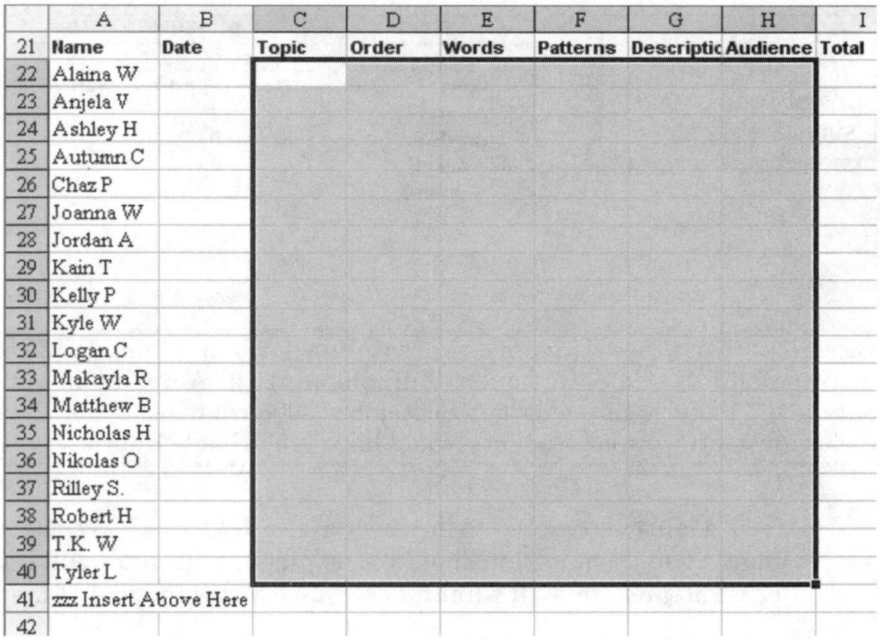

	A	B	C	D	E	F	G	H	I
21	Name	Date	Topic	Order	Words	Patterns	Descriptic	Audience	Total
22	Alaina W								
23	Anjela V								
24	Ashley H								
25	Autumn C								
26	Chaz P								
27	Joanna W								
28	Jordan A								
29	Kain T								
30	Kelly P								
31	Kyle W								
32	Logan C								
33	Makayla R								
34	Matthew B								
35	Nicholas H								
36	Nikolas O								
37	Rilley S.								
38	Robert H								
39	T.K. W								
40	Tyler L								
41	zzz Insert Above Here								
42									

3a. Type a zero and then Ctrl+Enter. All of the cells in the selection will fill with zeroes.

4. Next, select I22 down to the cell in column I that corresponds to your last student. Again, leave the zzz student unselected.

21

Figure 423

Selecting a range that includes the Total column

	A	B	C	D	E	F	G	H	I
21	Name	Date	Topic	Order	Words	Patterns	Descriptic	Audience	Total
22	Alaina W		0	0	0	0	0	0	
23	Anjela V		0	0	0	0	0	0	
24	Ashley H		0	0	0	0	0	0	
25	Autumn C		0	0	0	0	0	0	
26	Chaz P		0	0	0	0	0	0	
27	Joanna W		0	0	0	0	0	0	
28	Jordan A		0	0	0	0	0	0	
29	Kain T		0	0	0	0	0	0	
30	Kelly P		0	0	0	0	0	0	
31	Kyle W		0	0	0	0	0	0	
32	Logan C		0	0	0	0	0	0	
33	Makayla R		0	0	0	0	0	0	
34	Matthew B		0	0	0	0	0	0	
35	Nicholas H		0	0	0	0	0	0	
36	Nikolas O		0	0	0	0	0	0	
37	Rilley S.		0	0	0	0	0	0	
38	Robert H		0	0	0	0	0	0	
39	T.K. W		0	0	0	0	0	0	
40	Tyler L		0	0	0	0	0	0	
41	zzz Insert Above Here								
42									

5. With this range selected, press the AutoSum button in the Standard toolbar. (The AutoSum button looks like a Greek letter Sigma.)

Because you selected a range, Excel will automatically enter a formula to sum columns C through H for each student. Initially, these totals will all be zero.

Figure 424

Initial Total column sums are zeros

I22   fx =SUM(C22:H22)

	A	B	C	D	E	F	G	H	I
21	Name	Date	Topic	Order	Words	Patterns	Descriptic	Audience	Total
22	Alaina W		0	0	0	0	0	0	0
23	Anjela V		0	0	0	0	0	0	0
24	Ashley H		0	0	0	0	0	0	0
25	Autumn C		0	0	0	0	0	0	0

 Note:

Be careful to use the AutoSum *before* entering dates in column B. Microsoft considers dates to be numeric data. If a date were entered in column B, the AutoSum in column I would probably add the date to the scores. Since a date in September 2006 is almost 39000 days after the start of the twentieth century, your students would have remarkable Rubric scores of 39002!

You might be tempted to enter a date in B22 and leave the remaining cells in column B blank. This temptation should be avoided. Your data will later be sorted by various criteria, and you will want a date in each row instead of many blank cells.

6. Select B22:B40. Type the date in the format of 9/3/2006 and type Ctrl+Enter to fill this date in all cells.

Tip:

Excel 2002 or Excel 2003 will display a green error triangle in each total in column I. Select a cell in I and open the Information button to see Excel's warning that the Total formula omits adjacent cells. Excel wants to include the numeric date in the total. It would take forever to choose "Ignore this error" throughout the life of this worksheet, so simply ignore the green error cells in this case.

Figure 425

Excel 2002/2003's warning that adjacent numeric cells are not included in the Total formula

7. This would be a good time to save the workbook. Use File – SaveAs and give the file a useful name.

Using Trickery to Double the Value of the Worksheet

Currently, the workbook is designed to show the progress of a single student. While that will be useful after a few rubrics, you might also want to show the scores for all students on one particular rubric.

This is basically pretty difficult. If you build a chart with the X-axis based on the dates in column B, it is very hard to later change the source data to use names in column A. Editing source data is possible, but it is not something that you would want to do every time that you want to analyze student data.

 Note:

There are some Excel features that are hard to remember. My rationale throughout this book is that if you need to use one of these features every day, you will learn that feature. However, if you only need to use a feature once a month, you will be frustrated trying to remember it. On the other hand, the following approach uses a really hard feature just once, after which you will never have to touch the feature again for the rest of your teaching career. Follow the steps in the book and the chart will be much easier work to work with throughout the rest of the year.

Understanding the Basics of Chart Ranges

Default charts have rectangular source data ranges. The left column and the top row of the chart contain headings. If you based the chart on the range of B through H, you would have a valid chart with dates along the X-axis. As with the chart shown at the beginning of the chapter, this chart will do a great job of showing trended scores by student. However, you might want to show all of the scores for all of your students on one writing prompt. In this case, the chart would need to point to column A instead of column B.

The Trick – Base the Chart on a New Column C

It would be really cool if you could have a new column C that could show either dates or names, based on your need. With the flip of a switch, the column would change to include names or dates and the chart would flip to have either names or dates.

Setting up the Trick

1. Select any cell in column C. From the menu, select Insert – Column. Enter a heading of "Chart" in cell C21.

Figure 426

Inserting a Chart column

	A	B	C	D	E	F	G	H	I	J
21	Name	Date	Chart	Topic	Order	Words	Patterns	Descriptic	Audience	Total
22	Alaina W	9/3/2006		0	0	0	0	0	0	0
23	Anjela V	9/3/2006		0	0	0	0	0	0	0
24	Ashley H	9/3/2006		0	0	0	0	0	0	0
25	Autumn C	9/3/2006		0	0	0	0	0	0	0
26	Chaz P	9/3/2006		0	0	0	0	0	0	0
27		9/3/2006		0	0	0	0	0	0	0

2. Move off to the right side of your worksheet. In column L, at the top, enter text as shown in Figure 427. For now, enter a "2" in cell L4.

Figure 427

Entering the key to using the chart off to the right

	L	M	N	O
1	Chart Trick: Use cell L4 to control the chart			
2	Enter a 1 for charts by date			
3	Enter a 2 for charts by name			
4	2			
5				

Using the Seemingly Useless OFFSET Function

When people read about the OFFSET function in Excel help, they generally agree that this seems like a seemingly useless function. In my personal experience, with over 40,000 hours of spreadsheet use over the course of 20 years, I have used OFFSET less than a dozen times. The OFFSET function allows you to start with one cell address and to move a certain number of rows and columns away from the original cell.

In the language of an OFFSET formula, a positive number of rows moves down the spreadsheet. A positive number of columns moves right across the spreadsheet. Conversely, a negative number of rows moves up the spreadsheet. A negative number of columns moves to the left across the spreadsheet.

How can this function help us in cell C22? The first part of the function tells Excel to start from a particular cell. In the case of cell C22, you want to start with that cell. From cell C22, you want to move zero rows, but either one or two columns backwards to grab the date or the name. The function of =OFFSET(C22,0,-$L$4) will achieve this.

3. Enter =OFFSET(C22,0,-$L$4) in C22. It is very important to add the dollar signs around L4 so that the formula will always point to L4 as it is copied down.

Figure 428

Adding dollar signs to make the L4 row and cell references absolute

	A	B	C	D	E	F	G	H	I	J	K	L	M	N
2												Enter a 1 for charts by date		
3												Enter a 2 for charts by name		
4												2		
5														
6														
7														
8														
9														
10														
11														
12														
13														
14														
15														
16														
17														
18														
19														
20														
21	Name	Date	Chart	Topic	Order	Words	Patterns	Descriptio	Audience	Total				
22	Alaina W	9/3/2006	=OFFSET(C22,0,-$L$4)			0	0	0	0	0				
23	Anjela V	9/3/2006	OFFSET(reference, rows, **cols**, [height], [width])			0	0	0	0					
24	Ashley H	9/3/2006		0	0	0	0	0	0	0				

4. Type Enter. Cell C22 will show the name in A22, because the name is two columns to the left of C22.

Figure 429

OFFSET formula points to the cell two columns to the left

21	Name	Date	Chart	Topic
22	Alaina W	9/3/2006	Alaina W	0
23	Anjela V	9/3/2006		0
24	Ashley H	9/3/2006		0
25	Autumn C	9/3/2006		0

5. Change the value in L4 to a 1 and L22 will change to point to the date in column B.

6. Select cell L22. Double-click the fill handle (the square dot in the lower right corner of the cell) to copy the formula down to all of the students.

If you have done this correctly, column L will show the dates from column B when L4 contains a 1. If L4 contains a 2, the column will contain the names.

Caution!

Entering a 3 in L4 will point to a column that is three columns to the left of column C. This column doesn't exist, so entering anything greater than a 2 in L4 will result in a reference error.

Setting up the Chart

1. Excel's intellisense technology really needs the top left corner of the chart range to be blank. Temporarily, clear the value from cell C21 by selecting the cell and typing the Delete key on the keyboard.

   This is a bit tricky, because you are going to be ignoring adjacent data on two sides of your range and including an extra row on the bottom of the range.

2. Very carefully, select from C21 down to one row below the last student in column I. Do not select the Total column and do not select columns A or B. Be sure to select the zzz row.

Figure 430

Selecting the range

	A	B	C	D	E	F	G	H	I	J
20										
21	Name	Date		Topic	Order	Words	Patterns	Descriptic	Audience	Total
22	Alaina W	9/3/2006	Alaina W	0	0	0	0	0	0	0
23	Anjela V	9/3/2006	Anjela V	0	0	0	0	0	0	0
24	Ashley H	9/3/2006	Ashley H	0	0	0	0	0	0	0
25	Autumn C	9/3/2006	Autumn C	0	0	0	0	0	0	0
26	Chaz P	9/3/2006	Chaz P	0	0	0	0	0	0	0
27	Joanna W	9/3/2006	Joanna W	0	0	0	0	0	0	0
28	Jordan A	9/3/2006	Jordan A	0	0	0	0	0	0	0
29	Kain T	9/3/2006	Kain T	0	0	0	0	0	0	0
30	Kelly P	9/3/2006	Kelly P	0	0	0	0	0	0	0
31	Kyle W	9/3/2006	Kyle W	0	0	0	0	0	0	0
32	Logan C	9/3/2006	Logan C	0	0	0	0	0	0	0
33	Makayla R	9/3/2006	Makayla F	0	0	0	0	0	0	0
34	Matthew B	9/3/2006	Matthew]	0	0	0	0	0	0	0
35	Nicholas H	9/3/2006	Nicholas I	0	0	0	0	0	0	0
36	Nikolas O	9/3/2006	Nikolas O	0	0	0	0	0	0	0
37	Rilley S.	9/3/2006	Rilley S.	0	0	0	0	0	0	0
38	Robert H	9/3/2006	Robert H	0	0	0	0	0	0	0
39	T.K. W	9/3/2006	T.K. W	0	0	0	0	0	0	0
40	Tyler L	9/3/2006	Tyler L	0	0	0	0	0	0	0
41	zzz Insert Above Here									
42										

3. From the menu, select Insert – Chart. In the Chart type box, select Column chart. In the sub-type selection, choose the Stacked Column chart from the top row, second column of options.

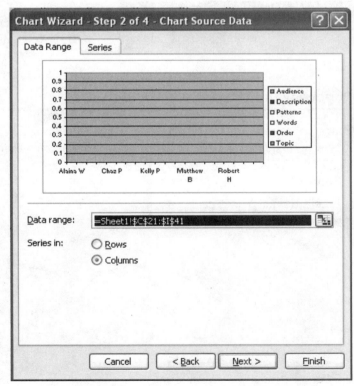

Figure 431

Selecting chart and chart sub-type options

4. Click Next to proceed to the second step of the wizard.

    4a. Take a moment to study the second step of the wizard. The wizard should indicate that your data is in columns.
    You should see a few student names across the bottom axis of the chart and the list of Rubric topics in the legend of the chart. If you have numbers instead of names along the bottom of the chart, cancel the wizard and check that cell C21 is actually blank.

Figure 432

Step 2 of the wizard should have names, not numbers, along the bottom

 Caution!

Use care with Step 2 of the wizard.

5. Although this chart will require a lot of customization, none of it can be done in the wizard. Click Finish to create a chart embedded in the current worksheet.

21

The chart will be created at the wrong size and in an inconvenient place in the worksheet.

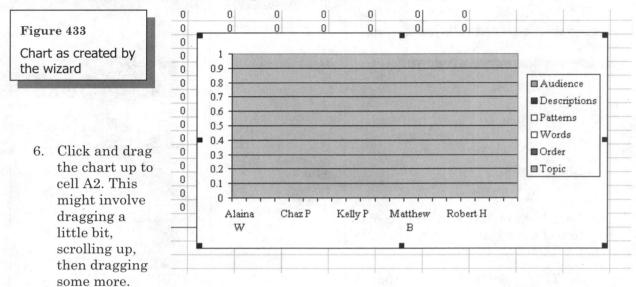

Figure 433

Chart as created by the wizard

6. Click and drag the chart up to cell A2. This might involve dragging a little bit, scrolling up, then dragging some more.

7. Once the chart is in A2, it may not extend far enough down. Click on the bottom right handle and drag to stretch the chart down to cell J20.

Figure 434

Moving and resizing the chart

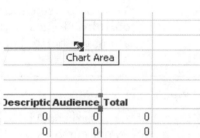

Correcting the Y-Axis

Since there is no data in the chart, Excel does not have a good sense of how to scale the Y-axis. The axis is currently scaled from 0 to 1 in 0.1 increments.

Figure 435

Excel's default Y-axis scale

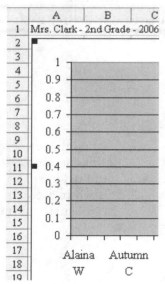

1. Right-click any number (such as the 0.2) and choose Format Axis. Go to the Scale tab. It initially is set up to automatically scale and the dialog confirms that it is currently displaying from a minimum of 0 to a maximum of 1.

Figure 436

Accessing the Format Axis dialog

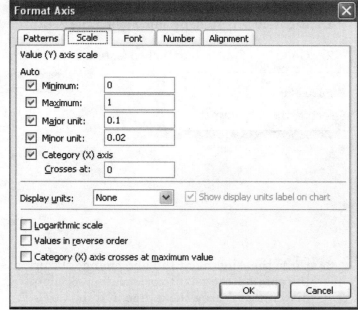

When you change the values in the textboxes, the checkboxes in the Auto column will automatically uncheck.

2. Change the Maximum to 6.
Change the Major unit to 1 and the Minor unit to 0.5.

Figure 437

Changing the Y-axis scale values

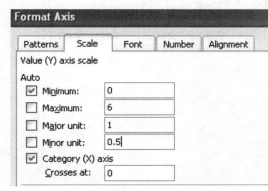

3. Move to the Number tab of this dialog. Choose a Number format with zero decimal places.

Figure 438

Selecting zero decimal places

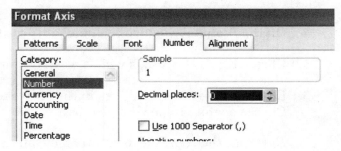

4. Click OK to close the Format Axis dialog for the Y-Axis.

Correcting the X-Axis

The X-axis is also a mess. The chart shows every third student and leaves the other student names blank.

1. Right-click a student name along the X-axis and choose Format Axis.

2. Go to the Font tab and choose an 8-point font.

Figure 439

Selecting the font format

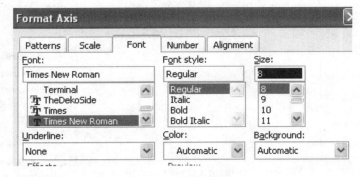

3. Go to the Alignment tab and change the orientation to 90 degrees. You can either use the spin button next to orientation, or simply grab the red diamond in the Orientation diagram and drag the diamond from 3 o'clock to 12 o'clock.

Figure 440

Changing the text orientation

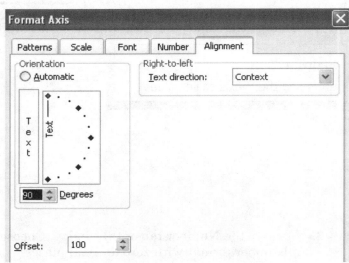

4. On the Scale tab, change the number of categories between tick mark labels to 1.

5. Click OK and the X-axis will show all of your students.

6. Right click between gridlines in the center of the chart and choose Format Plot Area. Choose a white fill for the plot area.

7. Now that the chart has been created, you can re-enter the heading in cell C21.

8. Select a cell in row 22; from the menu, select Data – Filter – AutoFilter.

Using the Application

After the first writing prompt, enter the rubric scores for the students. The chart will reflect the results. It is very helpful if you can print the chart on a color printer. In the chart below, both Kelly P and Logan C scored a three on the rubric. However, Kelly scored a point for Patterns while Logan scored his third point for Descriptions. Seeing the colors that make up the bar tell which items the students have mastered.

Figure 441

Student mastery indicated by bar color

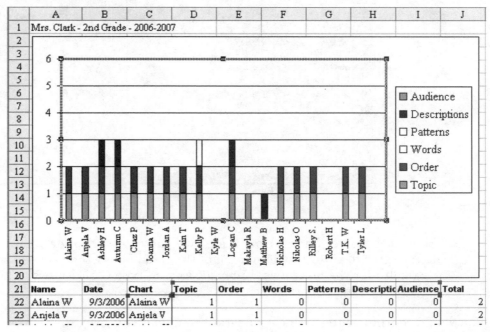

Entering a Second Rubric

When you want to add scores from an additional rubric, you should insert them before the zzzInsert row. One way is to follow these steps.

1. Select cells A22 through J40. This selection contains names through total columns for each student in the class. Type Ctrl+C to copy. Select the zzzInsert Above Here cell. From the menu, select Insert – Copied Cells – Shift Cells Down.

Figure 442

Inserting scores from an additional rubric

The result is a second set of scores identical to the first.

40	Tyler L	9/3/2006	Tyler L	1	1	0	0	0	0	2
41	Alaina W	9/3/2006	Alaina W	1	1	0	0	0	0	2
42	Anjela V	9/3/2006	Anjela V	1	1	0	0	0	0	2
43	Ashley H	9/3/2006	Ashley H	1	1	0	0	1	0	3
44	Autumn C	9/3/2006	Autumn C	1	1	0	0	1	0	3
45	Chaz P	9/3/2006	Chaz P	1	1	0	0	0	0	2
46	Joanna W	9/3/2006	Joanna W	1	1	0	0	0	0	2
47	Jordan A	9/3/2006	Jordan A	1	1	0	0	0	0	2
48	Kain T	9/3/2006	Kain T	1	1	0	0	0	0	2
49	Kelly P	9/3/2006	Kelly P	1	1	0	1	0	0	3
50	Kyle W	9/3/2006	Kyle W	0	0	0	0	0	0	0
51	Logan C	9/3/2006	Logan C	1	1	0	0	1	0	3
52	Makayla R	9/3/2006	Makayla F	1	0	0	0	0	0	1
53	Matthew B	9/3/2006	Matthew]	0	0	0	0	1	0	1
54	Nicholas H	9/3/2006	Nicholas F	1	1	0	0	0	0	2
55	Nikolas O	9/3/2006	Nikolas O	1	1	0	0	0	0	2
56	Rilley S.	9/3/2006	Rilley S.	1	1	0	0	0	0	2
57	Robert H	9/3/2006	Robert H	0	0	0	0	0	0	0
58	T.K. W	9/3/2006	T.K. W	1	1	0	0	0	0	2
59	Tyler L	9/3/2006	Tyler L	1	1	0	0	0	0	2
60	zzz Insert Above Here									
61										

Figure 443

Second set of scores added

2. Select the range of dates from the newly pasted data. Enter a new date and type Ctrl+Enter to enter the date in all of the cells. Select the range of scores in columns D through I for the new rows. Enter a zero and type Ctrl+Enter to change the scores back to zero. Key in the correct scores.

You would continue entering new rubrics throughout the year. In the following example, one rubric score has been entered for each of the months from September through March. Data extends from row 21 through row 154. The chart is unreadable.

Once you have more than one set of rubric data in the table, you can combine the AutoFilter and the value in L4 to quickly display some interesting charts.

Displaying a Trend for One Student

1. From the dropdown in cell A21, choose the student in question. Make sure that L4 contains a "1".

   The chart will redraw to show that student's progress throughout the year. The X-axis will show dates. You can choose successive students from the A21 dropdown to print charts for each student.

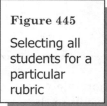

Figure 444

Single student selected

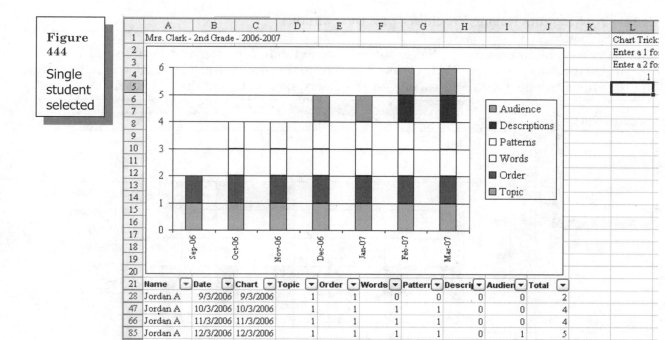

	Name	Date	Chart	Topic	Order	Words	Pattern	Descri	Audien	Total
28	Jordan A	9/3/2006	9/3/2006	1	1	0	0	0	0	2
47	Jordan A	10/3/2006	10/3/2006	1	1	1	1	0	0	4
66	Jordan A	11/3/2006	11/3/2006	1	1	1	1	0	0	4
85	Jordan A	12/3/2006	12/3/2006	1	1	1	1	0	1	5
104	Jordan A	1/5/2007	1/5/2007	1	1	1	1	0	1	5
123	Jordan A	2/5/2007	2/5/2007	1	1	1	1	1	1	6
142	Jordan A	3/5/2007	3/5/2007	1	1	1	1	1	1	6
156										

Displaying All Students for the Most Recent Rubric.

Change cell L4 to a 2. From the dropdown in A21, select (All). From the dropdown in B21, select the most recent date. The chart will redraw to choose the scores of your students in the most recent rubric. With the exception of Kyle, it looks like they are ready to pass the state test.

Figure 445

Selecting all students for a particular rubric

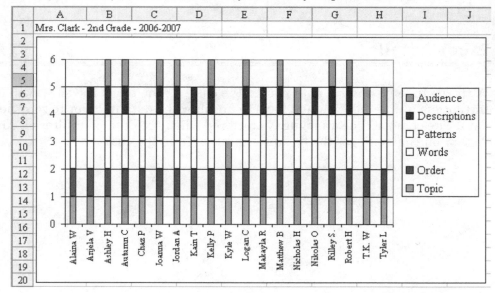

21

Displaying Students Having Problems with Descriptions

Make sure that L4 contains a "2". Select the most recent date from the dropdown in B21. The description dropdown is in cell H21 – select a zero from this dropdown. The chart will redraw to identify students who did not score a one for the description portion of the last rubric.

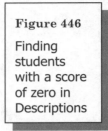

Figure 446

Finding students with a score of zero in Descriptions

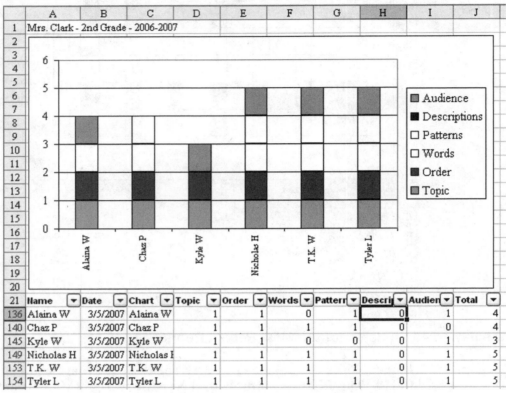

	Name	Date	Chart	Topic	Order	Words	Pattern	Descri	Audien	Total
136	Alaina W	3/5/2007	Alaina W	1	1	0	1	0	1	4
140	Chaz P	3/5/2007	Chaz P	1	1	1	1	0	0	4
145	Kyle W	3/5/2007	Kyle W	1	1	0	0	0	1	3
149	Nicholas H	3/5/2007	Nicholas H	1	1	1	1	0	1	5
153	T.K. W	3/5/2007	T.K. W	1	1	1	1	0	1	5
154	Tyler L	3/5/2007	Tyler L	1	1	1	1	0	1	5

21

Excel Details

With 20 students and six data points, the chart at the top of the sheet will look horrible when the data is unfiltered. You will have to un-filter the data in order to copy new rows in to the data. The chart will be annoyingly cluttered when the data is unfiltered. Always filter to one date or one name to get the best presentation from the chart.

Chapter 22 – Organizing Vocabulary Lists

Opportunity

My middle school students gather many vocabulary words throughout the year. They are required to identify the word, the part of speech, the definition, the chapter/topic, and to write a sentence that clearly demonstrates the meaning of the word. Currently, they are keeping them on index cards or in a notebook. By the end of the year, when it is time for them to study for their final exam, they often have incomplete lists, lost cards, ripped notebooks, etc. I would like them to be able to create an electronic version of their list so that they can organize it by chapter or topic. Because many of them are accustomed to using flash cards, they will need to be able to hide either the definition or the word as a way of testing themselves.

Solution and Overview

Each student will create a workbook that contains all of the vocabulary words learned throughout the year. They will be able to organize their words in a way that is meaningful to them and to use this list as a study guide. Once vocabulary text is entered, they will be able to test themselves by hiding the terms or the definitions. In addition, they can add notes to their spreadsheet that will help them identify which words they have mastered and which are more difficult. They will also be able to print various parts of the workbook to better help them study.

Creating the Solution

You will instruct the students to create a workbook for their vocabulary words. Some students will prefer to have one worksheet for each subject area, while others will want to put all vocabulary into one worksheet and identify them with a column heading called "Subject." Because this is a study guide for them, allow them to organize it in whatever way that is most meaningful for them. The instructions that follow will set up the workbook with a different worksheet for each subject area.

1. Start with a workbook with a single worksheet. Enter the following headings in row 1:
   - A1: Term
   - B1: Chapter
   - C1: Definition
   - D1: Part of Speech
   - E1: Notes/Clues
   - F1: Mastery Y/N

Because this is a worksheet in which some columns will contain a large amount of text, you will want to use the Wrap text feature. Look at the columns and determine the type of content that each will contain. For example, column D, Part of Speech, will contain only a few characters and therefore can be relatively "skinny."

2. Click on cell D1 and select the Format menu and choose cells. Select the Alignment tab and check the Wrap text box. Do the same for columns C and E, selecting the entire column when formatting by clicking on the gray "C" and the gray "E" rather than in a cell.

Figure 447

Formatting all the cells in a column at once

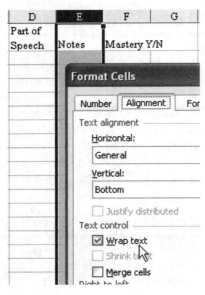

3. After the columns are set up for wrap text, click on the line between each column letter and drag the column to adjust its width to fit your needs.

Column D will be skinny while columns C and E will be wider in order to accommodate paragraphs. You may need to adjust these as you enter data. Remember that you can also double click between each column to use the AutoFit feature. This is useful when you know your content will contain fewer characters than your column heading, such as in B and D.

Figure 448

Adjusting column widths

	A	B	C	D	E	F
1	Term	Chapter	Definition	Part of Speech	Notes	Mastery Y/N
2						

4. To finish the formatting, select row 1 by clicking on the gray "1" and make the text bold by selecting the Bold icon on the Formatting toolbar. Next, determine which columns should contain centered text, probably B, D, and F; select each column by clicking on the gray letter and then on the Align Center icon.

Figure 449

Formatting text to be bold and centered

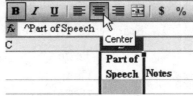

5. Once the formatting is complete, you will want to copy the worksheet, making one sheet for each subject area. Control click on the "Sheet 1" tab and choose Move or Copy. Check the Create a copy box and choose move to end. Once you have enough worksheets, rename each for the appropriate subject areas.

Figure 450 Copying and renaming worksheets

Note:

When you try to name a worksheet "History", you will get a pop up window that tells you "History" is a reserved name." Click OK and name the worksheet History Vocab or something similar.

You are now ready to begin entering information into the spreadsheet. When writing paragraphs, as may be the case here, it is natural to want to use the Enter key. Doing so in Excel will move you to the cell below. Instead, just type continuously and use the Tab key to move across each row. Shift+Tab will move you backwards from cell to cell in a row.

Using the Application

There are various ways to organize information. One might choose to sort by chapter, or alphabetically, or maybe by those words that are not yet mastered. If you wanted to sort first by chapter and then by those words that are not mastered, you can easily do so.

1. Start by clicking on the gray box to the left of column A. This will select the entire spreadsheet. (This is important; otherwise, you may sort only part of your information and end up with a big mess.)

2. Next, select Data, Sort. A window appears that asks you to identify the sorting criteria. First, make sure that the button next to Header row is checked. This tells Excel that the headings should *not* be included in the sort. Once this is done, you can choose your criteria from the pull down menus. In this case, choose Sort by Chapter and Then by Mastery.

Figure 451

Selecting sorting criteria

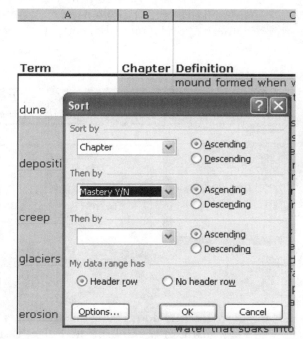

Because there are several ways to look at information such as this, the Custom Views tool is a great way to set up different views to serve different purposes. Students may want to hide the definition column to test themselves, or to hide the term column. Using custom views will allow them to set the worksheet up in a certain way and then easily move back and forth between particular views.

3. Before doing a lot of formatting, set up a Basic view to remember the original worksheet view. From the menu, select View – Custom Views – Add. Give the view a name such as Basic. Leave the two boxes checked and click OK.

Figure 452

Setting up a Basic view

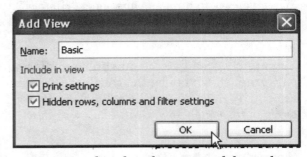

Determine your needs and set up the spreadsheet in the way that will fit those needs, including sorting, filtering, printing, etc. Let's take a look at filtering by terms not yet mastered and make a spreadsheet that will allow us to look at the term and fill in the definition.

4. Click on any cell in the worksheet and choose Data, Filter, AutoFilter. Go to the Mastered Y/N column and use the pull down menu to select "n". This will show you all of the rows that contain n.

Figure 453

Selecting a criteria from the Mastery dropdown

5. Next, prepare a view that will allow you to print out a spreadsheet that can be used as a self-test. Highlight column C and choose Format – Column – Hide.

 Tip:

If you are working on a Macintosh, you will notice that the column letters surrounding the hidden column are blue. This is Excel's way of letting you know that there is hidden information.

22

Figure 454

Selecting sorting criteria

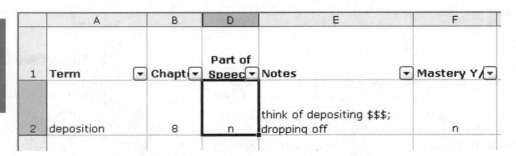

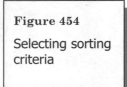

6. Now that the definitions are hidden, you'll want an extra column on the printer version for writing in the definition. Select column G and choose Format – Column – Width. Adjust the width to about 40. Do the same for the row height by choosing Format – Row, Height. 40/50 will work here. You are trying to give yourself enough room to write.

7. Now you'll want to set it up for printing. Highlight the area that you will want to see; in this case, A1:G13. Go to File – Print – Set Print Area. Now go to File – Page Setup. On the Page tab, decide if you want portrait or landscape. For something like this, landscape is the better option.

8. Go to the Margins tab and adjust the margins so that the entire print area will fit on the page. Go to the Sheet tab and check gridlines. Doing this will show the lines that separate each cell.

Figure 455

Worksheet set up for printing and showing gridlines

Term	Chapter	Part of Speech	Notes		Mastery Y/N	
deposition	8	n	think of depositing $$$; dropping off		n	
creep	8	n	think of creeping across the floor		n	
aquifer	9	n	aqua = water		n	
unconformity	13	n			n	

Whew! That was a lot of work. The beautiful thing is that you can now create a Custom View to save all of the settings for this worksheet.

9. Go to View, Custom Views and click on add. Give a name to this view, such as "Self Test." Leave the boxes checked that say "Print Settings" and "Hidden rows, columns and filter settings." This will save all the settings that you just took the time to create.

Your student can now switch between Basic and Self-Test views by using the View – Custom Views dialog.

10. Choose the correct view name and choose the Show button.

Figure 456

Selecting between the Basic and Self-Test views

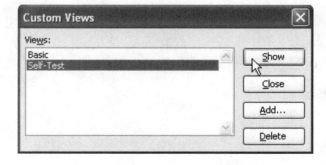

To test that it works, unhide the columns by highlighting the surrounding columns and going to Format – Columns – Unhide. Undo the filters by clicking on Data and un-checking AutoFilter. Go to View, Custom Views, highlight the view that you want, in this case, Self Test, and click Show. Your view will appear like magic!

22

Chapter 23 – Reading Journal

Opportunity

My students are required to keep a journal of the books they read for pleasure throughout the year. They are asked to list the title, author, genre, main characters, and plot. In addition, they are asked to rate the book on a scale of 1 – 4 as a way of recommending it to other students. Currently, they create this journal in a notebook that I collect at the end of the year. I find that I end up re-typing much of their work so that I can compile a list of recommended reading for future students. I would like the final product to be a combined list of all student work from which someone could easily locate books by their ratings, genre, or author. In addition, I would like to be able to print out the summary for any given book.

Solution and Overview

You will create a shared workbook that you will save onto the network so that multiple students can enter data at the same time. This solution assumes that your students have access to your school's network and can save to it.

Creating the Solution

Start with a workbook with a single worksheet. Eventually, you will copy this single worksheet so that you have multiple worksheets into which several students can enter data at the same time. First, you want to set up one in a way that is most useful for your purpose.

1. Enter the following headings in row 1:
    - ➢ A1: Student Name
    - ➢ B1: Title
    - ➢ C1: Author
    - ➢ D1: Main Characters
    - ➢ E1: Summary
    - ➢ F1: Rating
    - ➢ G1: Comments by other readers

2. Make the headings in row 1 bold. Start by clicking on the row heading "1" to highlight the entire first row. On the Formatting toolbar select the Bold icon to make the column headings bold.

Figure 457

Making column headings bold

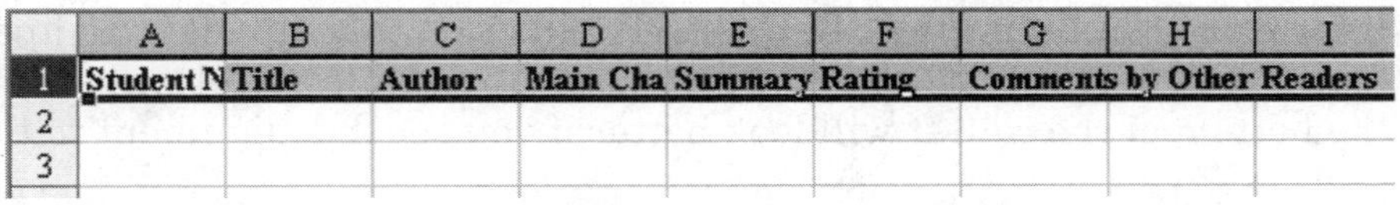

	A	B	C	D	E	F	G	H	I
1	Student N	Title	Author	Main Cha	Summary	Rating	Comments by Other Readers		
2									
3									

Format each column so that it will be able to hold the content that it requires. Columns D, E, and G will each hold a large amount of text so you should format them for wrap text.

3. Highlight column D by clicking on the gray "D". While holding down the Ctrl key, select columns E and G. From the menu, select Format – Cells. In the window that appears choose the alignment tab and check the box marked Wrap text.

Figure 458

Selecting Wrap text cell format

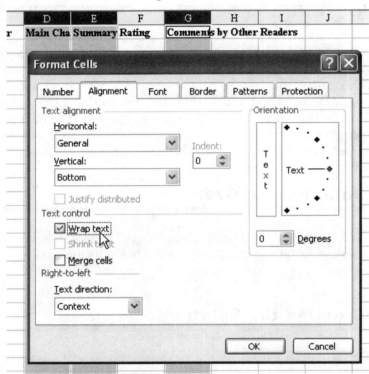

 Note:

There is a bug in Excel. When you turned on Wrap text, the row height in row 1 became tall enough to hold four lines of text in column G. Even after making column G wider, Excel fails to resize row 1 back to a normal height. To correct this problem, double click the line between row 1 and row 2 in the row number section of the worksheet.

4. Adjust the width of each column by clicking and dragging on the line between each gray column heading. A tool tip window appears that indicates the column width. There is not way to know exactly how wide each column should be, but you can estimate for now.

Figure 459

Estimating column widths

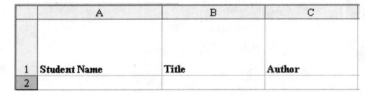

23 The students may need to adjust these
column widths as they enter information. If the title they enter does not fit into the cell, instruct them to double-click on the line between the gray "A" heading and the gray "B" heading. Doing this will perform an AutoFit and adjust the width to fit the cell with longest title. The same may need to be done for columns B and C.

Information in columns A, B, C, and F will often take up just one line, while columns D, E, and G will spill over into several lines of data. By default, Excel will align all of these entries with the bottom of the cell. It will look better if you set the alignment to the top of the cell.

5. Select cell the gray box above and to the left of cell A1. From the menu, select Format – Cells. On the Alignment tab, set the Vertical alignment to Top.

Figure 460

Changing Vertical cell alignment to Top

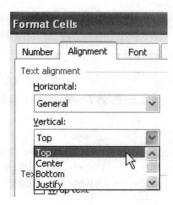

So that you don't have to repeat yourself 30 times for every student that sits down to enter information, can add comments to individual cells that explain your expectations.

6. Select cell C1 and go the menu and choose Insert – Comment. A small window will appear. Type a short description of what you require the students to enter into that particular column. Choose Insert – Edit Comment to return to a comment for editing.

Figure 461

Adding explanatory comments

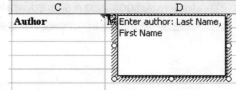

A red triangle appears in the upper right corner of any cell that contains a comment. When the students sit down to enter information, the comment will appear whenever the mouse scrolls over that cell.

Figure 462

Comment displays when a student scrolls over a target cell

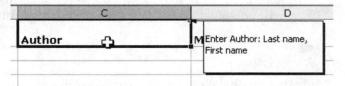

7. Enter comments for the other heading cells.

8. Once the formatting is complete, you will want to copy the worksheet, making one sheet for each genre. Control click on the Sheet 1 tab and choose Move or Copy. Check the Create a copy box and choose (move to end). Repeat this until you have enough worksheets for each genre.

Figure 463

Copying the necessary number of worksheets

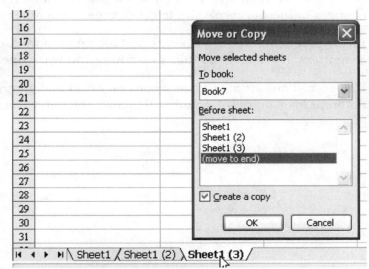

23

9. Once you have enough worksheets, rename each for the appropriate genre by double-clicking on the sheet tab.

Figure 464 Renaming worksheets

10. Now that the workbook has been set up to fit your needs, it is time to make it a shared workbook. Go to the Tools menu and select Share Workbook. On the Editing Tab, check "Allow changes by more than one user at the same time."

Figure 465

Making a workbook into a shared workbook

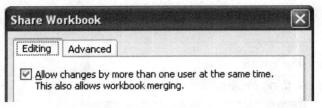

11. Next you will be prompted to save. Give the workbook a name and save it to a shared space on your network. Once the workbook is shared, the Change History feature is activated. This will allow you to track changes made to the workbook. Multiple students will now be able to open the spreadsheet and enter information simultaneously.

 Note:

Students must have read-write privileges in order to make changes.

Using the Application

Shared workbooks sound like a good idea, but in practical usage, they are difficult to manage. After entering their title for a book, the student should immediately click Save to post their changes to the workbook and to get changes from other students.

Ideally, students would cooperate and all agree to work on a specific row on their individual computers. If students do this, everything will work fine.

However, if one student types a book on row 4 and another student on another computer types a different book on row 4, chaos will follow. The entry from the first student will be written to the file.

23

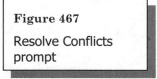

Figure 466

First student's entry written to file

	A	B	C	D	Summ;
1	**Student Name**	**Title**	**Author**	**Main Characters**	
2	Josh Moorhead	A World of Difference	Galada, Lee	Derek	Humans fellow m conscrip attack t
3	Tessa Hershberger	Bakers Dozen	Asimov, Asaac		
4	Ashley Henneman	For All Time	Cooney, Caroline	Annie, Strat	Annie s(pyramid working dig. But up in ar tomb as

In the meantime, the second student has entered his information on row 4 on another computer. When that student clicks Save, the information from the first student will be bumped to row 5. This will be fine.

However, if both students attempt to simultaneously enter a comment in the same cell, the second student will get this message. Although the students have the option to Accept Mine or Accept the Other student's comment, most will choose to Accept Mine and arguments will ensue.

Figure 467

Resolve Conflicts prompt

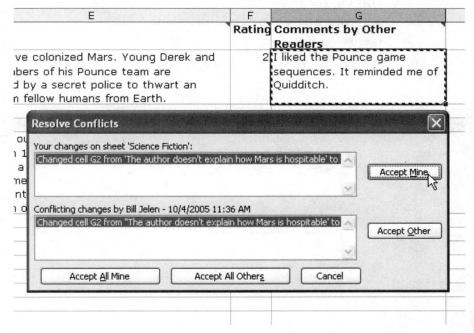

Excel Details

Be careful when setting up shared workbooks. Many types of Excel functionality are turned off when the workbook is shared. Specifically, the following features will be unavailable:

- ➢ Merged cells
- ➢ Conditional formats
- ➢ Data validation
- ➢ Charts
- ➢ Pictures
- ➢ Objects, including drawing objects
- ➢ Hyperlinks
- ➢ Scenarios
- ➢ Outlines
- ➢ Subtotals
- ➢ Data tables
- ➢ Pivot table reports
- ➢ Workbook and worksheet protection
- ➢ Macros

23

Chapter 24 – Demonstrating Fractions with Charts

Opportunity

In order to teach math standards, students need to be able to visualize fractions.

Solution and Overview

Use an Excel pie chart to draw a circle with a fraction of the circle drawn in. A pie chart is a circle broken up into wedges. Business people typically use pie charts to show the percentage of sales by product line.

You can use pie charts to represent fractions for your students. In the solution, you will create a pie chart with two wedges. One wedge will be colored in to represent the fraction. The other wedge will be formatted to be transparent.

Creating the Solution

1. Start with a blank worksheet. In B1, enter the word "Value" as a heading. In A2 and A3, enter the letters A and B. The worksheet will be flexible enough to show any fraction. To begin, start with 0.25 in cell B2 in order to represent 1/4.

Figure 468

Entering a decimal value to be represented as a fraction

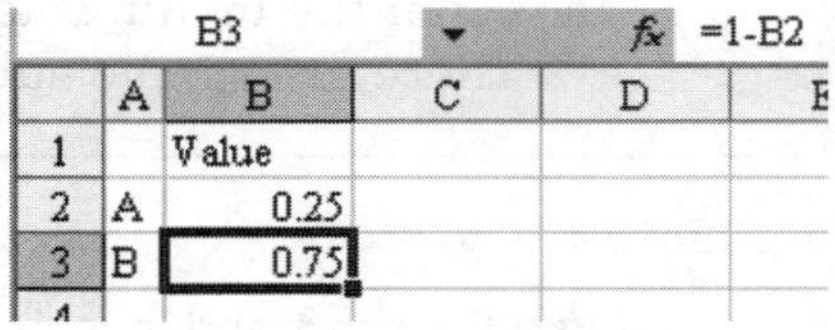

	A	B	C	D	E
1		Value			
2	A	0.25			
3	B	0.75			

B3 f_x =1-B2

2. In cell B3, enter a formula of =1-B2. A pie chart must be comprised of 100% or 1. As you change the fraction in B2, the formula in B3 will ensure that the total value for the pie chart adds up to 100%.

Older students may understand that 1/4 and 25% are the same thing. However, it would be better if the pie chart could have a label of 1/4.

3. Select cell B2. Type Ctrl+1 to display the Format Cells dialog. In the Category list, choose the option for Fraction. If you will only be displaying fractions such as 1/2, 1/3, or 3/8, then it is OK to use the option for Up to 1 Digit. If you might be displaying 1/16 or 1/32, then you might want to use the option for up to two digits.

24

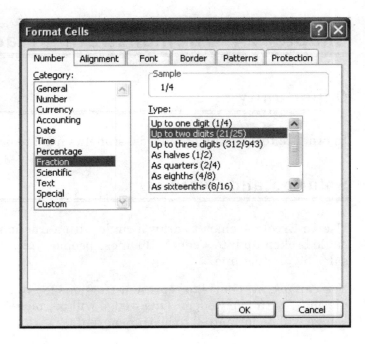

Figure 469

Selecting number of digits for fractions

4. Select the range of A1:B3.

Figure 470

Selecting a range to be represented in a chart

4a. From the menu, select Insert – Chart. In the chart type selection, choose Pie chart. There are six pie subtypes. Select the first type.

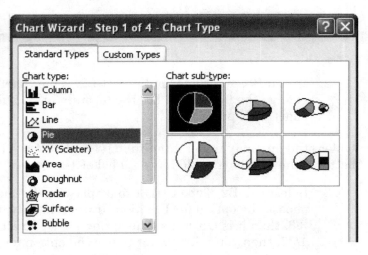

Figure 471

Selecting a Pie chart and its sub-type

5. Click Next twice to move ahead to Step 3 of the Chart Wizard. On the Title tab, clear out the title. On the Legend tab, uncheck the Show Legend box. On the Data Labels tab, choose Value.

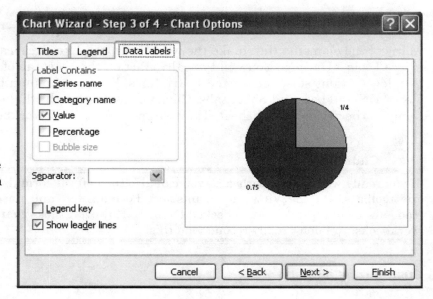

Figure 472

Selecting data label value

6. Click Next to move to Step 4. Choose to create the chart as an object in the current sheet and click Finish.

You will turn your attention back to the chart in a minute, but first let's hide some of the extraneous information on the worksheet.

7. Select the Value heading in B2. In the Formatting toolbar, there is a Text Color icon. The icon contains the letter A over a small (usually red) rectangle. Next to this icon is a dropdown arrow. Click the arrow to display a pallet of available colors. Choose white from the pallet.

Figure 473

Choosing a color from the Text Color icon

Note that the color of the rectangle of the A icon is now white. You can format additional cells to the same color by simply clicking on the icon.

8. Select cells A2:A3. Click the white text icon. Select the formula in B3. Click the white text icon. If you wish, select the fraction in B2 and change the font to 24 point using the font size dropdown.

Figure 474

Changing font size

Although row 1 and column A now appear to be blank, you can completely hide that row and column.

9. Select a cell in row 1. Select Format – Row – Hide from the menu. Type the Down-Arrow to move to A2. Select Format – Column – Hide to hide column A.

Making a Worksheet Not Look Like Excel

Many of the elements that make the worksheet look like Excel can be hidden. From the menu, select Tools – Options. You will typically start on the View tab of the options menu. In the Window Options selection, uncheck Gridlines, Row and Column headers, Horizontal Scroll bar, Vertical Scroll bar, and Sheet tabs. Click OK to dismiss the dialog. These settings will only apply to the selected worksheet. They will not affect other workbooks that you might open.

 Caution!

If you really want to go overboard, you can also turn off the formula bar, status bar, and hide most of the toolbars. On the View menu, unselect Formula bar and unselect Status bar. In the View – Toolbars menu, unselect any checked toolbars. However, these changes will globally affect all future workbooks, so I don't really recommend this!

Customizing a Chart

By default, Excel will draw the chart to take up a certain amount of space on the worksheet. If you are going to be projecting this worksheet onto a screen, you will want the chart to be as large as possible. The chart is comprised of the pie, surrounded by white space and then a black border.

1. Click inside of the white space and eight black handles will appear on the border. You can now click and drag on the white space to move the chart up to just below the fraction.

Figure 475

Moving the chart

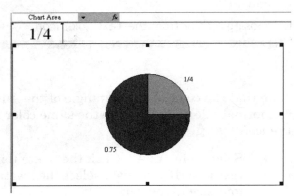

2. Click on square dot in the bottom right corner of the chart and drag down and to the right so that the chart fills the entire screen.

For some reason, Excel allocates a lot of room to the white space around pie charts. You can make the plot area of the chart take up more of the chart area.

3. Select the dropdown on the Charting Toolbar and change the selection to Plot Area.

Figure 476

Increasing plot area size

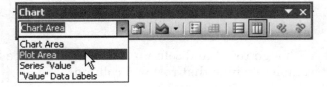

This selection will draw a new bounding box just around the pie.

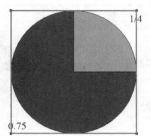

Figure 477

New bounding box eliminates excess white area around pie

4. Click on the white space inside this bounding box and drag the pie to the top of the chart area. Next, click on the dot in the bottom corner and drag down and right to make the pie fill most of the height of the worksheet.

5. Now remove the large rectangle from around the chart area. In the Chart toolbar, select Chart Area from the dropdown. Right-click on the white space in the chart and select Format Chart Area. Change the Border selection to None.

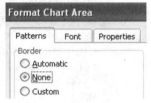

Figure 478

Removing borders from rectangle around pie

Currently, both wedges of the pie are labeled. The blue wedge is labeled with 1/4 and the other wedge is labeled with 0.75. You want to hide the second label. When you click on the 0.75 label, all of the data labels will be selected. Each label will have a square dot on either side, including the 1/4 label.

Figure 479 Locating square dots on either side of labels

· 1/4 ·

6. After clicking on the 0.75 label, wait a moment and then do a second single click on the 0.75 label. Now – the 0.75 label is the only label selected and there is a bounding box around just that label. Type the Delete key to remove this label.

Figure 480 Deleting labels

0.75

Finally, you will want to change the colors of the pie wedges.

7. Click on the pie once to selected the entire pie. There will be just two square dots on the perimeter of the pie. Wait a moment, and perform a second single click on the larger pie wedge. The wedge will now be outlined with six square dots. Right-click the larger pie slice and choose Format Data Point.

Figure 481

Format Data Point dropdown menu

8. Choose a white color for the Area of the data point.

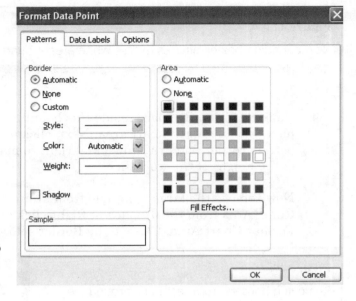

Figure 482

Formatting pie data point color

9. Click OK to close the Format Data Point dialog. Single-click on the smaller wedge to switch the focus to that wedge. Right-click that wedge and choose Format Data Point. Change the color to a bright red or yellow color.

10. While you are in the dialog, choose the Options tab. The options tab for pie and donut charts have an interesting setting called angle of first slice. Typically, the first slice will start at the 12 o'clock position. If you would like to rotate the position of the first wedge, you can do so here.

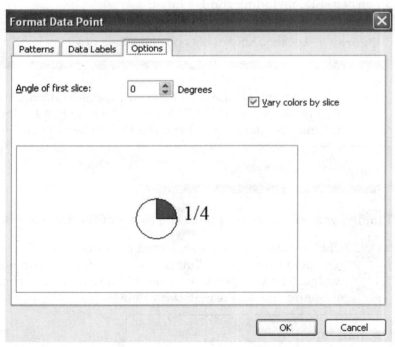

Figure 483

Rotating position of pie wedge

24

11. Click OK to close the dialog.

Using the Application

Select the cell containing the fraction in the upper left corner of the worksheet. Type any fraction here and the pie chart will redraw with that fraction of the circle highlighted.

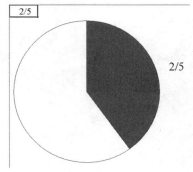

Figure 484

Typing a fraction in the target cell causes the pie chart to redraw to represent that fraction

Excel Details

It is also possible to build a pie chart with four equal wedges and only one wedge filled in. Base the chart on a series with four cells, each one containing 0.25. You will have to repeat the steps to delete the data labels for the second, third, and fourth ranges. You will have to individually format the second, third, and fourth slices to change their color to white.

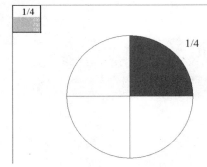

Figure 485

Formatting a pie chart to have four equal wedges but to show only one

24

Chapter 25 – Bar Charts

Opportunity

For math class, teach the students to use a bar chart to graphically represent survey questions. Ask your students how they came to school this morning. Have the class tally the number of students who arrived by bus, car, walking, or bicycle. You will then have the students create a bar chart to visually represent the data.

Solution and Overview

Excel is fantastic at creating charts. You can easily create bar charts, column charts, or pie charts, among many other types.

Creating the Solution

1. Type values into a blank worksheet as shown in Figure 486.

Figure 486

Setting up the worksheet

	A	B	C	D
1	How did you get to school this morning?			
2				
3		Responses		
4	Bus	12		
5	Walk	3		
6	Bike	1		
7	Car	6		
8				

 Caution!

In the image above, cell A3 is the corner cell of your data table. Although it is usually advisable to have a heading above every column, when creating charts, you will want to leave the corner cell empty. This is particularly crucial if the answers in A4:A7 contained dates or numeric data such as ages.

2. To create a bar chart, select the range A3:B7. Find the Chart Wizard tool in the Standard Toolbar.

Figure 487

Selecting the Chart Wizard tool

3. Choose the Chart Wizard button to begin making the chart.

25

In Step 1 of the wizard, you are given a list of several chart types. The right side of the dialog shows a number of subtypes. You may initially see a variety of column charts.

Figure 488

In most cases, column charts are the initial default

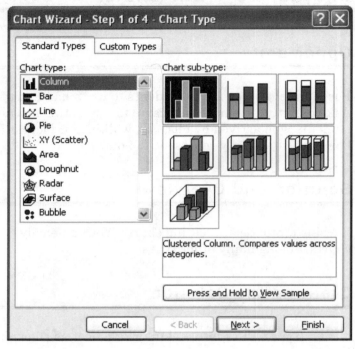

4. Select Bar from the Chart Type list. You are offered six varieties of bar charts. Since your data only has one series, your only real choice is if you want a 2-dimensional graph (first choice in the first row) or a 3-dimensional bar (first choice in the second row).

Figure 489

Choosing a bar chart

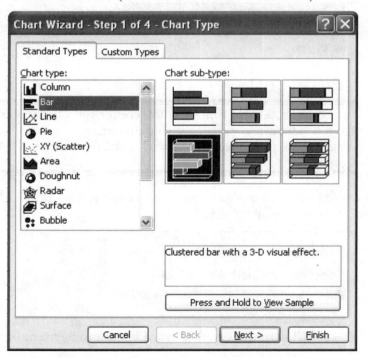

5. After choosing the chart type, choose Next to proceed to Step 2 of the Wizard.

6. The second step of the wizard offers a preview of your chart. If you were plotting two series of data, you might need to specify if the data should be plotted by rows or by columns, but in this case, you can choose Next to proceed to step 3.

Figure 490

Previewing the chart

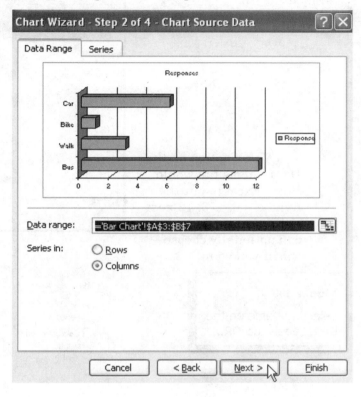

It is ironic that Microsoft says that you can create a chart in three steps, but the third step of the wizard actually contains six different tabs to which you must attend. I guess these are really steps 3a, 3b, 3c, 3d, 3e, and 3f.

7. On the Titles tab, Excel put in a default title of Responses based on the data in cell B4. Type a better title.

Figure 491

Changing the chart's title

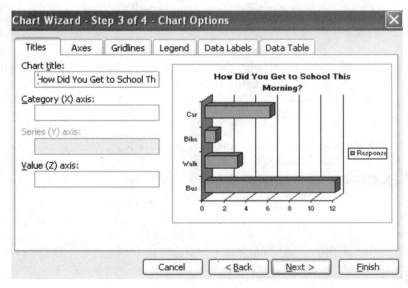

8. The legend box showing that the blue bars stand for responses is not necessary with a single data series. On the Legend tab, uncheck the box for Show Legend.

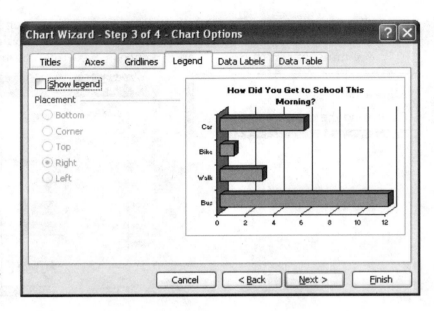

Figure 492

Hiding the legend

9. The Value option on the Data Labels tab would cause Excel to put the numbers 6, 1, 3, 12 next to the various bars. You can optionally choose this if you want.

Figure 493

Selecting Value on the Data Labels tab OR...

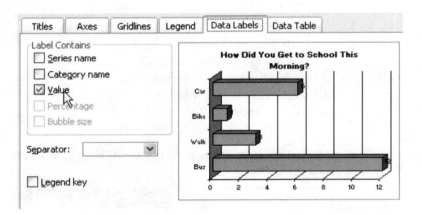

9a. Alternatively, you can use the Show Data Table option on the Data Table tab to add a numeric table below the chart.

Figure 494

... Selecting Show Data Table on the Data Tables tab

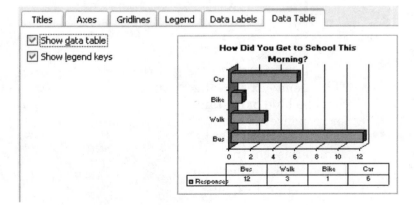

9b. In the example for this book, we are going to leave the data table and data labels unchecked.

10. Choose Next to move to Step 4 of the wizard. In this step, you can specify if the chart should be a full screen chart on a new sheet or if it should be embedded in an existing worksheet.

Figure 495

Choosing whether to embed the chart in an existing worksheet or to place it in a new one

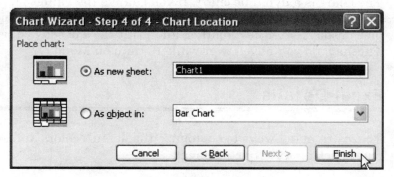

11. Click Finish to create the chart. In this case, you chose to create the chart on a new chart sheet. This creates a chart that will take up the entire printed page and project to fill the screen on the overhead projector.

Figure 496

Finished chart takes an entire page for printing or displaying on a projector

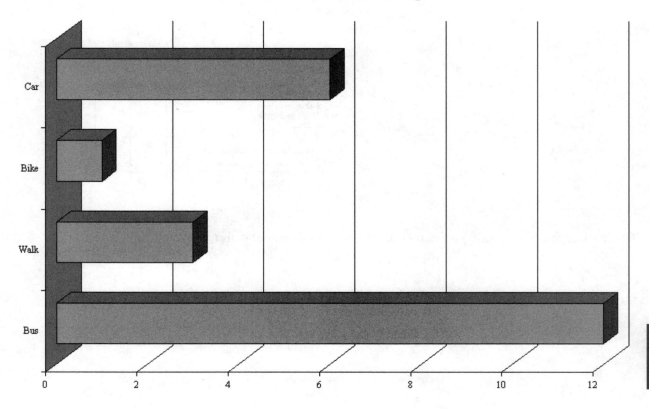

Using the Application

The chart is a dynamic chart. If you change the values on the original worksheet, the chart will redraw. Perhaps you can take the survey on Monday and print the chart. Take the survey again on Tuesday, enter new figures, and print the Tuesday chart to compare. If it is raining on Tuesday, do you have fewer walkers than on Monday?

Excel Details

There are many ways to customize the default colors and styles used in the chart. The trick is to right-click on any chart element.

 Tip:

Macintosh owners should Ctrl+Click to simulate a Windows Right-Click.

1. Right-click any bar on the chart. Choose Format Data Series. There are five tabs in the Format Data Series dialog for a bar chart. On the Options tab, you can check the box to Vary Colors by Point. This will replace the blue bars with varying colors.

Figure 497

Using the Bar right-click dialog to change the colors of the bars

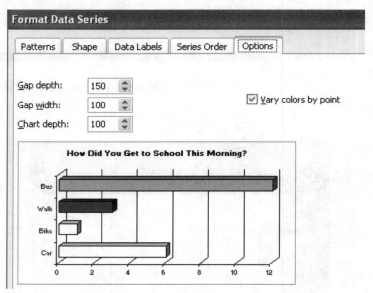

2. On the Shape tab, you can change the bars from cube shapes to cylinder shapes.

Figure 498

Using the Bar right-click dialog to change the shape of the bars

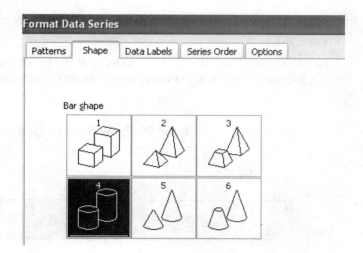

The resulting bars will have a round shape.

Figure 499

Resulting cylinder-shaped bars

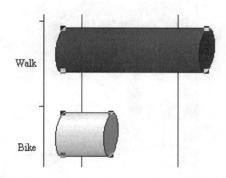

3. Right-click the chart title and choose Format Chart Title. You will access a Format Chart Title dialog where you can select the font size and color for the chart.

Figure 500

Using the Title right-click dialog to change the font and color of the title

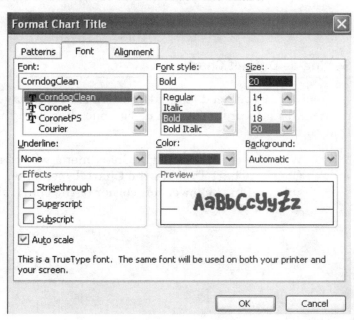

Everything on the chart can be formatted by right-clicking. You can change the gridline color, the walls, the floor, the x-axis labels, and the y-axis labels. Students love to use their creativity to jazz up the charts.

25

Figure 501

Thoroughly formatted bar chart by using the right-click dialog boxes

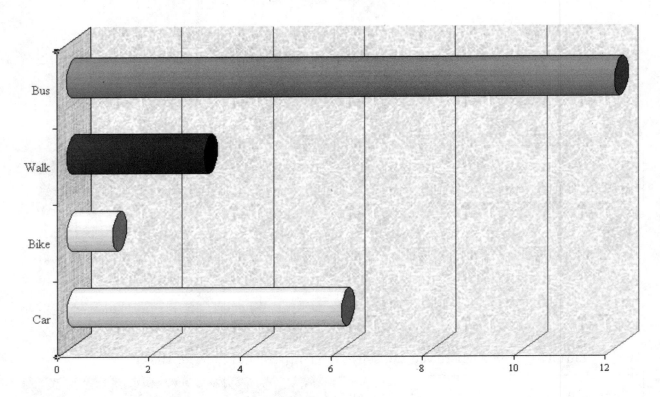

Setting as Default Chart

Let's say that you need to create bar charts every day for the next two weeks during a particular math unit. You can design one chart and then set that chart as the default chart for that computer.

1. With the chart selected, a Chart menu will be available in the Excel menu bar. Choose Chart – Chart Type. In the Chart Type dialog, choose a bar chart and the appropriate subtype. In the lower left corner of the chart, choose the button for Set as Default Chart.

25

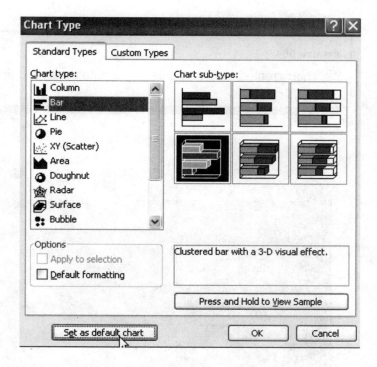

Figure 502

Selecting a Default Chart Type

2. Excel will remember the default chart type on that computer. When you have data on a new day, you can select the data and press the F11 key to create the default chart on a new chart sheet with a single click.

Figure 503

Using F11 to create a new chart using the default configuration

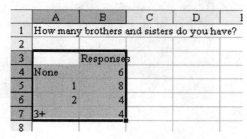

	A	B	C	D	
1	How many brothers and sisters do you have?				
2					
3		Responses			
4	None	6			
5	1	8			
6	2	4			
7	3+	4			
8					

After pressing F11, you will have a bar chart.

25

Figure 504

Bar chart created simply by selecting a data range and pressing F11

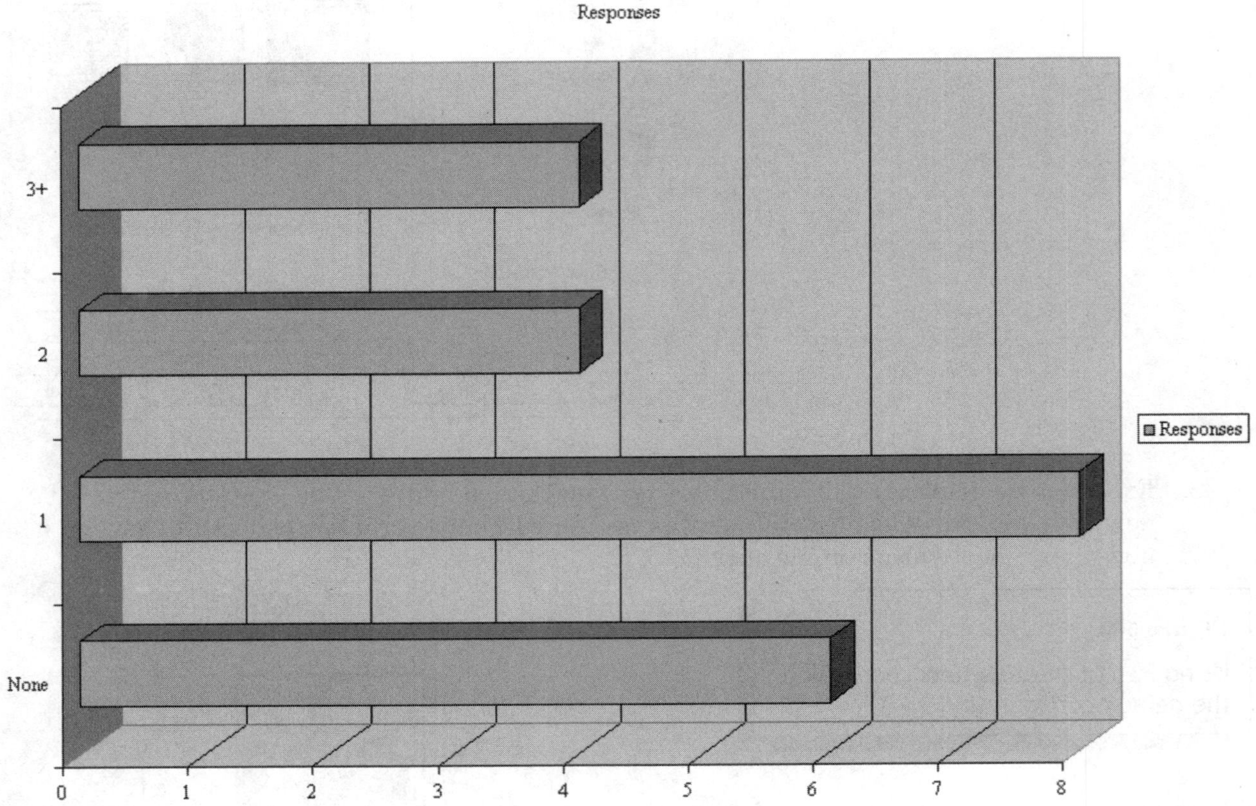

Responses

Index